P9-BZU-465

DATE DUE

KCN PL. Kansas City, KS

MAY 1 1 '89

SEP 1 3 '88

JUL 2 1 '89

DEC 01 '95

RT'D NOV 28 '95

GAYLORD

PRINTED IN U.S.A.

THE
FOUNDATIONS AND PRACTICE
OF
ADULT RELIGIOUS EDUCATION

THE
FOUNDATIONS AND PRACTICE
OF
ADULT RELIGIOUS EDUCATION

by

John L. Elias, Ed.D.

Fordham University
Bronx, New York

ROBERT E. KRIEGER PUBLISHING COMPANY
MALABAR, FLORIDA
1982

BL
42
E39
1982

#8280947
DLC

9-16-82 JH

Original Edition 1982

Printed and Published by
ROBERT E. KRIEGER PUBLISHING COMPANY, INC.
KRIEGER DRIVE
MALABAR, FL 32950

Copyright © 1982, by
Robert E. Krieger Publishing Co., Inc.

All rights reserved. No part of this book may be reproduced in any form or by any electronic or mechnical means including information storage and retrieval systems without permission in writing from the publisher.

Library of Congress Cataloging in Publication Data

Elias, John L., 1933-
    The foundations and practice of adult religious
education.
    Bibliography: p.
    Includes index
    1. Religious education of adults. I. Title.
BL42.E39   207   81-19327
ISBN 0-89874-339-7   AACR2

Printed in the United States of America

In Memory of my father, George Elias

For my mother, Josephine Elias

467714

ALUMNI MEMORIAL LIBRARY
Creighton University
Omaha, Nebraska 68178

PREFACE

For the past five years my major academic endeavor has been in the field of adult religious education and development. The exploration of this field has enabled me to pursue a number of disciplines that have occupied me over the period of my professional life. Philosophy and religion are my first loves, the areas of undergraduate, professional and graduate study. They are also a lifelong personal pursuit. A deep appreciation for intellectual history, inspired during graduate study, has accompanied my philosophical interest and religious quest. In more recent years an interest in psychology and social sciences has grown with the realization of the need for a broader base upon which to theorize and teach.

What has enabled me to interrelate these interests are various fields of education: adult education, religious education, and adult religious education. What attracts me most to the study of education is that it is a field which combines the theoretical and the practical, the humanities and the sciences, the cultural past and the present situation. I am attracted in a special way to religious education because of its potential to raise issues of ultimate value and meaning and inspire personal and political action. I focus mainly on adult education because this area has long been neglected both in religious bodies and in society in general.

My academic interest in adult education has been accompanied by practical involvement in this field. In 1964 I gave my first course to adults in Bethlehem, Pennsylvania, and was exhilarated by the experience. Later when I was director of Religious Education for the Catholic Diocese of Allentown, Pennsylvania, I organized programs for adults in a five county area and continued to teach many courses. For the past three years I have been a volunteer director of adult religious education in the church of St. Vincent Martyr, Madison, New Jersey. These practical involvements have greatly aided my teaching and writing in this field.

i

I am indebted in the writing of this book, first of all, to my colleagues and students in the Graduate School of Religion and Religious Education of Fordham University. I am especially grateful for the support of Vincent Novak, S.J., Dean of the School. In his usual foresight he recognized a decade ago the need for a graduate program in adult religious education, used a sabbatical leave to pursue studies in this area, and introduced the program of adult studies of which I am now the director. The students in the program from past years will recognize themes, ideas, proposals which I hope are presented more clearly here than in earlier classroom efforts.

A glance at the references and indexes of the book reveals a second indebtedness. I have freely made use of the ideas of many excellent scholars in a number of fields. My chief sources in adult education are the works of Malcolm Knowles, Cyril Houle and Leon McKenzie. In religious education I have learned most from Gabriel Moran, Maurice Monette and James Schaefer. I hope that these persons are not displeased with the use I have made of their work.

My last, and undoubtedly greatest indebtedness, is to my family. I have learned much about both adulthood and religion through joyful involvement in Rebecca's and Rachel's growth toward adulthood and religious faith. My deepest personal support comes from my wife, Eleanor Flanigan. A decade ago in dedicating her dissertation to me she wrote that I made all things worthwhile for her. It is she who makes the completion of this work and whatever else I do worth the effort.

John L. Elias
Fordham University

CONTENTS

INTRODUCTION
THE CENTURY OF
THE ADULT

In his introduction to the *Daedalus* studies on adulthood Stephen Graubard suggests that we may be entering the century of the adult. He asserts that this event is not simply a function of changing demographic trends in developed nations; nor does he feel that this necessarily means a lessening of interest in childhood or adolescence. We are entering the century of the adult, he believes, because many academic disciplines and fields of practice are focusing more and more on adults, and adult problems and issues: medicine, literature, psychology, sociology, anthropology, history, religious studies, and education. The *Daedalus* studies are the first interdisciplinary effort to bring these various disciplines to focus on adulthood as a particular stage of life (Graubard, 1978).

It is my aim in this book to present an interdisciplinary approach to the field of adult religious education. I intend to do this by drawing on the various disciplines that have made significant contributions to our understanding of adulthood. An approach to adult religious education from the vantage point of one discipline, be it psychology, educational theory, or any other discipline, will necessarily omit many essential viewpoints that need to be considered. In this introduction it is my purpose to indicate briefly the disciplines that will make up this interdisciplinary approach to adult religious education.

Both biology and medicine have begun to enhance our knowledge of adulthood. Now that neonatrics, pediatrics, and adolescent medicine have become separate specialties, more attention is given to the study of adult problems. The distinctive aspects of adult sexuality and reproduction have become the focus of medical studies. Geriatrics has been established as a separate specialty. The biological factors involved in various transitions from puberty to young adulthood, young adulthood to middle adulthood, and middle adulthood to late adulthood have been examined.

Menopause, male climacteric, and the process of aging are the subjects of extensive study. In psychiatric medicine the work of Jung and Erikson, joined to the earlier work of Freud, who treated almost exclusively adult patients (though interested more in determining the influences of the earlier years on adulthood), has given strong impulse to impressive developments in psychiatry and psychology (Katchadourian, 1978).

Extensive theory and research in the psychosocial development of adults have appeared in the past decades. Jung was the first psychologist to treat explicitly the second half of a person's life. As will be seen, he found strong evidence of religious needs in this period of life. He challenged the great religions to become the schools for adults that they were in previous centuries (Jung, 1933). Erikson built on the psychosexual stages of Freud a theory of human development which includes stages into adulthood and to the very end of life (Erikson, 1963; 1978). Neugarten, Havighurst, and their associates have developed a theory of developmental tasks that have to be faced throughout life (Neugarten, 1968; Havighurst, 1972). In the past decade important studies by Levinson (1978), Gould (1978), and Vaillant (1977) have added considerably to our knowledge of adult development. Various efforts have been made to highlight the religious significance of this research (Whitehead and Whitehead, 1979; Elias, 1979a; 1979).

A fertile source for the study of adulthood has been the study of works of literature. According to Lynn (1978) the classic American authors—Cooper, Irving, Melville, Hawthorne, and Poe—were curiously insensitive to the dramatic possibilities of the human life cycle and made only crude attempts to distinguish among the various stages of life. The result is that their literature is considered more appropriate for juveniles than for adults. A change came about, he contends, in Melville's *Bartleby the Scrivener* and Hawthorne's *The Scarlet Letter*. Ever since the publication of these works authors have treated adult themes more seriously in literature. Beginning with Hemingway, Faulkner, and Fitzgerald, and down to Bellow, Updike, Heller, and others, adult themes, especially sexuality, development, meaninglessness, career dissatisfactions, and changed life dimensions have increasingly found their way into novels. In a fascinating study Merriam

(1980) has studied the mid-life crises of males in American literature of this century and has contended that it gives a number of insights not otherwise found in psychological literature. Also, a study of Tolstoi's novels by Malia (1978) has shown developments in Tolstoi's life and novels in areas of love, marriage, pacifism, religion, family, and state.

An interdisciplinary approach to adult religious education looks to historical studies that show how the concept of adulthood is largely an artifact of the twentieth century American culture (Jordan, 1978). The concept of adulthood emerged as a result of a process of exclusion, as a final product resulting from prior definitions of other stages in the human life cycle. Infancy, childhood, adolescence, and youth have been identified and researched separately in many fields of study. In the past, by focusing on these, less attention was given to adults. For example educational psychology began with a study of processes in children that are important in their education. Thus psychology first discovered the child, then the adolescent, then youth. In our time it has discovered the adult. A number of historical studies such as Aries on childhood (1962), Hall on adolescence (1904), and Keniston on youth (1970) have shown the various forces— religious, educational, social, cultural, and economic—that have been influential in this development.

Besides history, the social sciences of sociology and anthropology have begun to focus more on adult issues and problems. Knox (1977) and Kimmel (1980) review much of the literature on adult socialization. Issues discussed in these studies include work and career, leisure and technology, various forms of family life, sexuality, living arrangements for the aged, and influences of cultural factors on adult development. Among studies of a sociocultural nature can be included those that study the factor of religion in the socialization of adults (Greeley, 1976).

The emerging interest in adult studies has also had an impact in the field of religious studies. The past decade has seen an increased awareness that religious faith is normatively an adult activity. In the recent past religious bodies have been so interested in the transmission of faith to children that almost exclusive attention was paid to the educational needs of young people. In religious studies a great interest has developed in exploring the concepts of adulthood in various religious traditions. In the *Daedalus* studies edited by Erik Erikson (1978), the greatest number of articles were explorations of the concept of adulthood in religious traditions: Christian, Islamic, Confucian, Japanese, and Indian. These articles represent only the beginning of study in this area. In the first chapter we will examine these traditions for the rich wisdom they afford us for understanding and conducting adult religious education.

A final academic discipline that has developed considerable interest in adults is education. Since the 1920s there has been a slowly growing field of adult education or continuing education in many parts of the world. Increasingly the terminology "lifelong learning" is used. The advantage of this term is that it maintains a continuity between the education of pre-adults and adults. It appears that formal and informal adult learning has greatly increased in many countries. Efforts have been made to develop a distinct field of adult education with its own philosophy, history, psychology of development and learning, program planning, institutions, and organizations. Opinions differ on the success of these efforts but the efforts have been great.

Within the field of adult education a sub-field of adult religious education has slowly developed. The Johnstone and Rivera study (1965) showed that large numbers of persons in the United States participate annually in adult religious education. The three major faiths, Protestantism, Judaism, and Cahtolicism, have increased their efforts in reaching adults. A growing number of educators identify themselves as primarily adult educators. Philosophical issues in this field have been discussed by Westerhoff (1976) and Moran (1979). Important work in faith development has been done by Fowler (1981) and Simmons (1978). Schaefer (1971) and McKenzie (1977) have published valuable books for program planning. A body of serious literature is now available for examination and assessment. The purpose of this work is to add a comprehensive and interdisciplinary approach to the entire field of adult religious education.

It is clear that a strong case can be made that we are truly at the beginning of a new educational era within our culture. Entitling this era "the century of the adult" may be more a hope than an existing reality. But this hope is not without its foundations as this brief introduction has shown. The hope of this new era will not pass the religious bodies by if they seriously take up the challenge of adult religious education. The argument of this book is that history, culture, and faith make this both possible and necessary at this time.

PART I
THE FOUNDATIONS OF ADULT RELIGIOUS EDUCATION

CHAPTER I

TOWARD AN UNDERSTANDING
OF ADULTHOOD

No approach to adult religious education is possible without some clarification of the concept of adulthood and maturity as it is used in contemporary society. The word adult is used in different ways in our language and it is important to understand these various usages. This clarification can be done only by looking at a number of disciplines that have grappled with the problem of definition. Light is shed on the meanings of this term by looking to history, law, philosophy, and religious traditions. The primary purpose of this chapter is to develop a concept of adulthood which can form the basis or constitute the ideal toward which a religious education can be directed.

HISTORICAL AND LEGAL ASPECTS
OF ADULTHOOD

The concept of adulthood in American culture is clearly a product of nineteenth and twentieth century developments. Adulthood has emerged as a distinct stage of life because other stages have been separated from the entire life cycle for special treatment by academic disciplines and the general culture. Adulthood clearly developed as a separate stage of life when G. Stanley Hall wrote his two psychological works on adolescence and senescence (old age). This separation of two stages from the life span left a middle stage to be explored by psychologists and other scholars. The separation of these two stages in the life cycle (childhood having become a separate stage in the nineteenth century) is connected with the development of institutions to house adolescents (high schools) and older persons (retirement homes). The development of childhood in the previous century was connected with the development of primary schools. The case has also been made that a separate stage of youth has developed in past decades because of the large number of young people who attend colleges (Keniston, 1970).

In his historical essay on adulthood Jordan (1978, p. 196) notes that as of 1968 the *International Encyclopedia of the Social Sciences* had articles on adolescence and aging but none on adulthood. Since that time numerous books, articles, conferences, and symposia have had adulthood as the primary theme. What is clear from Jordan's study is that adulthood, which was once described as a condition or a status in life, has become a process that needs explanation. This historical development results from a number of causes: technology, geographical and social mobility. As will be seen in a later section of this chapter, it is the human sciences of psychology, social psychology, and sociology that have been responsible for the concepts of adulthood that are in current usage.

Within adulthood the first stage to be demarcated historically was *old age*. Hall (1922) viewed old age as a stage of development rather than one of decline and decay. In the twentieth century social reformers, popular writers, and policy makers have been influential in making old age a separate stage of life with regard to academic study. Old age has clearly emerged as a social, cultural, and biological phenomenon. A number of factors have been responsible for this development. Hareven (1978) gives these as the major ones: demographic changes in numbers of old persons and their life expectancy; the increasing proportion of older persons in the population; decreasing job opportunities for older persons in a production-oriented society; the technological revolution; different living arrangements for older persons. Old age became a clearly differentiated stage historically when there was introduced a clear transition from a stage of productive life to a life of retirement. This constituted a separate group of people who make up a cohort or peer group. Once people were segregated and treated in a special manner because of advanced age, a separate stage of old age developed.

Historical development has been such in recent decades that at least two other stages of adulthood can be delineated. The transition from school to work and family responsibilities is so clear in most societies that *young adulthood* has emerged as a separate stage of life. *Middle adulthood* has emerged as a separate stage in psychological and popular literature mainly because of discussions about mid-life crises. This stage is the least delineated socially, at least at its beginning point. The end point of the stage seems to be the transition to old age through retirement from work. These latter two stages of adulthood have not developed as clearly as old age with regard to social status, though there is a growing consensus about them in psychological literature. No separate discipline such as gerontology has emerged to treat the problems and concerns of either young adults or middle-aged adults. We can certainly look forward to developments such as these if past history is to be a guide in these matters.

Some light on the concept of adulthood in modern society is shed by a consideration of *laws* that pertain to adults. At the outset it appears that secular law systems do not set up ideals for being adult in society as do psychological and religious traditions. Rather the law fixes the minimum standards for acquiring the status of adult and for maintaining this status. Goldstein (1978) has examined the processes in secular law for determining the status of adulthood. Secular law is most concerned with determining adulthood in the sense that persons are free from the coercive intervention of the state in pursuing their particular goals in life.

In law chronological age is important in determining adulthood. This age is usually set around eighteen to twenty-one and varies with regard to particular rights and obligations accorded to adults. The law also sets ages for older adulthood through mandatory retirement laws and social security laws. This impersonal process of determining adulthood avoids making decisions on particular religious or psychological theory.

Though the law sets up chronological age as the norm for adulthood, particular laws contain exceptions and limitations to the rights of adults in society. Goldstein speaks of the general limitations on being an adult. For example, a tension in law exists when a person wants to act as his or her own counsel. Courts have decided that a person has this right, though lawyers have argued that the state should intervene to protect an individual by providing legal counsel. Another case where the state will intervene is where parents are deemed incompetent to take care of their children. Courts have decided that medical care should be given to children even if the giving of this care is against the religious principles of the parents. There are also other areas where the law restricts the free expressions of adults: to form or join unions in some cases; to marry more than one person at the same time; to declare a homosexual preference and remain in the armed forces.

In law adult status is modified in two main ways: personal exemption and personal disqualification. Adult freedom and autonomy is recognized through laws protecting conscientious objectors. During the Vietnam war this freedom was extended to persons who had a merely moral belief in the immorality of war as opposed to the religious belief that was previously demanded for exemption. Also, the courts have exempted Amish parents from the general obligation to send children to school. This exemption pertains to high school and not to primary school attendance. Goldstein sees these cases as examples of the law becoming more secular in its treatment of adults.

The second exemption to adult status comes through personal disqualification. The burden is upon the state to prove that a person should not be accorded adult legal rights. In effect the state has established psychiatry as the judge in these cases of personal disqualification. Psychiatrists declare that persons are incapable of committing crimes, marrying, caring for their children, standing trial, making valid wills, or facing execution.

In the conclusion to his essay Goldstein indicates the value and the limitations of the legal system in defining a concept of adulthood. The value of the law is that it defines a status and does not set up an ideal of adulthood that persons should attempt to achieve. Goldstein concludes that:

> To be an adult in law is not necessarily to be an adult. And to be a child or dependent in law is not necessarily not to be an adult. But to acknowledge this is not to suggest that law makes no difference or that legal systems cannot be distinguished in terms of the extent of their secularity. Rather such an observation should serve to emphasize the importance of recognizing how complex and frail are the processes in secular law for both safeguarding societal needs and preventing one's personal truth from becoming another person's tyranny (pp. 249-250).

The case for secularity in law is well made by Goldstein. But what he does not make adequately clear is that the law does work with a normative concept of adulthood. It is true that religious traditions are less frequently appealed to in most legal systems. The replacement of religious concepts by concepts derived from human sciences still leaves the concept of adulthood in law with considerable difficulties. If psychology or psychiatry are to replace religion, it must be recognized that there are various psychological theories that can be appealed to in determining adulthood in particular legal decisions. Though law tends to become secular, it still needs normative values by which to make its decisions. Even in such a secular legal system as found in the United States the law must take into account religious convictions and concepts of adulthood as is clear in cases involving the Amish, Jehovah Witnesses, and other religious groups.

PHILOSOPHICAL ANALYSIS OF ADULTHOOD

Some clarity comes to the concept of adulthood through a philosophical analysis of this concept. The British analytic philosopher of education R. W. K. Paterson (1979) has provided a clear delineation of a number of ways in which "adult" is used in ordinary langauge. Common to all the usages of the concept is the contrast between adult and child or juvenile. Central to the concept is the idea of growth. Adulthood is the end state for a human person. Though various stages of adulthood are now differentiated, these are still stages of adulthood.

Paterson's analysis of adult comes to the same conclusion as Goldstein's legal analysis. He contends that in calling someone an adult we do not usually ascribe certain empirical characteristics to that person; we merely confer on the person "a certain *status*, a status which derives its significance from contrast with the status of a child and which the person gains only after relinquishing the status of a child (Paterson, 1979, p. 5)." The status of adulthood is in this sense one which can never be revoked and which is not relinquished for another status.

What Paterson makes clear, in contrast to Goldstein, is that adult is preeminently a *normative* concept. The status of adulthood presumes certain qualities in persons, certain rights they possess and certain obligations that others have toward them. We have the right to presume that adults will care for themselves, be responsible parents if they have children, and have the right to exercise free choice in a large area of life. It is true that these rights may be overridden by other considerations, but the ascription of these rights to adults is fundamental.

The philosophical problem that Paterson grapples with is the nature of the criteria for conferring rights and obligations on adults in contrast to children. In his view the status of adulthood presumes that persons possess certain ethical qualities and personal capabilities. These include experience, power of judgment, altruism, a sense of responsibility, and a balanced approach to life and its problems. Paterson recognizes that many adults do not manifest these qualities. Yet he contends that the ascription of the status of adulthood is based on the presumption that these qualities exist in adults. If a person does not possess these qualities we are justifiably disappointed. In Paterson's words, "an adult may not be morally and emotionally mature, but we are entitled to expect him to be so, and he is an adult because he is a rightful object of such expectations (p. 10)."

As for the grounds of ascribing rights and obligations to adults, Paterson's analysis is deceptively simple: "adults are adults, in the last analysis, because they are older than children (p. 10)." Age thus has ethical and existential relevance for the status of adulthood. It is our expectation that with the passage of time persons will have gained the qualities and the experiences that justify ascribing the status of adulthood to them. Age indicates the time they have had to develop and to gain the necessary qualities. The passage of time engenders objective presumptions of moral and emotional maturity.

The philosophical analysis of adulthood that Paterson gives leaves two major issues unanswered. What are the personal qualities and moral attainments that we presume adults to possess by virtue of which we ascribe the status of adulthood to them? A further question, one that is not within the scope of Paterson's work, is about the qualities by virtue of which we presume adults to be mature religious persons. To seek answers to these questions we look first of all in this section to contemporary philosophers of religion. In later sections of this chapter we will examine psychological and religious traditions.

Moran (1979, ch. 2) distinguishes four operative meanings of adult in contemporary language: adult as pornographic, as a chronological point of development, as an ideal of rationality and productivity, and as an ideal of maturity and integrity. Moran's main effort is to critique the ideal of adulthood which stresses rational maturity and productive ability. He argues persuasively for an ideal of adulthood which entails the integration of opposites. In his ideal of adulthood persons integrate within themselves rationality and non-rationality, dependence and independence, life and death. Moran's theory of adulthood includes older persons, while the rational-productive view of adulthood tends to exclude them.

The Jungian influence on this theory is clear, as will be seen in a later section of this chapter. Also, this theory has implications for the models of education that are developed for adult religious education. What this model makes clear is the continuity that exists throughout the life cycle between childhood and adulthood and between the earlier stages of adulthood and old age. Religious education to be truly effective must take cognizance of this continuity and of the consequent implications for an intergenerational education alongside programs of education that separate persons by reason of age.

In a later chapter of his work Moran incorporates his integrated model of adulthood into a description of a religious journey to adulthood (Ch. 4). Moran sees the religious journey not as a transcendence of the ordinary or as a journey into the depths of the self to find the sacred within the person. He images the religious journey as going out, over, back, and down. In Moran's words:

> A person doesn't pass once in a lifetime to a non-ordinary world; instead, a person moves constantly toward some center that always eludes a clear location. Religious is not coextensive with non-ordinary or exclusive of the ordinary. Moving "beyond the ordinary" is intrinsic to the religious journey, but one never actually leaves behind or leaves out the ordinary (p. 60).

According to this image of the religious journey, God is to be found in a journey which is both transcending and immanentizing.

In developing his image of mature religious adulthood Moran highlights a number of important elements. Integrated adulthood focuses upon the individual within a communal setting.

Discursive speech or religious language has meaning only if rite, paradox, and silence are appreciated. Points of time gain their value from the presence they contain. Seriousness is sensitive to the value of irony. Death as the end of life is seen in context of a life which has been lived and a life yet to be lived. In this integrated view of adulthood Moran describes a view of religion that implies that the sacred or extraordinary is found within the profane or ordinary (ch. 4). Though a person must go out of self and over into another sphere, it is primarily in the coming back to the ordinary sphere of life and going into the center of one's being that the encounter with the sacred takes place.

Moran's analysis of mature religious adulthood is clear and profound. His thought is informed by religious, philosophical, and psychological thought. The Jungian influence is decidedly strong in this treatment. His analysis parallels that of the theologian, John Dunne (1978). Within religious thought and psychological theories there are other strands that must be examined in a search for a concept of mature religious adulthood. First we will examine concepts of adulthood in religious traditions. Then will follow an exploration of adulthood in dominant psychological theories.

ADULTHOOD IN RELIGIOUS AND CULTURAL TRADITIONS

Though the concept of adulthood as such is not a concept found in the great religious traditions, all religions and cultures have developed the ideal of the good and just person who is mature or complete in the practice of religious faith. This description is usually cast in terms of religious beliefs, behavior, and worship. The value of examining these religious traditions is that they continue to have a formative power in the socialization of many individuals. The traditions present the ideals that many persons attempt to attain. Most often the ideals represent a description of the founder of the religious tradition as this person is remembered. In developing a concept of mature adulthood for purposes of religious education, it is important to examine what religious traditions present as the image of maturity in faith.

The *Jewish Scriptures* present an ideal of maturity. These

writings tell us as much about human persons as they do about God. A fundamental theme of this literature is that through membership in the Jewish people, a person enters into a covenant relationship with God. It is this relationship of covenant which provides many of the characteristics of spiritual maturity. The mature person is faithful to the covenant and this entails faithfulness to God, God's law, the people, and the leaders of the people. The spiritually mature person is one who is faithful in keeping the law which is summed up as the love of God and the love of neighbor.

Within the prophetic tradition of Israel another dimension to spiritual maturity is found. The prophets emphasized the close connection between the love and worship of God and the doing of justice in the social and political order. The prophetic message is that one is not truly just and mature in doing the law unless care and love are expressed for the poor and destitute members of the community. The prophets recognized that it was not through worship or ritual alone that one becomes good and just but rather through walking in the ways of justice. Thus the maturity of love manifested in action is the highest spiritual ideal.

The wisdom literature of the Hebrew Scriptures presents the spiritually mature person as the person who is wise in relations with God and with others. The wise person has achieved an insight into the deeper meaning of life, in its practical and theoretical dimensions. The most powerful element of this tradition is found in the book of Job. Here it is clearly stated that a person's relationship to God and a person's spiritual maturity are to be judged in the face of sickness, suffering, and fear of death. Thus the experiences of the second half of life are those that ultimately determine a person's spiritual maturity. It is through these experiences that a person comes to view both God and life in ultimate and meaningful terms.

It is clear from a reading and studying of the Hebrew tradition that maturity is a lifelong task. Maturity is forged in one's life with God in communion with a group of people with like-minded ideals. Maturity is both the task of human persons and the task of the God whom they encounter in life. The meaning of spiritual maturity is not to be found in a status once achieved or in legal and ritual observances. It is rather to be found in a life lived in faithful love and obedience to the God that one encounters in daily experiences and in prayerful union and worship.

Christian Adulthood is indebted to the Jewish tradition for its concept of spiritual maturity as it is indebted in many other areas. The Christian Scriptures present the spiritually mature person as the person of faith, one who is faithful to the law, one who does justice, and charity, and one who is spiritually wise in relationships with God and all of life. Besides these ideals Christianity has emphasized a number of other ideals as it has developed historically.

In the Gospels the spiritually mature person is preeminently the person of faith who trusts in and depends upon God in Jesus. This faith entails a basic humility, a love for others, a life of conversion and repentence, and the willingness to forgive others. Jesus presented himself to his disciples and to others as the mature person whose life and virtues are to be standards by which maturity is to be judged. The Beatitudes with their emphasis on internal states and external actions represent the fullest expression of this ideal. Jesus continues the prophetic emphasis on the doing of justice in his parable on the final judgment, wherein the ultimate worth of persons is determined by their effective charity and justice to others. A number of parables indicate that the Christian life is a going back and forth between sin and repentence. Conversion or spiritual growth is a continuous process.

In his historical survey on Christian adulthood Bouwsma (1978) distinguishes between the historical concept of Christian adulthood and the normative concept. The *historical* concept, he contends, accepts the Greek distinction between mind as higher and body as lower. This concept is a source of:

> a Christian ethics of repression directed (like the pagan ethics of the Hellenistic world) chiefly against sexuality; of Christian distrust of spontaneity, a quality especially associated with childhood; and the notion of the mature Christian as a person who has successfully cultivated his own bad conscience, his guilt for his persistent attraction to lower things; that can only come to terms with his existence by a deliberate and rigorous program of self-discipline and self-denial in the interest of saving his soul (pp. 82-83).

This concept of negatively ascetical Christianity has been criticized by Nietszche, Freud, and others for its joylessness and its attempt to reduce adults to the status of children in the church and in society. It leads to a harsh, joyless, and guilt-obsessed religion that stresses unbalanced self-centeredness and authoritarianism. This concept of adulthood has been prevalent especially in those forms of Christian life where group solidarity and discipline are stressed over individual freedom to respond to God (McNeill, 1951, Int.).

In contrast to the historical concept of adulthood, Bouwsma delineates the *normative* concept of Christian adulthood. He sees the origin of this concept in Pauline literature. He contends that this concept has rarely been dominant in Christian history but that it is found in the mature Augustine, the more Pauline manifestations of the Protestant and Catholic Reformations, and in biblical theology and neo-orthodoxy with their sensitivity to history and culture. The classical text for this normative view is found in Paul's letter to the Ephesians. Paul speaks of the ultimate purpose of the gifts of the community as building up the body of Christ:

> until we all attain to the unity of the faith and the knowledge of the Son of God, to mature manhood, to the measure of the stature of the fullness of Christ; so that we my no longer be children, tossed to and fro and carried about by every wind of doctrine. . . . Rather, speaking the truth in love, we are to grow up in every way into him who is the head, into Christ, from whom, the whole body, joined and knit together by every joint with which it is supplied, when each part is working properly, makes bodily growth and upbuilds itself in love (*Ephesians* 4: 13-16).

The analysis that Bouwsma gives to this text brings out a number of prominent aspects of normative Christian adulthood. Maturity is associated with personal stability in contrast to the lack of such in children. Full maturity is identified with loving solidarity with a community of which one is a member; it is not a task that one achieves through rugged individualism. No Christian can be fully mature or adult, for growth is a lifelong process until one achieves the full growth that Jesus reached. The goal then of Christian life is a transcendent one. Bouwsma draws from this Pauline teaching the implication that there is a close connection between sin and refusal to grow or develop. Christian adulthood demands both dependence upon God and the spontaneous freedom of the child.

In another approach to Christian adulthood the sociologist of religion Robert Bellah (1978) contends that two elements must characterize the mature adult life: the passive life of contemplation and the active life of involvement in world affairs and transforming the world. Bellah finds this distinction not only in the Christian tradition but also in Greek philosophy, Buddhism, and Confucianism. In analyzing present industrial society Bellah contends that there has been an eclipse of the contemplative in favor of the active. This unbalanced situation will prevent individuals from reaching maturity in this culture. In Bellah's view the need for these two elements of life is biologically founded in the need for both action and rest. Bellah contends that Augustine best expresses this dual need when he writes that "we see then that it is the love of truth that looks for sanctified leisure, while it is the compulsion to love that undertakes righteous engagement in affairs (Augustine in Bellah, 1970, p. 70)."

It is clear that both Bouwsma and Bellah are dealing with ideal types of adulthood. Bouwsma has perhaps drawn too sharp a contrast between historical and normative adulthood in the Christian tradition. The Christian must ever deal with elements of sinfulness, weakness, finitude, and alienation. It is true that at particular times negative ascetical dimensions have been stressed over more positive dimensions of Christian life. But it must be remembered that the Christian tradition has developed within many different cultural situations. In fact the writings of Paul and John contain elements that support the ascetical view. The ascetical tradition within monasticism and reform movements often began as an indictment of moral laxity and conformity to values opposed to the teachings of Jesus and the Christian tradition. Asceticism often brought into focus the need for greater moral discipline in crisis which particular Christians faced.

In a real sense the distinction between historical and normative Christian adulthood is not one between ideals but between ways of achieving those ideals. The ascetic also wants to grow up to the full personhood of Christ. But asceticism is sensitive to the forces within persons and the community that prevent this growth. At certain times in Christian history this has been more pronounced than at others. In many ways a profounder analysis of Christian adulthood for the present situation must await a dialogue among this tradition, other religious traditions, and present psychological theories that attempt to define adult maturity. But before turning to this task it is first necessary to examine a number of studies which present concepts of adulthood in other religious traditions and cultural situations.

In the *Islamic religious tradition* the concept of adulthood is presented in rather legalistic terms. The adult is the:

> legally and morally responsible person—one who has reached physical maturity, is of sound mind, may enter contracts, dispose of property, and is subject to the criminal law. He is responsible for the religious commands and obligations of Islam, for bearing the burden laid upon him by God . . . (Lapidus, 1978, p. 97).

The Koran describes the mature person as one who subordinates passion and impulse to ethical self-restraint. The mature person is one who has faith in Allah and in the will of Allah. Faith is viewed as a process of development throughout life.

According to Lapidus, in Moslem religious writings a crucial issue of adulthood is striking the balance between confidence and humility. Though the writings affirm that the human person is essentially helpless, they also hold to a measure of human strength and responsibility. In this religious tradition it is also recommended that a balance be struck between activity and passivity. Adulthood is to be achieved within the ordinary activity of human life and through a life of faith. It is recognized that in this life faith does not exclude all elements of doubt.

Lapidus defines the essence of spiritual maturity in Islam as the integration of the individual with the norms of the religion and culture. It is a personal reconciliation to the reality of the world and of the person's place in it as Allah has willed it to be. Spiritual maturity is peace expressed and achieved through living in the world according to the reality revealed by Allah in the Koran. Muslim literature agrees with Christian writings that one becomes an adult through a life of faith. Through a life of faith one is relieved of false maturity and of the anxiety of self-sufficiency to face the inadequacy of all that is merely human. "In Islam trust in

God and humility open the way to the inward healing and outward responsibility which is on the way to adulthood (Lapidus, 1978, p. 111)."

One major difference between adult maturity in Christianity and the same ideal in Islam is that in Christianity spiritual maturity is considered as transcending any given social situation. Christianity has attempted not to become committed to any particular cultural situation. Though this ideal has not always been achieved, it nevertheless remains an ideal. In fact very often Christians are called to reject particular cultural and social values in order to become committed to what are considered ultimate values. In Islam adulthood is realized in terms of a concrete culture, the Muslim way of life. The situation in Moslem countries today where religion exercises its full influence is no doubt similar to situations in medieval Christendom where religion and culture were so intimately connected.

The examination of spiritual maturity in Islam has introduced a new factor in our effort to arrive at a concept of adulthood. This factor is the influence of a particular culture in shaping the view of adulthood and maturity within that culture. It is clear that being adult in American culture is different from being adult in Islamic or another culture. While philosophers tend to look for ideals and concepts that transcend cultural contexts, social scientists increasingly make us aware of important differences that exist among cultures.

Another important implication of this inquiry into the concept of adulthood in Islam is that it should sensitize us to different concepts of adulthood within a given culture itself. We have in recent years become aware that within our general American culture there exist numerous subcultures. While the legal system attempts to work with a concept of adulthood that can be generally applicable throughout the culture, concepts of adulthood that come from other sources must be examined for the cultural conditions that gave rise to these concepts. In fact even the legal definitions of adulthood change with cultural change, as we have seen. This implication will become of more value to us when we examine in a later section various psychological concepts of adulthood and maturity.

Cultural influence on concepts of adulthood is seen in the

Confucian perception of adulthood. Wei-Ming (1978) has explored this concept in terms of "becoming" or "being on the way." Adulthood is not a state of attainment but a process of becoming. To become an adult in this culture is to steer the middle course in life. A person develops into adulthood through an inner direction and a knowledge of the established social norms. Adulthood entails creative adaptations to the inevitable process of aging. Within this cultural tradition old age is recognized as a delicate situation and often as a difficult problem. But the stage of old age is intrinsically valuable as a concluding chapter in personal self-realization.

Interestingly, Confucianism has recognized particular problems to be overcome during each stage of adulthood. On these problems Confucius wrote:

> In his youth, before his blood and vital humors have settled down, he is on guard against lust. Having reached his prime, when the blood and humors have finally hardened, he is on guard against strife. Having reached old age, when the blood and vital humors are already decaying, he is on his guard against avarice (Confucius in Wei-Ming, 1978, p. 117).

This strong biological approach to development is interesting. Psychoanalytic theory has attempted to build on a similar basis. Confucius was also not without suggestions for handling these problems. He recommended poetry to the young adult as a force for harmonizing the emotions. To the middle aged adult he recommended ritual for harmonizing human emotions to accord with cultural values. To the aged he recommended music for peace achieving and directing oneself to transcending interests (Wei-Ming, 1978, pp. 119-122).

Confucius recognized that though the goal of adulthood was self-realization, this goal could be achieved in a number of ways. The goal of the follower of Confucius was not to narrowly follow his example but to become a genuine human person. Confucius stated that he was still on the way to becoming a sage. Wei-Ming comments on this aspect of Confucian teaching:

> It is therefore conceivable that a person in his eighties or nineties may be able to advance further on the Way than Confucius had in his seventies. It is also conceivable that people under new circumstances may choose to pursue the

way in a mode which differs significantly from what has been traditionally sanctioned as authentically Confucian. After all, from the Confucian perspective, the approaches to sagehood are as many as there are sages. And by implication, although adulthood can be recognized it can never be defined (Wei-Ming, 1978, pp. 125-126).

It is not the purpose of this section to present concepts of adulthood in all religious cultures. The emphasis has been on the Judaeo-Christian tradition. A number of other cultures have been presented for purposes of comparison and to arrive at a richer perception of adulthood. Studies have also been made of traditional Japanese culture which places great emphasis on character development and improvement (Rohlen, 1978). A study of Indian culture by Rudolph and Rudolph (1978) contrasts the Brahmin ideal which is ascetical and Rajput maturity which is expressive and non-ascetical. This study shows how maturity can be achieved within the cultural situation of the extended family, a finding that appears contradictory to theories of adult development recently published in the United States which postulate leaving the home as the first step in achieving adulthood (Levinson, 1978; Gould, 1978). Malia (1978) has examined Russian concepts of adulthood by exploring the life and writings of Tolstoi and has shown that adulthood is closely connected to political rights and duties.

To summarize and compare the insights from these various religious traditions, perhaps we may fruitfully use the concept of dialectical tension. To become an adult means to hold together two divergent tendencies. Adulthood might be best described as the delicate art of balancing various needs, tendencies, instincts, or demands upon the person. It is a time for stability but also a time for changing and becoming. It is a state that one achieves but never realizes fully. The religious adult balances trust and dependence upon God with reliance on one's own powers and abilities. The adult must hold in tension personal initiative with necessary conformity to societal norms and rituals. The active life must be embraced but not at the expense of the contemplative life. One must be both mystical and practical. Mature religious adults attend to personal growth and development but are also actively engaged in affairs of the world. Mature religious adults imitate and learn from the founders and heroes of their religious tradition but they also develop their own styles of maturity and spirituality.

The richness of these religious traditions compares favorably with what psychologists in this decade have found to be true of mature adults. On the other hand, insights from modern psychology certainly enrich the religious traditions and challenge them at many points. Yet it is also true that psychologists have very often rediscovered in this century some of the wisdom that religious traditions contain. It is to these psychological theories that we turn in the next section.

PSYCHOLOGICAL THEORIES OF ADULT MATURITY

The purpose of examining psychological theories in this section is merely to indicate the normative concept of adult maturity that different theories contain. All psychological theories presume an image or norm of the mature adult around which the theory is based, and toward which persons should develop. It is important to examine these normative concepts because it is to psychological theory that most people look to discover what it means to be mature or adult in our culture. No full treatment of psychological theories will be given here; a fuller discussion will be found in a later chapter. In this chapter we will describe briefly the concept of the mature adult person that important theories propose. In this chapter I will also indicate the basic attitude that these theories take toward the religious dimension of life.

Psychoanalytic Theories

For Freud (1953) adult maturity is described in both a negative and a positive manner. Negatively, a mature person is one who does not become fixated at lower stages of development. Positively, the mature person is the stoical individual who faces the reality of the world and human life without recourse to any higher being. The mature person accepts the human helplessness and insignificance that are part of the human condition. In his view the mature person depends on the power of reason to face up to the contradictions and disappointments of life. Freud's trust is in scientific reason for it is the power that explores the world.

In Freud's view religious faith is a major obstacle to achieving adult maturity. Religion in his theory is viewed as the flight from the frustrations of this life to the illusory security of belief in a father who can deliver us from all evil. Religion is the purely human response to helplessness and insignificance. It serves to exorcise the terrors of life and to reconcile humans to cruelty and death. Religion as the projected father image is responsible for most of human weakness. Religion is ultimately an illusion, a wish for help from an almighty father.

Carl Jung (1938), Freud's disciple, took a more positive view of religion in his description of the mature adult person. For him the mature person is the individuated person, the whole person, the integrated person. Mature persons integrate a number of opposites in their personalities: masculine and feminine; darkness and light; the roles of parent, worker, neighbor, and citizen; the conscious and the unconscious. In Jung's view the work of maturity is accomplished in the second half of life when a person faces suffering, illness, and death. Wholeness is usually found in the neglected, inferior, and underdeveloped side of the personality.

Religious faith plays an important part in the development of maturity. Religion is a natural human response, for it arises from an inborn need and desire to enter into a relationship at a level beyond ordinary life. Religion supplies a satisfying form of expression for human needs. The great religions provide the symbols which enable people to express their deepest needs and desires.

One of the most respected views of adult maturity comes from the psychoanalyst Erik Erikson (1963; 1978). Mature persons are those who have successfully responded to a number of life crises concerning trust, autonomy, initiative, industry, identity, imitacy, generativity, and integrity. The last four crises are encountered in the adult years. Erikson has given an important role to religion in achieving the inner unity and integrity which neither nature nor society can provide. He contends that it is:

> the world religions which have striven to provide an all-inclusive world view for the containment of such human extremes as self-seeking, vanity and self-abnegating humility, ruthless power-seeking and loving surrender, a search for beliefs worth dying and killing for, and a wish to empathize and understand (Erikson, 1978, p. 21).

As will be seen in a later chapter, Erikson sees a strong potential for religious faith in aiding persons to achieve maturity in the culture in which they find themselves.

Erikson's description of mature adulthood comes through in his description of the virtue of wisdom which he suggests as the final human task. Wisdom is the detached and yet active concern with life in the face of death, and the maintaining and conveying of the integrity of experience in spite of decline in mind and body. Wisdom is the attempt to put order in one's life. It is the love of the ego in a spiritual sense. Wisdom is marked by the acceptance of one's life cycle and a defense of its dignity (Erikson, 1964, p. 112).

The recently deceased psychologist, Erich Fromm, has also presented in his works a view of the mature adult person. According to Fromm the mature person has met existential needs. This entails the overcoming of the horror of separateness, powerlessness, and lostness and the finding of new forms of relation to the world in order to feel at home in the world. Existential needs are satisfied in passions such as love, tenderness, striving for justice, and independence. The mature person has achieved a character: the relatively permanent system of all non-instinctual strivings through which a person relates to the human and nature world (Fromm, 1973).

Fromm retains the symbols of religious faith but gives these symbols a humanistic interpretation. Religion for him becomes the ecstatic love of human persons for other human persons. God is the symbol of the highest human values. It is the symbol in which one expresses the "totality of that which man is striving for in the real of the spiritual world, of love, truth and justice (1956, pp. 70, 71)."

Maturity for Fromm is achieved through self-awareness, resolution of conflicts, active involvement in life, and striving for justice. The emphasis in his writings is upon doing truth and justice in the world. The stress is here because for him there is no spiritual realm outside or transcending human existence. Thus the primacy is upon ethical development which includes love, justice, and reason. The mentally healthy person lives by love, faith, and reason, and reflects upon the life of all mankind.

In the past decade a powerful description of adult maturity

appeared in the writings of the psychologist and cultural anthropologist, Ernest Becker (1973). In his view the mature person is the heroic individual who lives without shrinking from life in the face of the certainty of death. This person has the personal power to avoid the pitfalls of mental illness and the danger of unrepression. Becker expresses clearly the irony of the human condition: we strive to be free from the anxiety of death and annihilation but at the same time we live a life that awakens this anxiety and causes us to shrink from being fully alive (1973, pp. 9, 61). In order to overcome this dilemma human persons need, according to Becker, to develop character defenses—secret neuroses, repressions—that enable them to look upon the futility and ambiguity of life without despair.

Becker appeals to religious faith to aid persons in this tragic human condition. Yet religious faith in his view gives no easy solutions to the problem of death and life. Drawing on the religious writings of Otto Rank, Paul Tillich, Sören Kierkegaard, and William James, Becker grapples with the deepest problems of human life. He finds none of their solutions completely satisfactory; but he finds the solutions of scientists and psychotherapists even less satisfying. He ends his work bravely believing that humanity is neither to be lost nor to be thrown away. He is a believer who possesses a large amount of uncertainty and doubt. But curiously he also dares to speak of hope and heroism. A revolutionary optimism characterizes this brave and honest work.

Becker's optimism comes from his belief that the orientation of human persons is beyond their bodies, grounded in healthy repressions, and towards explicit immortality-ideologies which are myths promising the possibility of heroic transcendence. Becker concludes his work by stating that in the human condition:

> the most that any one of us can seem to do is to fashion something—an object of ourselves—and drop it into the confusion, make an offering of it, so to speak, to the life force (1973, p. 285).

The descriptions of the mature adult in the psychoanalytic tradition have strongly influenced our understanding of the human person. The tradition has provided much of the vocabulary that we use in speaking of human problems and their solutions. The tradition is a mixture of hope and despair, reason and instinct, growth and stability, freedom and determinism, and other dialectical tensions. Religion is variously regarded in this body of literature. Both positive and negative views are expressed. The negativism of Freud has been countered by the more positive views of Jung, Erikson, Fromm, and Becker.

One strong current permeating all of psychoanalytic theory is that powerful forces in the depths of the person's being are responsible for growth and development. These forces are shaped by the earlierest experiences in life. The struggle for maturity is the attempt to direct these forces in positive and fruitful ways. Environmental forces are not considered determinative factors in shaping the mature person. Intrapsychic struggles determine the maturity that a person will achieve. This distinguishes this tradition from the behaviorism we now discuss.

Behavioristic and Social Learning Theories

The second major force in psychology that addresses in some degree the issue of the mature adult is behaviorism. Assimilated to this theory are a number of social learning theories which attempt to combine insights from behaviorism and psychoanalysis or from behaviorism and cognitive-developmental theory. What unites all of these views is the belief that in the ultimate analysis the environment or social forces are determinative in shaping human behavior.

Radical behaviorism is best represented in the works of the contemporary behaviorist B. F. Skinner (1971). In Skinner's view the mature person is one who engages in socially acceptable behavior. The mature person is controlled through the forces of the environment. Skinner prefers to look at external behavior and not at any internal processes in individuals. Controlled behavior is to be achieved through an elaborate system of behavioral modification wherein positive rewards and not punishment are used to change behavior.

In this theory there is little room for individual maturity and freedom as opposed to group socialization. In fact it is Skinner's contention that our insistence on speaking of individuals as free and autonomous persons is what is responsible for the evils and tragedies of modern life. Group socialization is described in a utopian manner by Skinner:

> People live together without quarreling, maintain themselves by producing the food, shelter, and clothing they need, enjoy themselves and contribute to the enjoyment of others in art, music, literature, and games, consume only a reasonable part of the resources of the world and add as little as possible to its pollution, bear no more children than can be raised decently, continue to explore the world around them and discover better ways of dealing with it, and come to know themselves accurately, and therefore manage themselves effectively (1971, p. 205).

In Skinner's view, through behavioral modification we have the human technology to make this vision a possibility.

Skinner sees little place for religion in his controlled society, though he admires the controls that some forms of religion have over people. He indicts religions for readiness to use fear and punishment to gain control over individuals. Skinner skillfully interprets religious doctrines and practices along behavioristic lines (Elias, 1979a, p. 23).

A modified form of behaviorism is found in a number of psychologists who classify themselves as social learning theorists (Bandura, 1977). These theorists modify radical behaviorism either with psychoanalysis or more cognitively oriented approaches. Their image of the mature adult does not come clearly through in their works, for they are more interested in explaining human learning and socialization than they are in describing the ultimate goals of this socialization. Their differences with behaviorist theory are located in the areas of freedom and those internal states of the mind that influence individuals.

Some social learning theorists have shown an interest in the religious sphere, for example, Hoffman's work on the learning of internal moral standards by children (1971). More recently socialization theory has become a helpful paradigm in the hands of a number of religious educators (Nelson, 1967; Westerhoff, 1976; Marthaler, 1978). These educators, however, have drawn more on sociological and anthropological theory than on psychological theory.

Behaviorism and social learning theories sensitize us to the fact that individuals fashion their mature selves in specific contexts and that these contexts help shape the mature adult. We do not have to accept the extreme position of Skinner to be impressed by the influence of social learning on adult maturity because in its basic outlines social learning theory has established a number of important principles. Modeling, imitation, identification, internalization are all important principles of learning. In a chapter on adult learning and socialization we will explore at greater length some of these important issues.

Cognitive-Developmental Theories

The major thrust of cognitive-developmental theorists is to explain how human persons develop in their rational understanding of themselves and the world. The image of adult maturity found in these psychologists is that of the fully rational, autonomous, and principled individual. Mature persons are capable of abstract thinking, symbolic understanding, and principled moral reasoning. The genesis of this theory is in the extensive research on children and adolescents that has been done by Piaget (1948) and many others who have utilized his approach.

In more recent years this theory has been extended to adults through the research of Kohlberg (1976), Fowler (1981), and Peatling (1976). This research presents adult moral maturity in terms of principled moral reasoning. Individuals are mature in their moral reasoning if they appeal, not to the conventions of society but to universal principles of justice, reciprocity, equality, and the dignity of human beings as individual persons. Mature religious faith has been described by Fowler as a universalizing faith that moves beyond the paradoxes of life to embrace a vision of a world community and to express loyal commitment to this vision. In a recent article Fowler (1980) has attempted to present the image of living in the Kingdom of God as a particular expression of adult mature faith in the Judaeo-Christian tradition.

No extended treatment of these developmental theories is presented here for they will be treated later in this book. What is stressed here is the norm that these theories present as the goal for adult intellectual, moral, and religious maturity. The theory focuses on an important element in human life, the power of rational understanding. Greater emphasis is placed on the conscious and rational processes of human life than on emotional and environmental factors. This is both the strength and the weakness of this approach. We now turn to a group of theories which attempt to integrate these various emphases in unified theories of personality or human maturity.

Existential and Humanistic Theories

No psychologists have devoted themselves more to exploring adult maturity than a number of psychologists loosely grouped together under the label of humanistic, existential, or Third Force psychologists. Among this group are included Carl Rogers, Abraham Maslow, and Gordon Allport. The term Third Force has been used of this group because they represent an alternative to behaviorism and psychoanalysis. The influence of this group in the field of adult education has been extensive since their ideas have been incorporated into the work of two prominent adult educators, Malcolm Knowles (1980) and J. R. Kidd (1973).

Rogers (1969) explicitly addresses himself to the issue of describing the mature adult. For him, the mature adult is the fully functioning person who is open to all experiences, both joyful and painful. This person attempts to remove barriers and inhibitions to consciousness and communications. Living in an existential manner is another characteristic, meaning a willingness to remain in a process of becoming. Fully functioning persons trust themselves, even though they recognize that they may make mistakes. Finally, these persons are creative, in that they do not easily conform to the culture and are not readily predictable.

Though Rogers does not include a religious dimension in his personality theory, his thought does not preclude adding a religious dimension. His emphasis is on values that are esteemed in most religious traditions: freedom, value, autonomy, will, trust, love, and respect. Rogers began studies for the ministry but abandoned them when he experienced a crisis of faith. Though he was never ordained, Rogers's work has influenced two generations of pastoral counselors, teachers of religion, and religious ministers. A theory of the mature religious adult that utilizes his work must grapple with the optimistic view of the human person contained in it, which appears to minimize or ignore the influence of the dark side of human nature.

For Abraham Maslow the mature adult is best described as the self-actualized person (1954). Persons reach this state after meeting progressively a number of deficiency and growth needs: sheer survival needs, physical safety, belonging and love needs, the need for self-esteem rooted in competence, and the need for insight. Self-actualization entails that persons become what *they* can be. They fulfill personal potential in all its aspects. They are free from cultural and self-imposed restraints. Only a small group of people reach this state—Lincoln, Beethoven, Jane Addams, and Einstein are among the examples given. To be self-actualized means to identify with mankind through peak or mystical experiences.

Maslow has explicitly treated the role of religion in his personality theory. Religion is identified with peak experiences that self-actualized persons have. Religion is given a naturalistic interpretation since peak experiences are not experiences of a Being apart from the self and the world. Peak experiences, however, are not only of beauty, cosmic unity, and benevolent love, but also of evil, disease, and death. Through these experiences "the bad things about life are accepted more totally than they are at other times. It is as if the peak experience reconciled people to the presence of evil in the world (Maslow, 1964, p. 64)." Maslow's view of religion is similar to Fromm's naturalism.

While Maslow assigned only a few individuals to the highest stage of adult maturity or self actualization, Gordon Allport (1955) contended that many persons can achieve fully integrated personhood. In his creative eclecticism he described a number of influences that bring about the mature person. These include the satisfaction of organic desires and needs, temperamental factors, psychogenic and spiritual needs—truth, beauty, goodness, holiness, self-expression, power and personal integrity, the pursuit of meaning, and a proper response to the surrounding culture.

In Allport's view mature persons have three chief attributes. They possess *expanding selves* in that they have a widening number of higher or psychogenic values. Secondly, they are marked by *self-objectification*. They can look at themselves honestly and assess their strengths and weaknesses. A sense of humor is a good sign for Allport that this quality exists. The final attribute is *self-unification* or integration. Mature persons have some unifying philosophy of life that supplies direction and coherence in their lives.

In Allport's personality theory religion is given a potentially prominent role in developing the mature person. In his classic work on religion, *The Individual and His Religion* (1950), he contends that religion can be a creative force in a person's life; he also recognizes that it can also be a crutch that prevents a person from fully developing. Allport carefully describes the characteristics of a mature religious faith. This faith is well-differentiated since it is critically held and reflected upon. This faith is dynamic in controlling and directing the motives and activities of the person. Mature religious faith is consistently directive in transforming character and aiding the person to make moral and religious decisions. Mature religious persons have a faith that is comprehensive and integral in that it relates to all aspects of their lives and puts a certain order into their life and their values. Finally mature religious faith is heuristic since it is held only with a high degree of probability and as a working hypothesis to help people find better and fuller answers to problems in their lives.

The concept of adult maturity presented by humanistic or existential psychologists is an influential one in American culture. The optimism of this view is consonant with strong elements in our national culture. Self-help movements which are pervasive in our culture assume that indivduals have control over their destinies and are not at the mercy of environmental or intrapsychic conflicts. This view has been especially attractive to religious persons for precisely these same reasons, though some have attempted to temper the optimism of this position with traditional religious teachings on sin, weakness, finitude, and alienation (Oden, 1968). So modified this theory forms a powerful basis for adult religious education.

CONCLUSION

This chapter has developed the concept of adulthood or adult maturity from a number of perspectives: history, law, philosophy, religion, and psychology. These disciplines do not include all the elements necessary to form a concept of adult maturity for religious education, but they are certainly essential ones. In succeeding chapters a number of other disciplines will be explored, especially those concerned with adult socialization and development.

The disciplines thus far explored sensitize us to a number of important considerations. Historical studies make us realize that adulthood is a rather recent concept and that its meaning differs in different cultures and at different historical periods. The historical perspective enables us to see the present situation as the result of forces that have operated in the past to bring about the present awareness of adulthood as a separate stage in life. Yet history also contains a warning. In the past when there was extreme focus on one stage in life, for example on childhood or adolescence by psychologists, the study of this stage was often cut off from other stages and the continuity of the life cycle was lost. Focusing on one stage tends also to exaggerate the differences between this stage and others. While adult studies and adult education need their separate identities, these fields of study must continue to look to the entire life span and to the continuities between the various stages of adulthood and the earlier stages of life.

An examination of legal studies makes us aware of the complex issues involved in determing the rights, responsibilities, and duties in society. The law is less concerned with internal growth than it is with external actions that have a bearing on the rights of others. In most countries the development of law has meant an increase in areas where persons can exercise responsible freedom. The law is also deeply concerned with cases where the freedom of adults is to be qualified or infringed. In these cases some psychological norm is utilized to determine what constitutes adult rights and responsibilities. In some societies religious traditions still exercise influence in determining standards of adult behavior.

Philosophical analysis of adulthood comes to a conclusion similar to that of legal studies. What is needed are some normative criteria for determining the ethical and psychological demands for adulthood. Different ethical systems can be utilized in this analysis as can differing psychological theories. Philosophical analysis provides a necessary clarity to our thinking in this area but important normative or value questions will still have to be addressed.

A study of religious traditions reveals a rich wisdom on what it is to be adult in a religious manner. Religious traditions are strongly influenced by the cultural circumstances in which they developed and were refined. A number of major tensions are found within these traditions. How can persons reconcile faithfulness to the norms of mature faith found in the traditions with the demands of contemporary society life? How do persons live the tension between conformity to the norms of society and individual choice in the direction of their lives? How do persons balance the calls in religious traditions for asceticism and discipline with summons to personal freedom and autonomy? How do people responsibly balance in their lives personal growth, commitment to love others, and the formal religious activities of prayer and worship? No easy solutions are possible for the questions; but it is around questions like these that religious maturity revolves.

In the past century our views of maturity have been heavily determined by the theories and findings of psychologists. Psychology has presented different models for understanding human maturity: psychodynamic, behavioristic, cognitive, and existential. Religion has begun to enter into a fruitful dialogue with psychology through the work of theologicans or religionists and psychologists who attempt to forge relationships between the two disciplines. This dialogue attempts to avoid both extremes of excessive pietism and unwarranted reductionism. In the work of Becker, Allport, Erikson, and Fowler we see the fruitfulness of this dialogue.

From the preliminary concepts of adulthood and the adult maturity explored in this chapter we move to a consideration of the social and development factors in adult religious growth. Our knowledge of these factors has increased considerably in recent years. A sound adult religious education must be based upon an understanding of the developmental stages of adulthood, the social contexts in which adults develop, and the processes of socialization in adult life.

CHAPTER II
SOCIAL CONTEXTS OF ADULTHOOD

From the treatment of adulthood in the first chapter it is clear that adulthood differs according to the social contexts in which adults live and develop. Within each socio-cultural situation there are forces which influence the ways in which individuals express their adult maturity. For example, Malia (1978) in his study of nineteenth century Russia argued that adulthood was defined in terms of citizenship and freedom for social and civic action. In his historical treatment he also raised the issue of differing concepts of adulthood among the various social classes of society.

From the historical analysis of the first chapter it was concluded that adulthood has meant different things at different times in American history. Changes in family organization, work practices and mores, and community expectations have been important factors in bringing about the present conception of adulthood. Preoccupation with social and personal changes in society have brought about a view of adulthood that is dominated by the image of psychological change. New social roles for young adults and the elderly have determined the meaning of adulthood for these groups.

The purpose of this chapter is to examine more carefully the present social context in which persons came to adulthood in the United States. The general social context will be examined first and then the social context of religious bodies will be explored. What is said of the United States situation may be generalized to other industrial nations but only with careful qualifications. The social science research presented will come almost exclusively from studies done in North America.

THE GENERAL SOCIAL CONTEXT

Demographic Changes

There are some basic characteristics of the population of the United States. To some degree these characteristics can be applied to other industrialized countries. The population has become more *heterogeneous* with the emergence of greater ethnic, racial, and regional differences. Though diversity has always been a characteristic of the population, the social changes in the 1960s and 1970s produced an increased awareness of differences among the population. More than at any time in our history the issue of cultural pluralism is seriously debated. Old images such as that of the melting pot are questioned and efforts have been made to allow for diversity without losing the benefits of unity (Gordon, 1964).

A second characteristic of the population of this country is that it has become increasingly *urbanized*. It is in the urban areas that the diversity of peoples is greatest. Urbanization has produced both positive and negative effects. Cities have industrial, cultural, and educational advantages; but these benefits have to be balanced with economic, environmental, and social problems. American cities since the middle of the nineteenth century have had both these advantages and disadvantages. But in recent years the problems of the deterioration of the cities have become a great concern both to the cities and the federal government.

A third characteristic of the population is that in recent years there has been increased *geographical mobility*, especially among young adults in the population. Modern corporations have been the primary force in promoting this mobility among aspiring executives and managers. Mobility also exists among blue-collar workers because of the shifting of factories and home building from one part of the country to other parts. Mobility has meant upward mobility and broadening perspectives for some, while for others it has entailed the painful dismantling of support systems for individual and family needs.

A higher degree of *educational attainment* characterizes the adult population of this country. More persons complete high school each year and a larger proportion of high school graduates receive post secondary education of some kind. The phenomenon of middle-aged adults returning to educational institutions for advanced learning has become more common than in previous decades. Adult education programs of both a degreed and a non-degreed nature have grown considerably in the past two decades.

A final general characteristic of the population is the *increased age of adults* in this society. The number of older persons has increased. This has been accompanied by fewer births in the population and a lessening mortality rate for children. Life expectancy for both men and women is around the age of seventy. This situation gives society an untapped resource for many sectors of our culture. But it also has created strains in the social security system, Medicare, and the proper care of the elderly.

There are a number of implications for adult religious education in these general demographic trends in the population. Adult religious education must have a diversity and a flexibility that will make it relevant to the different groups in the population. Special attention in programming must be paid to the needs of adults in the urban areas. To meet the needs of a highly mobile society adult religious education must provide for community and fellowship needs of individuals. Religious organizations in areas of high mobility should program in a special manner for newcomers along the lines of such community organizations as Newcomers Clubs and Welcome Wagon Clubs. Higher educational attainments among the population call for programs in religious education beyond the basics of faith. Finally, the special needs of the young, middle-aged, and elderly need to be addressed. Studies have shown, however, that it is young adults and older adults who feel most alienated from ordinary church life (Gray and Moberg, 1977). Concrete suggestions on programming for these groups will be presented in a later chapter of this book.

The Changing Character of Work

Knox (1977) reports on studies which show how the United States has changed from a manual work society to an industrial or machine society. There are important differences between the two types of societies. The rate of change is greater in an industrial society than in a manual one. Because of the existence of written materials in industrial societies older persons are less important as sources of knowledge. More recognition is given to economic success than to community service. Persons are judged more in terms of economic productivity than in terms of personal worth and length of service. These differences increase in post-industrial societies.

In industrial and post-industrial societies economic power is usually in the hands of younger men—middle-class managers. Job demands include speed, strength, and flexibility—attributes that tend to diminish with age. In an industrial society job entry tends to be on an impersonal and competitive basis with formal education serving as a powerful screen for admission to higher level jobs. Educational institutions have the task of preparing persons for entry into advanced positions in corporations.

In an industrial society there is little intergenerational contact in the work world. The young are excluded because they are in training for the job world. Coleman (1974) has documented the many problems that arise from separating the young from the work world and segregating them in age-specific groups. The elderly are excluded through laws of compulsory retirement and the nature of the work demands. In manual or pre-industrial societies such separations did not exist.

In modern industrial society there is a clearcut distinction between work and leisure. Weekends, holidays, and vacations are the times for leisure and recreation. Work is more on a nine-to-five basis. In some types of work in industrial society more leisure time is available to individuals. Studies have appeared documenting a great deal of worker dissatisfaction in industrial societies. Other studies show the difficulties that some workers have adjusting to leisure time (Kimmel, 1980, ch. 6). Many people tend to see leisure in a negative context, implying doing nothing productive.

A major change in the world of work in recent years is the large number of women, especially mothers of small children, who have entered the work force. Women today tend to enter the work force earlier and to stay longer. Many family tensions arising from this situation, especially in the case of working class women, need to be resolved. These tensions concern the husband's sense of personal worth and the quality of child care (Rubin, 1976; 1979).

Social scientists have reported a number of crisis points in the work cycle of individuals. Generally speaking, people have either orderly or disorderly work histories. More stability is correlated with orderly work history. Other crises arise at the time of entering a job and deciding on its worth, the decision to change jobs, unemployment and realization that one has gone as far as one will in a particular job, and the years of retirement (Kimmel, 1980, ch. 6). How work is integrated into the religious development of the person will be included in the following chapter.

One aspect of work that has received extensive treatment by sociologists is the problem of alienation. Blauner (1964) has found much of modern work alienating. Feelings of domination, futility, isolation, and discontent are pervasive in the work world. In his study he also found that the nature of work also affects a person's social character and personality, the manner in which a person participates or fails to participate as a citizen in the community, and the overall sense of worth and dignity of a person. Freedom, meaning, and self-expression are increasingly found to be rare elements in a person's work life.

The effects of the modern corporation upon the lives and families of its workers and managers has long been studied by sociologists (Whyte, 1961). A recent work by Kanter (1977) has extended this research into the lives of women in modern corporations. Her work is an argument for changes in the organizational climate and structure of work in order for more humanistic and personalistic values to emerge. She also called for changes that would better integrate women and minorities into the modern corporation. Her work is a warning to corporations that do not embark upon immediate changes. She contended that:

> The costs to organizations in productivity and effectiveness of routinely producing such [frustrated] people are considerable, in the sheer waste of potential human talent. Even more serious—and harder to measure—are the costs to those people as individuals. Work, which should be energizing and enlivening, which can be a vehicle for discovering and testing the limits of one's capabilities, for contributing and being recognized, becomes instead a source of strain or dependency or limitation (p. 287).

A final issue connected with the world of work is the important milestone of retirement. Retirement is a critical event in the life of individuals. It introduces a person into a new status or social position. Studies have shown that persons who retire voluntarily make a better adjustment than those who are forced to retire. Retirement brings reduction in economic power and an increase among some retirees, but not the majority, of a sense of uselessness. Studies have also shown that successful retirement is related to family relationships and community support for the new role in society (Kimmel, 1980, ch. 6).

Though more research relating to work could be reported, this sampling of findings from the social sciences provides material for reflecting upon the role of adult religious education with regard to the changing world of work. Religion has not been strong in addressing problems relating to work. While the Roman Catholic bishops in the United States have designated the 1980s as the decade of the family, it would be very surprising for a religious body to designate a decade for giving serious attention to problems concerning work. Religion and family have had strong ties over the years. But ever since the revolutions that swept over Europe in the eighteenth, nineteenth, and twentieth centuries, there has been a growing cleavage between religion and the economic sphere. The worker-priest movement in France has had limited support and success. Though some industrial chaplaincies exist in this country, these are meager in comparison to chaplaincies for other groups of the population.

Serious adult religious education should take into account the work dimension of life. It can challenge working persons to a deeper understanding of the religious implications and spiritual dimensions of work. It can raise people's consciousness of how they are affected by the ethos and values of the work world. Serious consideration should be given to the ethical problems that exist in various occupations. Religious bodies through educational efforts can make their members and the general community more sensitive to problems and issues that relate to the humanistic and personalistic values of the work world. Issues relating to the hiring of minorities and women need the educational forums that religious bodies can provide.

Areas where adult religious education can be especially valuable certainly include the healthy use of leisure time and the process of retirement. Religious activities and religious study are valuable forms of leisure. A profound understanding of worship sees it as a leisure activity in which one renews the human spirit through union and fellowship with God and with a community of believers. The Judaeo-Christian tradition of the Sabbath or Sunday rest, together with religious holidays and festivals, are leisure activities which show that the healthy human life needs times of rest, refreshment, and renewal.

In recent years religious bodies have attended more to the care of their elderly members. The crisis of retirement is one in which the religious community can be supportive of individuals. While communities and work organization at times provide help in these areas, persons with religious orientations can be especially supported in transitions from work to retirement by a consideration of those deeper dimensions of human life that transcend earthly work. A religious support group at this time of life can help a person overcome personal difficulties. An honest sharing of problems with others gives deeper insight and a broader vision of life.

Socialization Through Family Life

As the world of work has changed drastically in recent decades, significant changes have also taken place in family life. These changes in family life influence the way in which adults achieve maturity and consequently have an important bearing on efforts to educate adults in many areas, including religion. A number of these significant changes are reported in social science literature.

The modern family differs greatly from the family of a century ago. At one time the family had functions of protection, education, training for work, and religious formation. Other institutions of society have developed which now provide these services for children. One of the only remaining functions of the family with regard to children is socialization into the values of the society. Yet even in this function the family may be losing ground to media and peer groups.

In a careful analysis of historical developments in the family since the nineteenth century Lasch (1977) developed the theory that the modern family experiences emotional overload. People expect more satisfactions from the family than it can give. The family can less and less provide for its members the "haven in a heartless world." Women who remain in the home to raise children get little emotional help from the outside. They increasingly have to live vicariously through their husbands and children. At the same time institutions like schools, social agencies, and even churches make greater demands upon the family. Husbands tend to compartmentalize their domestic and occupational lives. They have difficulties balancing the needs of both and often fall either into a familism that seeks all satisfactions at home or a compulsive careerism that invests total self in work (Lasch, 1977, p. 145).

The modern family exists in many forms. There are nuclear families—made up of mother, father, and children. Extended families exist in some cultures. There are also modified extended families where there are interlocking networks of relationships with relatives. Increasingly the pattern of single parent families has become common in the United States. In many families a grandparent is present to give a three generational pattern to the family. The presence of a grandparent often makes it possible for the mother to work outside the home. Rarer family patterns include communal marriages and homosexual marriages. While at present the nuclear family remains dominant, other family patterns are increasingly found in this society.

Our understanding of families has increased through developments in the field of family therapy. Family therapy views the family as a system of interlocking personalities. An individual's problem is treated not in isolation from the family but in connection with the role that the client plays in the family. In this theory a disruption in any member of the family will have damaging repercussions on the family as a whole. Family members each have a concept of the family, a distinctive way of interacting in the family, and crucial roles to play within the family (Kimmel, 1980, ch. 5).

Not only have different patterns of family emerged in society, but also increasing attention is given by social scientists to the cycle through which families pass. Typically, families develop progressively through a series of phases. These stages include: premarriage, establishment of the marriage, new parents, preschool family, school-age family, family with adolescents, families as launching center, postparental family, and the aging family (Kimmel, 1980, ch. 5). It is clear that adult deveopment and education will be greatly influenced by the dynamics of particular stages. Each of these phases entails difficulties and issues which can be addressed in an educational setting.

Before marriage couples face the issue of marriage choice and the formation of an ideal of love that will characterize their marriage. When marriage is entered, personal relations, sexuality, and decisions about parenthood are faced. New parents face both joy and stress in their new roles. The rearing of children in the preschool years, school years, and adolescent years brings the problems of values, peer relationships, preparation for careers, the generation gap, and many other sensitive issues. Children leaving home create the well-known "empty nest syndrome." Aging families must face retirement, loss of income, separation from children, sickness, and finally the death of a spouse.

Though marriage is typical in our society, there are also a large number of persons who are not married. Many persons remain unmarried throughout their adult lives for various reasons. This group is increasing in the population. There are persons who are separated and divorced, widows and widowers, and single parents. Many groups in society have given increasing attention to these persons in recent years. Research has shown the painful experience that divorce and separation is for such individuals. These difficult transitions entail change in status and resocialization. Widowhood is marked for many by loneliness as a central experience.

Adult religious education to be truly effective must show an awareness of patterns, cycles, and problems that families face in contemporary society. Not all issues pertaining to family are educational ones. Very often family and family-related problems call for individual, family, or group counseling. Yet all adult religious education must be seen as family oriented in the sense that education is directed to individuals as they actually are. Most adults live in some form of family. It is interesting how often in religious discussion groups persons bring up family concerns, most often relating to children. In a religious book club that I presently conduct nearly every session contains some discussion of the relevance of the book's insights to family situations.

Not only is the family a general context and frame of reference in which adult religious education takes place, but it also provides a valuable part of the scope or content. The decision of the

Roman Catholic Bishops to designate the 1980s as the year of the family is a response to a need not only in the Catholic community but also in the general community. For sure, many groups and organizations of society are deeply interested in problems and issues that pertain to the family. In this area, as in many other areas, only a cooperative effort among many organizations and professions in society can adequately address the problem.

The U.S. Catholic Bishops' *A Vision and Strategy* (United States Catholic Conference, 1978) is a plan for family ministry that shows an awareness of the many forms of families that currently exist in our culture. No longer should the nuclear family dominate the thinking of religious bodies. Special attention is given to "hurting families" in this pastoral plan. The concerns and needs of single parents are also recognized.

Successful adult religious education at the local church level will always include a strong component on family and parent education. The distinction between education and therapy is not always easy to maintain, but certainly education has a legitimate role to play in dealing with families. In any case educational efforts must be realistic in assessing the actual situation that exists among families in the particular culture.

At the present time in many religious bodies some tensions exist between adult educators and family life or counseling personnel. The latter tend to come from a counseling orientation. Efforts have to be made at regional levels to coordinate activities between the two groups. There are obvious areas of overlap between the two endeavors since both include education as an essential component and both are directed at basically the same clientele. The future of work by religious bodies in the area of family will depend on cooperative efforts between educators and counselors in dealing with the problems that families face in our society.

The Conditions of Social Class

An important element that constitutes the context of adult religious education is social class. Studies have shown that white-collar workers and educated persons are well-represented in adult education activities. Blue-collar workers and members of the lower socioeconomic classes are not highly represented among adult learners. These facts present a challenge to adult religious educators, who should attempt to meet the needs of persons of all social classes.

Social classes are usually determined by income, education, and occupational prestige. Social classes are also distinguished by *life space*—the scope and complexity of the social environment of the person: network of friends and acquaintances with whom regular contact is maintained. *Life-style* refers to the quality of those interactions as reflected in the individual's specific interests, activities, and commitments (Knox, 1977, p. 59).

The life-style of the blue-collar worker revolves around work, home, and informal activities with family, friends, and neighbors. This worker pays little attention to national or international issues and problems. Rubin (1976) has carefully described the life of members of this class in her study of working-class families. Rubin was directly concerned with class differences between working-class and middle-class families. She discovered different ways of being in the family, different child-rearing patterns, and different orientations toward work and leisure. Her book is a persuasive argument for changing the socioeconomic realities that bring about such situations. Though she found evidence of some good times in these families, she contends that these were exceptional. She concludes on this note: "For, in fact, in the working class, the process of building a family, of making a living for it, of nurturing and maintaining the individuals in it costs worlds of pain (Rubin, 1976, p. 215)."

Another perceptive observer of class difference among adults is the psychologist Robert Coles. In his article on work and self-respect among the working classes (1978), he points out some of the main characteristics of this class in a tone less accusing of society than Rubin's. Working-class persons have family and religion as main concerns. Adulthood for them means growing up. Work entails the exertion of great energy and thus to be adult means to be hard-working, dedicated, and self-sacrificing without demonstrations of self-pity. Being adult means to be busy, to have found a mission in life, a purpose: the bills are to be paid and the children raised.

In Coles's interpretation working-class life is clearly a mixture of Christian fatalism and acquiescence to the prevailing social and economic system. He explicitly rejects the Marxist view, which

Rubin appears to accept, that the working class is necessarily alienated from work and society. Coles comments on the life of the working class:

> Freud's emphasis upon "love and work" as criteria for a person's relative normality and maturity is quite in keeping with the stress put on both by these not especially psychologically minded men and women, who almost never gauge their own "success" as persons without reference to their jobs and their family life: does he or she work well and hard, no matter what the job pays, status or demands, and does he or she have a good family to come home to (Coles, 1978, p. 225).

Adult religious educators need to be more sensitive to issues of working-class participation in educational programs. This can be done at a number of levels. Programs need to focus on concerns that are of interest to all members of society. Issues such as family, work, leisure time, religion, parenting, and the search for meaning in life need to be explored. But beyond this, education needs to develop a critical consciousness among all members of society concerning social and economic conditions that produce alienation from the structures and powers of society. An educational method that proposes to do this is the method of conscientization developed by Paulo Freire (1970) which is described in another chapter of this book.

Other things can be done to make educational programs appealing to all classes of society. Some suggestions are given in the chapter on program planning. For the moment it should be noted that attention should be paid to the physical, personal, and institutional climate within which education takes place. Programs should be conducted and advertised in such a manner that their appeal is clearly to all members of the organization.

Effects of Living Environment on Adults

Though the major factors in the general social context for adult religious education—demographic changes, family life, world of work, and social class—have been treated, a number of other factors can at least be mentioned briefly. One factor that can be considered is the effect of the living environment upon adult learning in our society.

Research has been reported on the effects of various living arrangements on adult learning. Knox (1977, pp. 62ff) reports on the effects of *college campuses* on young adults. Generally the life chances of an individual—richness of available opportunities—are increased by attendance at college. College has an impact on students who are open to the experience. In colleges students tend to become less authoritarian, less dogmatic, less prejudiced, more conservative towards public issues, and more sensitive to aesthetic experiences. There is also evidence that commitment to religious institutions decreases. Yankelovich (1975) reports that research on the young college and non-college student populations shows minor differences between the two. In his analysis of studies over the past decades he has discovered a trend among younger adults, somewhat higher among college students, for greater freedom in sexuality, a distaste for authority, greater religious individualism, and reduced patriotism. His studies also show that after the 1960s the political attitudes of college students have become less radical. Little research exists on the effects of college on older adults who attend them.

A second environment that influences adult learning is *the middle-aged household*. Research indicates that it has a number of characteristics that are positively associated with adult learning and development: an expectation of growth and development, familiarity with a number of adult role models, availability of learning resources in the home, awareness of opportunities for learning outside the home, and involvement by children in the learning activities of parents (Knox, 1977, pp. 66-67). What is found in this research pertains more to middle-class families than to lower-class families. Differences also exist where there are no children present, or only a single parent, or the presence of elderly persons in the home.

Finally, *housing for the elderly* takes many forms in our society. In past years there were three arrangements: maintaining one's home, moving in with family, or going to the old folks' home. Today there are other possibilities: retirement hotels, public housing, and retirement communities. Each of these forms has advantages and disadvantages for adult learning and development. Options are greater for those who can afford them, but many of the aged are poor and have limited opportunities. Those with higher levels of education and good health are better able to cope with living arrangements and other problems. One issue that is raised concerning living arrangements for the elderly is the extent to which they foster docility and prevent individual vigor and competence. Institutionalization often has the effect of programming people and thus not providing for their individual development.

Practitioners in adult religious education need to take account of the effects of these and other living environments on adult religious learning and development. Those who have worked with college students are keenly aware of the effects that the college environment with its peer pressure, academic and social life, and expectations has on the young adults who live there. It is not to be assumed that this environment will always be detrimental to religious learning and growth. Many young students have experienced religious awakening during their college years. Much depends on the quality of religious life on the campus, the previous religious experience of the students, and the particular values that motivate students during these years.

Young adults are also found in environments other than college campuses. Unfortunately, these environments have not lent themselves to the researchers' scrutiny. Young adults live at home with their parents, take apartments of their own, enter marriage and begin to raise a family, or serve a number of years in military service. The challenge of developing an approach to meet the religious needs of these adults has been felt with increasing urgency in recent years.

Without a doubt, it is the middle-aged household that has received most attention from adult educators, including adult religious educators. Most programs, until rather recently, were developed with a view to meeting the needs of these households. What adult educators in religious communities need to be more attentive to are the varied needs of these households and the particular needs of households such as those headed by single parents, those without children, and those with elderly persons. Adults can be assisted to greater development if educators have a sensitivity to the varieties of arrangements that exist and call forth different responses from religious communities.

One of the greatest challenges for adult religious educators is dealing with the educational needs of the elderly, given the various living situations in which they are now found. The question is obviously broader than an educational one; but certainly the work of religious education and pastoral care of the elderly must adapt itself to the various arrangements in which the elderly are found in our society.

In summary, these are a number of the general social factors that help to constitute the context for adult religious education. Obviously, not all the social factors can be considered but demography, family, work, social class, and living environment would appear to be essential factors. We now turn to a number of social factors that are particular to religious communities and groups that more immediately form the context for adult religious education.

THE SOCIAL CONTEXT OF RELIGIOUS INSTITUTIONS

Adult religious education takes place in the social context of religious institutions and organizations. The field of sociology of religion has studied the social contexts in which religious persons live out their religious commitments. In this section a number of cultural factors specific to religious organizations and communities will be examined.

A Typology of Religious Organizations

The various types of religious organizations that are found in contemporary society have been described by Hargrove (1979). The classification she has developed includes primitive or folk religion, archaic religion, historical religion, early modern religion, and modern religion. Her work combines the work of Bellah on religious evolution (1970) with Wallace's typology of religions (1948).

Expressions of *primitive or folk religion* exist not only in pre-literate societies but also in many contemporary forms of religious behavior. Primitive religious elements include the distinction between sacred and profane; the notions of soul, spirits, and mythic personalities; ascetic cults; rites of communion, initiation, commemoration, and expiation. This form of religion finds its manifestation in three types of cults. *Individualistic cults* include private magical actions such as using a magical charm and private reading of sacred literature. *Shamanic cult institutions* are organized around faith leaders. Often in this country the shamanistic faith healer had added some practice or language of psychiatry. *Communal cult institutions* are organized around families, kinship groups, locality groups, and national groups. Activities include family prayer, celebrations of funerals, weddings, births, deaths, and other significant events in the life of the group. This form of religion is most open to losing the religious dimension of events and of the rites celebrating them. Communal religion easily comes under the influence of secularizing tendencies in a culture.

In this form of religion the major concern is with expressions of personal and corporate values, desires, and emotions. A common theology is less important. Religion is something to be used in personal or group crises. What some scholars in this country have called American civil religion has a number of elements of primitive religion in its organization and expression. Certain holidays such as Memorial Day, Thanksgiving Day, and Independence Day are celebrated with a certain degree of religiosity. The purposes of these celebrations are the promotion of such values as national unity, patriotism, and group solidarity (Bellah, 1970).

A second form of religious organization is found in *archaic religion* in which there is a greater differentiation between the human and the divine. The great gap between gods and humanity is filled through sacrifices and sacraments. Various social groups in society have their own gods as in ancient Greece and Rome. An organized priesthood is found in charge of the cultic worship.

Vallier (1970) in a study of Latin American Christian religions contended that archaic religion is prevalent there. The two-class society has given rise to two forms of religion. Alongside the official church worship and religion there exists a folk Catholicism among rural and lower-class poor. The official priests and cult remain largely inaccessible to these groups. The main focus of these groups is upon extrasacramental communal units. The effort to form basic Christian communities in Latin America, and to a lesser degree in North America, is an effort to respond to this sociological phenomenon. These small groups meet for purposes of prayer, mutual support, and common action in society.

Historic religion as realized in the established national church is the third form of religious organization. The god who is worshipped is usually a single being who rules over lesser deities. The transcendent world has preeminence over present experience. The social organization of the church is found in a hierarchical priesthood. The medieval Christian Church was the clearest expression of this form of organization. The religious organization became extensive with the society but was well differentiated from family, economy, and government. Hinduism, Buddhism, Islam, and Judaism have also developed as historical religions.

Changes within the historic religions have led to the next two forms of religious organization. *Early modern religion* takes the form of the sect. The sect first developed within Protestantism. The members of a sect refuse to accept the mediation of the official church and attempt to confront the divinity directly. In religious organization the sect is not coextensive with society and is not committed to its ideals. It is more of a voluntary association. Sects often tend to be other worldly. Sociologically sects develop among the disinherited, i.e., among those who feel in some way deprived—economically, socially, ethically, or psychologically. Sects provide moral discipline, a strong sense of fellowship, and social mobility. Niebuhr (1928) has shown the influence of social forces in the development of sects in American Protestantism. Wilson (1967) has developed a typology of sects according to whether they seek individual conversion (conversionist), great social change (revolutionist), withdrawal from the evil society (introversionist), or power and domination over others (manipulationist).

An interesting phenomenon in the development of religious groups in the United States has been documented by Greeley (1972). He contends that in this country sects grew not into churches because there is no possibility of an established church. They have rather become denominations, taking on the characteristics of bureaucracies—rationalized types of organization. Denominations have many of the characteristics of organized churches. They have abandoned sectarian stands in theology and social life. They no longer live in tension with the established powers and norms of society.

The final form of religious organization is *modern religion*. In Bellah's description of this form, religious organizations provide only the environments within which persons work out their own ultimate solutions to religious and spiritual problems. A new understanding of self is found in modern religions. Bellah describes the progression:

> The historic religions discovered the self; the early modern religion found a doctrinal basis on which to accept the self in all its empirical ambiguity; the modern religion is beginning to understand the self's own existence and so to help man take responsibility for his own fate (Bellah, 1970, pp. 371-373).

The intellectual foundations for this dimension of self-responsibility in modern religion are found in the theological writings of Paul Tillich, Dietrick Bonhoeffer, Harvey Cox, and other liberal theologians. In modern religion all assumptions are treated as tentative, including religious assumptions.

Organizationally, religions in the modern spirit began to coalesce into large organizations. Denominational reunion has become an important issue for many religious bodies. However, in the living spirit of modern religion the person's religious denomination takes on less significance. The traditional churches turn from places where ultimate meaning is sought to places where persons can become actualized. Such popular programs as Genesis II, Romans VIII, and other humanistically oriented adult learning are manifestations of this trend. Greeley's description of the "communal Catholic" fits in with this description of modern religion (Greeley, 1976).

In certain forms of modern religion the most acceptable institution of religion may again become the cult: the loosely organized group of adults with some leadership, less concern with beliefs, a sense of religious fellowship, and an eclectic universalism. However, modern religion of this type faces a number of dangers. It may be commercialized or prepackaged for particular groups. It can also be privatized by being relegated to only the private areas of life. There also exists the danger of mere ritualization where religion is isolated from the great issues of society and becomes part of the narcissistic culture analyzed by Lasch (1979).

It should be obvious that adult religious education differs according to the type of religious organization in which it takes place. In all forms of religious organization, however, some form of adult education will take place. In primitive and archaic religions some information must be possessed about particular cultic forms or rituals. It was in the great historic religions that education as a separate function of religion clearly developed. Learning was organized around classes for adults and then for children. Specific doctrines, ethical practices, and ritual observances are to be passed on. Early modern or sectarian religion also has used educational forms in the development of group identity and solidarity. Emotional or revivalistic forms of education prevail among sectarians, alongside traditional transmission of religious teachings. Finally, it would seem that adult religious education will take on added importance as modern religious forms begin to prevail in various cultures. With greater self-responsibility for decision making in the religious sphere comes the need for greater learning. The freedom to dissent from authoritative pronouncements of religious bodies on what to believe or how to behave entails the responsibility to seek the truth through one's own efforts or in conjunction with others.

Adult Religious Education in Modern Religious Bodies

The changes which have taken place in the *governance* of modern religious organizations necessitate more adult religious education. For example, in Roman Catholicism the introduction of the principle of shared authority or collegiality by Vatican II has created the need for more knowledge about church doctrines and practices at all levels of church life. All members of the church from ordinary parishioners to church leaders have involved themselves in educational efforts. It is now clear that the apparently simple structural change of introducing parish or diocesan councils entails an effort in adult religious education to equip members of these groups with the necessary knowledge to fulfill their functions competently. A similar phenomenon has prevailed in Protestant and Jewish religious bodies where ordinary members have had more power and control and thus have needed more knowledge.

An area of church life that has undergone change in recent years is *liturgy or worship*. Esoteric and clericalized worship in religious bodies has given way to more popular forms of worship which include more participation by all members of the church. Contemporary cultural forms have been introduced into worship services. More participation in worship and the joining of traditional forms with contemporary forms of worship have called for an education of all members of churches, both leaders and ordinary members. In religious bodies changes in worship have been accompanied by serious efforts in educating adult members about the theological meaning of worship rites. It is clear that efforts in this area need to be continued as worship takes on a life of its own and does not become fixed in changeless forms.

One of the chief changes in modern religion relates to the *doctrinal* or belief dimension of religious life. In modern religions the concept of doctrinal pluralism has been widely accepted. One of the major achievements of the Second Vatican Council was the acceptance of the distinction between the faith of Christians and the relative and culturally conditioned modes of expression of this faith. In theology today no one school prevails in either Catholicism or Protestantism. Pluralism in Judaism has long been a distinctive characteristic. Doctrinal positions are viewed as culturally conditioned statements that do not exhaust the mystery of religious faith that they interpret.

The doctrinal pluralism of modern religions increases the need for more intensive adult education among the members. The roles of doctrines or beliefs in modern religions are less the touchstones of orthodoxy as they are opportunities for individuals and communities to have some basis for their own thinking through and developing of personal and communal meaning systems. Knowledge of what religious persons have believed in the past and interpretations of these beliefs in the present are helpful for persons who are honestly searching for religious truth. It is only through serious education in adult life that individuals are capable of balancing traditional doctrinal positions with personal searches for religious meaning.

Anyone familiar with modern religious bodies knows that it is the area of *morality* that has witnessed the greatest changes among religious persons. Many national polls have shown that there is often a great amount of dissent among church members from the official positions of the leadership of religious bodies. Many have begun to look to church leadership not as an authority but as a guide in the moral sphere of life. The principle of individual freedom and responsibility has often been enunciated in moral teachings but it is usually connected with the injunction to submit to the authoritative teachings of the religious bodies.

It is clear that with the passing of an absolutist morality and the development of situational or presumptive moralities (Wogaman, 1976) there is greater need for adult religious education in religious bodies. Education in this area needs to take account of the many factors that are involved in moral decision making. Though religious bodies can no longer function for many persons as binding authorities, there is much that they can do for their members if they are willing to engage them in serious efforts at bringing religious traditions and principles to bear on moral issues and problems.

Another major change on the religious scene in this culture relates to the current emphasis on *personal and communal spirituality*. Some forms of religion in North American culture are more connected with movements of personal and individual liberation than with movements for social and political change in the culture. Personal spiritual devotions, Bible prayer groups, communal spiritual activities, serious reading and discussion of spirtual classics of both East and West, are some of the manifestations of this religious revival. Some have characterized this time as the Third Religious Awakening in United States history. Though a judgment on this recent awakening is difficult with our present perspective, anyone familiar with the contemporary religious scene can attest to the increased emphasis on spirituality.

Though the current interest in spirituality has been given a number of interpretations—narcissism, retreat from the social gospel, neo-conservatism, or search for personal and communal space in mass society—it is clear that the movement has implications for adult religious education. Many persons approach religious education with a hunger for ideas, attitudes, values, and experiences that will challenge them at a spiritual level. Intellectual discussions must lead to personal grappling for meaning in religious terms. There is an obvious danger of non-intellectualism or anti-intellectualism lurking in this current spirituality movement. Educators who are aware of this danger are best prepared to deal seriously with the more spiritual aspects of adult religious education.

A final change in religious bodies is the increased attention to *social and political action.* The move toward a more socially relevant religious faith began in the 1960s around civil rights, war and peace, ecology, and other major social issues. Challenging theologies of a political nature have been developed that see the major thrust of religion in its involvement in movements for social change. Black theology, feminist theology, and ecological theologies have arisen in opposition to the traditional theologies which dealt with but did not make social and political action major concerns for religious bodies. Religious traditions have been reexamined for politically liberating symbols, stories, teachings, and events. While social and political action developed in liberal religious bodies in the 1970s, in the 1980s conservative churches have become deeply involved in these issues.

It is clear that this new thrust has importance for adult religious education. Sociological and political analysis needs to become equally central with the teachings of the religious traditions. The complex issues that religious bodies deal with in this sphere—nuclear disarmament, abortion, laws on homosexuality, housing, etc.—have deep emotional overtones and are potentially divisive, as many religious bodies have discovered. The qualities of the educational process—rationality, understanding, examination of evidence, openness to differing viewpoints, and the patient search for the truth—are essential for political adult education.

The changes in governance, worship, doctrines, morality, spirituality, and social theology that have taken place in religious bodies form part of the social context in which adult religious education takes place. What may prove to be of more significance for adult religious education in the future may be the emergence of new religious movements among those who feel themselves alienated from traditional religious bodies, even if these have become modern. It is to a consideration of these movements that we now turn.

New Religious Movements and Adult Religious Education

Persons who experience a discrepancy between their own goals and the goals of their culture respond in a number of ways. They may simply conform to the cultural goals, conform to them in an innovative manner, go through the motions or rituals without inner meaning, or rebel against the cultural goals by positing new goals and new means of achieving these goals (Merton, 1968, pp. 185ss). This general theory of social deviance helps to explain some of the contemporary developments in religious movements. These movements are characterized by various degrees of conformity, innovation, ritualization, or rebellion.

Hargrove's analysis of the present religious situation is in terms of the temptation to lose faith. In the face of such a temptation persons have three solutions open to them: permanent uncommitment or loss of faith and alienation from any faith system; the creation of changes in symbol systems which make it possible to live in the changed environment, either through social reformism or charismatic activity; or an overcommitment to the present system through intensified religious activities (Hargrove, 1979, p. 284). This analysis is an extension of Merton's ideas into the sphere of religion.

The attempt of religious bodies to reach those who have *"lost faith" or become alienated* has intensified in recent years. What must be realized is that some who have become alienated from religion have embraced various forms of secularistic faith based on forms of humanistic psychology, such as the human potential movement, encounter groups, sensitivity groups, Transcendental Meditation, and Dianetics or Scientology. Where many in the past have turned to religious groups for personal salvation, a secular salvation is sought through different groups that have developed in our culture. Efforts of religious bodies to reach those who have turned to forms of secular salvation must come to terms with the power of humanistic forms of life over the individuals who are involved in them.

The second response to alienation from religion is *the innovative attempt to develop new symbol systems*. This innovation usually takes the form of the development of new cults. Many young and middle-aged adults in our culture have turned to new cultic forms of religious faith. Many of these cults are of Eastern origin. Cults tend to proliferate in times of cultural stress. Wallis has described the chief characteristic of cults. They are composed of seekers of salvation. They are typically service-oriented, offering experience or special knowledge. Thus charisma is dispersed throughout the group. Also, cults face the problem of commitment, for by definition they are the one way to salvation, and thus in time cults experience from members passive and limited commitment, apathy, and declining adherence (Wallis, 1977, p. 13).

Cults that succeed over a period of time do so because they are successful in becoming sects. Hargrove reports the research of James Richardson which outlines a number of factors essential in this process: strong leadership, definite boundaries between members and non-members, strong commitment by members, a sense of a need for order and an ethic binding members, and external pressures to become more acceptable to the greater society of which the cult is a part (Hargrove, 1979, pp. 280-281).

Adult religious educators need to be aware of the cultural situation that gives rise to cults and sects in society. Especially those who work with young adults need a sensitivity to the deeply personal experiences and meaning that persons involved in these cults seek. It is not to be expected that established religious bodies can meet all the spiritual needs of their younger members especially in times of great cultural stress. However, serious efforts should be made by the leadership of religious bodies to understand the nature and attraction of these cults and sects and to engage young adults in serious dialogue about them. Adult religious education which merely presents official teaching without allowing the freedom to explore and study cannot hope to meet the needs of many who want greater freedom and diversity in religious experience.

The third religious response to cultural change is *an increased or overcommitment to one's present religious body and its system of beliefs and rituals*. The movement of evangelical Christianity in North America is an example of such a response. Quebedeaux (1978) has stated the three basic theological principles of evangelical Christianity:

> 1. the full authority of Scriptures in matters of faith and practice; 2. the necessity of personal faith in Jesus Christ as Savior and Lord (conversion); and 3. the urgency of seeking the conversion of sinful men and women to Christ (evangelism) (p. 7).

Quebedeaux states that by sheer numbers evangelicism must be considered the mainline form of American Christianity since it includes at least 18 percent of the population.

Evangelical Christianity should not be viewed as all of one piece. Five different types have been distinguished. *Separatist fundamentalism* is found among the most overcommitted and has appeared in nativistic movements which attempt to concentrate on particular values that face a challenge. *Closed fundamentalism* is linked with certain movements of the far political right such as Carl McIntyre's American Council of Churches and Billy James Hargis's Christian Crusade. *Open fundamentalism* is more apolitical and more open to different life-styles as found in the Jesus movement. *Establishment evangelicism* is represented by such groups as the Missouri Synod and the Baptist Churches. Billy Graham is the foremost leader in this wing of evangelical Christianity. Another type of evangelical Christianity is found in the *charismatic movement*. This is both related to and separate from old-line Protestant Pentecostalism. As it exists today it is a middle-class phenomenon, found primarily within mainline Protestant and Catholic Churches. The focus in this movement is upon religious experience, baptism of the spirit, prophecy, healing, and speaking with tongues (Hargrove, 1979, pp. 283-286).

The charismatic movement in this classification represents a bridge to religious movements that come not out of alienation from traditional forms of religion but from *anomie*, the feeling that the social environment does not supply adequate social support for individuals to develop their own life-styles. The charismatic movement represents a politically conservative response in its attempt to establish clear goals and means to achieve these goals. Members no longer want to depend upon a vague divine inspiration but rather seek official guidance through "Life in the Spirit Seminars." Within the movement, charismatic leaders have developed, similar to shamans or prophets. Though denominations have attempted to maintain good relationships with charismatic groups, tensions do exist between the traditional church structures and the perceived experiences of the members. In some groups a strong authoritative structure has developed to meet the needs and goals of members. With the development of such strong authority figures the possibility of change from cult to sect becomes strong.

Anyone who attempts to do adult religious education at the local church level today comes face to face with members of religious bodies who are evangelically oriented in their religious faith and experience. Educators are likely to meet members of charismatic movements. Though these persons do have educational opportunities within their own groups—when organized outside official church structures—they often look for educational activities at local churches. It must be admitted honestly that at times they attend in order to convince others of the value of the religious movement they have embraced. At other times they bring healthy experiential concerns to the educational processes. Charismatics have great interest in adult education that focuses upon reading and praying the Scriptures and programs of personal spiritual growth. Adult educators face the challenge of interesting charismatics in other dimension of religious teachings.

A number of more sect-like groups have developed in the United States that respond to a basic feeling of lack of clear goals and means to achieve these goals. L. Ron Hubbard's Church of Scientology has developed tight doctrinal and organizational structures. Internal problems within the group and external pressures over fund raising techniques have brought about greater internal discipline and more demarcation from the general society. These are some of the forces that move a group from a cult to a sect. This church has become highly bureaucratized in its process of change from a cult which offered techniques by which people could be better able to function in daily life to a tightly organized religion.

The extreme of the sectarian response is found in the tragic James Jones's People's Temple. At the time of the startling mass suicide by members, the Temple was under centralized and authoritarian leadership, its members possessed the highest levels of commitment, and rigid boundaries were maintained. The group was made up of many who were deprived economically, socially, and psychologically. Though in the beginning the movement was greatly interested in social reform, in the end this goal was totally subordinated to maintaining group identity and solidarity.

Another religious group that has attracted many young adults from mainline Protestant and Catholic churches is the Unification Church of Sun Myung Moon. Young people who appear to be lonely are attracted to this group by the friendliness and concern of its members. Membership provides identity and a caring group.

This movement has strong political motivation, of which young members are not always aware. It is militantly anti-Communist and in the activity of its youthful zealots, it resembles a medieval Children's Crusade. Academic conferences have been sponsored by the church in order to acquaint outsiders with the beliefs of the church. Charges of brainwashing have been made against the church and well-publicized efforts have been made at "deprogramming" members.

Of all the sectarian religious responses perhaps the most interesting is "New Evangelicals" or radical evangelicals. This group offers a distinctive combination of traditional evangelical theology with radical social concern. Members often live in communes for social support and for demonstrating a life-style that is concerned about ecological and environmental excesses. They criticize liberal churches for their lack of clear theology and conservative churches for their failure to be socially concened and active in struggles against injustice. The ideas of this group are circulated through journals such as *Sojourners, Radix,* and *The Other Side*. The group is not large but its potential appears great since it challenges both liberal and conservative religious bodies. The group has maintained ties to insititutional Christianity and feels committed to its transformation. Thus a potential for broad revitalization exists within the group that is not present in other sectarian responses. Little evidence exists yet that such revitalization is taking place, but the movement is still young in its development.

CONCLUSION

To be truly effective adult religious education must be sensitive to the social context within which education takes place. In this chapter an attempt has been made to sketch some of the salient features of this cultural context. In the first part of this chapter characteristics of the general social context were explored. The nature of the population that is to be served was carefully examined. That the population has increasingly become heterogenous, urbanized, geographically mobile, older, and more educated has implications for adult education in religious bodies. A variety of forms of adult religious education must be developed to meet the needs of this population.

The changed condition of work, changes in family life, differences in social class, and changes in living environments are also important factors to be considered in the educational ministry of religious bodies. Religious education has rarely succeeded in grappling with issues relating to work. Changes in family structure and living call forth more creative responses from church bodies. Social class differences are real in the population. Adult education which has succeeded well among educated classes faces the challenge of reaching other social, racial, and economic groups. Finally, changes in the living environments of young adults, middle-aged persons, and the elderly call for adult education efforts that are sensitive to the particular environment in which people live.

Besides these social factors of a general nature, adult religious educators need also to be sensitive to certain social factors that relate particularly to religious bodies. Sociologists of religion have described a number of forms of religion that are found in contemporary culture. Elements of primitive and archaic religion exist in the culture, though these are not predominant forms. In this country where there is no established church, religious bodies are found in the form of denominations, sects, and cults. These three types of religious bodies differ in theology and organizational patterns. Modern religious bodies are thus highly complex in their social organizations and in the religious life of their members.

It is difficult to prescribe a single mode of adult religious education that would suit the different religious bodies found in this culture. Educational goals, values, needs, and life-styles of members of these bodies are highly diverse. Each group chooses the type of religious education that appears best suited to meet the needs of the group. Educators need to be aware of the traditions and social environments of the particular groups in which they work.

Though the social context is important in determining the forms of adult religious education, it alone does not supply adult educators with all they need to know to do effective programming. This awareness of social context must be supplemented by a knowledge of adult developmental theory and research and an understanding of adult learning theory. It is to these two areas of knowledge that we turn in the next two chapters.

CHAPTER III

DEVELOPMENT IN ADULTHOOD
PSYCHOLOGICAL AND RELIGIOUS

When developmental psychology is mentioned, a person usually thinks of theory and research on the cognitive, emotional, moral, and religious development of children and adolescents. Until recently development psychology has largely been restricted to the study of pre-adults. In the past two decades, however, psychologists and social psychologists have given increasingly more attention to development throughout the adult years. Much of this work reached the general public through the best-selling work of Gail Sheehy, *Passages: Predictable Crises of Adult Life* (1976). Since then a number of other works have appeared on this topic. It is clear that for many years to come we can expect more theory and research in the area of adult development.

The theory and practice of adult religios education need a strong grounding in adult developmental psychology. Just as the religious education of children and adolescents has been strengthened by the understandings that have come from developmentalists, so the religious education of adults can be improved by an awareness of the various developmental changes that adults undergo in their lives. Knowledge about the transitions from adolescence to young adulthood, from young adulthood to middle adulthood, and from middle adulthood to advanced adulthood is especially valuable for religious educators who want to develop programs to help adults through these transitions.

The purpose of this chapter is to review some of the significant theory and research in this area. Emphasis will be given to that research which has implications for religious education. Research specifically on the religious aspects of adult development is just beginning. Thus for the most part in this chapter implications will be drawn from the general research on adult development. Drawing such implications is legitimate for no clear-cut distinction can be made between the religious and non-religious spheres of life.

The approach in this chapter will be basically chronological. There are advantages and disadvantages to proceeding in this manner. The main advantage is that a focusing on one age group at a time gives a unified picture of the developmental challenges faced at that period. The chief disadvantage is that the developmental theorists will be presented in piecemeal fashion, for the findings of the researchers will be presented in different parts of the chapter. It is felt that the value of a concentrated look at an age group is of more advantage than the unified views of a number of development theorists.

The concept of development is one that comes from the biological and psychological sciences. Though the concept may be appropriate for describing religious or faith growth, a more fitting image for describing religious development might be *life story* or *life journey*. These latter images emphasize the personal, existential, and dramatic dimensions of human growth and change. Before treating the particular aspects of the religious journey of adults at the various stages of life, it might be helpful to get some clarity on such crucial concepts as religious faith and religious journey.

RELIGIOUS FAITH AND JOURNEY

Though religious faith can be viewed as an activity in which a person engages, it is better viewed as the personal story of an individual or a religious journey that a person travels with God, self, and others. The story and the journey are difficult ones because their ways, paths, perils, and final destination are not clearly known. One gets the strength to travel the religious journey because of the realization that one does not travel alone. Many millions of religious persons have traveled through this life before, aided by a spiritual vision. Also, persons of faith usually have the support of others in their religious journeys.

Religious or spiritual life is lived in a believing, worshipping, and loving community. To have religious faith is to have an understanding of self, world, others, and life-events in which one sees more than appears on the surface. Religious life is lived with the explicit consciousness that within all known reality and besides all experienced reality there is a reality that both exists in and transcends what we ordinarily experience. In Western religions this reality is encountered and addressed as the person of God.

Religious persons realize that no convincing proof can be given to non-religious persons for the existence of the person they address as God. This in no way diminishes for them the reality of this person. Faith is validated or confirmed in a number of ways. Some appeal to personal experience of the holy or sacred in their lives. Others attempt to give some reasons for the faith that they possess. Others put their faith in the religious revelation of founders of great religions. No matter what the reasons given for living the life of faith, the decision to believe is a deeply personal one that influences all aspects of life.

Religious faith not only gives an understanding of human life; it also provides basic and fundamental attitudes and values which shape responses to life events. Faith entails moral and ethical commitments that are based on religious grounds. It demands a commitment to a way of life which is presented in religious literature and traditions as consonant with the major values of the founders and chief leaders of the religious way of life embraced.

Though religious faiths provide for their members clear meaning systems and coherent codes of values, there is much that remains unclear and unresolvable in religious faiths and ethical systems dependent upon them. Religious bodies that attempt to provide simple answers to all problems of meaning and behavior do an injustice to the complexity of human life and provide false hope for their adherents. As will be seen in a later section of this chapter, the ability to live a life of faith without absolute certainty is one of the characteristics of mature religious faith.

A good model for viewing the life of faith is provided in the concept of human relationships. We grow and develop in our relationships with one another. Our lives together are often a series of conversions from one level of relationship to another. In personal relationships not all is positive growth. There are times of regression, pain, conflict, and confrontation. These times may prevent further growth or they may be occasions for deeper insight and appreciation. So it is in spiritual life. Light and darkness, joy and sorrow, growth and regression are part of the story and journey. What distinguishes the life of religious faith from our ordinary human relationships is the experience of the loving fidelity of God in the face of human weakness and rejection. This is the experience of the grace of God for those who live the life of religious faith.

The journey of faith is a dimension of the human journey. Faith development and psychosocial development are not separate and opposed concepts. Also, they are not to be seen as identical. How faith is related to other dimensions of human life is a theological problem to which many solutions have been given. Attempts are made to build syntheses between faith and ordinary human life. A more appealing approach is to see the relationship between the two in a tension-bearing and paradoxical relationship. In this view faith at times makes demands that go counter to what persons naturally desire. Another way to see the relationship is to see faith as a power that transforms or changes ordinary human life by accepting what is good in it and bringing it to fuller development by adding the dimensions of depth and the holy to what is common and ordinary.

What we refer to as psychosocial development refers to the development of physical, intellectual, emotional, moral, and social capacities of persons. Faith development is included in all these forms of development but it is also attentive to the dimension of the holy and the transcendent in all of these human areas of growth. The journey of faith is one in which a life with God colors, influences, and gives deeper meaning to all human activities. All aspects of life's journey are religious. The religious person makes this dimension an explicit one and through this faith transforms all of human life and culture.

THE FAITH JOURNEY OF PRE-ADULTS

While this book is concerned with adult religious education and thus with adult faith development, both of these cannot be separated from development that precedes adult life. There is not a great separation but rather a continuity between the development in adulthood and the development of infants, children, and adolescents. Thus the major areas of faith development in these earlier years will be sketched before giving a fuller treatment to adult faith development.

It is in *infancy* that the journey of faith begins. Psychologists have described the rapid development that takes place physically, cognitively, and emotionally in the first two years of life. According to Erikson, it is at this time that the roots of faith are developed. Religious faith in his view builds upon the trust developed in infants through the loving care of parents. It is upon the loving and trustful relationship with parents that religious faith builds. Faith development at this time is spontaneous and involuntary, and largely undifferentiated from other aspects of human life. Only with later development does faith development have the potential of becoming an explicit and separate dimension of life (Erikson, 1963, p. 249).

Erikson's rooting of the origins of faith in infancy are expressed in powerful words:

> Trust born of care is the touchstone of religion. All religions have the periodical childlike surrender to a Provider of fortune and health; some demonstration of man's smallness by reduced posture and humble gesture, the admission in prayers of misdeeds and evil intentions; fervent prayer for unification by divine guidance; the insight that faith must be a common faith with ritual practice. . . . The clinician can only observe that many are proud to be without religion whose children cannot afford to be without it (Erikson, 1963, p. 250).

Erikson's words remind us that the powerful religious symbol of relating to God as parent originates in childhood and continues throughout life. The appropriateness of this symbol for adult life will be explored later in this chapter.

The life of faith nurtured in infancy comes to conscious expression in *childhood*, when besides physical, emotional, and intellectual development there also appears a development of a consciously religious dimension of life. Psychoanalytically oriented psychologists point to the beginnings of a personal relationship with God through prayer. Erikson relates religious growth to development of autonomy and respect for law, including God's law; the development of initiative in play and fantasy which lays the basis for participation in ritual and mythic stories; and the development of a sense of industry which gives children a sense of competence to act in the broader community, including religious bodies (Erikson, 1963, p. 255).

Extensive research has been done on the religious understanding of children. Goldman's studies report that children pass through three stages in their understanding of the religious: a *pre-religious stage* (before age ten) in which there is no real insight into the religious point of view; a *sub-religious stage* (before the age of thirteen) in which a materialistic, physical, and anthropomorphic religious orientation prevails; a *religious stage* (after age thirteen) in which real religious insight is found. The latter stage is more appropriately an adolescent stage of development (Goldman, 1964).

The most recent research on the faith development of children has been reported by Fowler (1981). He has described two faith stages in childhood. Between the ages of four and seven the faith of the child can be characterized as *intuitive-projective*. Faith is intuitive because the young child engages in immediate knowing and exercises little logical activity. The young child's faith is more a projection of the faith of significant others in the child's life. The faith of the older child (ages seven to eleven) is characterized as *narratizing* or *mythic* faith. At this stage children tend to interpret religious myths, stories, and doctrines in a literal and anthropomorphic manner. At this stage of development they are still largely under the influence of parents and significant others.

Psychologists concerned with religious development have insisted on the importance of childhood for the development of mature religious faith. It is in this period of life that the first images of God are formed. A prayer life develops in children; feelings of guilt and repentence arise. Children come into contact with the reality of suffering, pain, and death. Religious interpretations of life-events are presented and internalized. Children are introduced into the myths, rituals, doctrines, ethics, and organization of religious bodies. The development of positive and healthy religious attitudes during this period are essential for future faith development (Nelsen et al., 1977).

The period of *adolescence* has received great attention from psychologists and sociologists interested in religious development. Research indicates that adolescence is a time of religious awakening, often accompanied by sudden conversion experiences. In psychoanalytic theory this religious awakening is connected with a number of adolescent conflicts. These conflicts center around the increased emotional life of the adolescent, a heightened awareness of personal sin and evil in the world, conflicts between religious faith and sexual impulses and desires, conflicts between religious faith and personal power, and intellectual doubts concerning faith (Gruber, 1957).

The cognitive aspects of adolescent faith have been studied by Goldman (1964) and Fowler (1981). Goldman has found that the adolescent is capable of true religious understanding, especially as this pertains to the myths and symbols of faith. He does note, however, that religious thinking develops later than ordinary thinking, presumably because of the nature of religious experience in which symbols, myths, parables, and allegories abound. Fowler describes typical adolescent faith as *synthetic-conventional*. Faith is synthetic in that it provides a synthesis of beliefs which enables young people to achieve a personal and group identity. Faith is conventional because it is still largely dependent on what the reference group or religious body believes.

Though the research of cognitive developmentalists like Goldman and Fowler gives some understanding of the dynamics of faith development, it is especially the psychoanalytic tradition that provides the richest understanding of the adolescent experience of faith. This tradition explains more fully the dynamics of religious conversion and adolescent rejection of religious faith. In both of these there are elements of a rejection of a former self and an adherence to a new faith or ideology, often embodied in some charismatic person. Writing a number of years ago, Erikson gave reasons for faith rejection by adolescents which are still valid today:

> Young people in crises of faith chose to face nothingness rather than submit to a faith that to them had become a cant of pious words; a collective will that cloaked only collective impotence; a conscience that expended itself in a stickling for empty forms; a reason that was a chatter of commonplaces, and a kind of work that was meaningless busy work (Erikson, 1964, 1958, p. 99).

Of the special religious rituals that are presented to adolescents, Erikson found that "many young people, eager for an image of the future, find the confirmations and ceremonies offered by their parents' churches designed more for parents' uplift than their own good (Erikson, 1958, p. 99)."

In recent years religious bodies have awakened to problems that adolescents experience in religious faith. Potvin (1978) sounded a warning in reporting that it is during the high school years that young people make a decision for or against the religious faith in which they have been socialized. Sensitive to this problem religious bodies have developed programs of ministry to youth during this critical period of religious development.

FAITH DEVELOPMENT IN YOUNG ADULTHOOD

A number of approaches are found among social science attempts to understand development among young adults. Havighurst described developmental tasks that young adults face: learning to live with a marriage partner, starting a family, rearing children, managing a home, getting started in an occupation, taking on civic responsibility, and finding a congenial social group (Havighurst, 1972). In examining these tasks it is clear that the period of young adulthood would roughly span the ages from eighteen to thirty-five or forty. Tasks directly related to religion are not found in Havighurst's list of tasks. This description also presumes that the young adults become married and raise families.

A more appropriate model for examining young adulthood is found in Erikson's treatment of the crises of *identity* and *intimacy*. The first task of young adulthood is to resolve the crisis of identity that was first met in adolescence. An identity crisis has phases or dimensions. First of all, there is some rejection of a past identity, usually one associated with parents. Very often the rejection process entails a rejection of the religion in which one was socialized. Secondly, many young people go through a moratorium stage where they try out various identities without becoming committed to any particular identity or cause. Finally, the identity crisis is resolved when the young person makes some commitment to what Erikson calls an ideology, but which may better be termed a somewhat permanent way of life, meaning system, or set of values (Erikson, 1963, p. 43).

Erikson's research on identity has been developed by Marcia (1967) into a classification schema. Young adults are to be found in one of four categories with regard to achievement of personal identity. They may have neither experienced a crisis nor made any commitment. They may be in the state of acute crisis, or identity diffusion, not having made any form of commitment. Thirdly they may have made commitments without experiencing any type of crisis—what Marcia terms foreclosed identity, since it has not been worked out at a personal level. Finally, the young person may have made a commitment after experiencing a personal crisis. This is the state of achieved identity.

At this point it is important to clarify the meaning that psychoanalytic writers give to the word *crisis*. It is not used in the sense of catastrophe but in the sense of a time of judgment or choice. In young adulthood persons often for the first time experience opportunities for real freedom of choice when they must make decisions for themselves for which they are responsible. These moments of decision can be grouped around the central decision of deciding what one will be and what one will do with one's life. Psychoanalytic writers by using the word crisis emphasize how emotionally charged these decisions are and the contexts in which they are made. Erikson uses the word crisis to mean a "turning point, a crucial period of increased vulnerability and heightened potential (Erikson, 1978, p. 5)." Obviously, the amount of emotional crisis experienced varies among individuals, acute in some and almost nonexistent in others.

The resolution of the identity crisis, according to Erikson, demands the development of what he calls the virtue of fidelity. This he describes as "the ability to sustain loyalty freely pledged, in spite of inevitable contradictions and confusions of value systems (Erikson, 1964, p. 125)." The religious connotations of the terms "virtue of fidelity" are striking. Fidelity entails understanding what one is doing, a freely embarked-upon commitment to do something, and the resolve to do this even though one is aware that one has personal weaknesses and that there are alternative choices that can be made. This interpretation of fidelity closely parallels religious faith: understanding, freedom, commitment and loyalty, personal weakness, and an awareness of alternative faiths or meaning systems. For the religious person the identity crisis entails a crisis of faith, a time to make a free choice about the religious dimension of life.

In a masterful interpretation of Bergman's film *Wild Strawberries*, Erikson reveals the religious dimensions of the identity crisis in young adulthood. Three young people are in the car with Dr. Borg as he travels to get his high honor. In these three young people are represented modern youth in search of something worthy of their awakening sense of loyalty and fidelity. Religious arguments take place during the car trip, as one would expect in a Bergman film. According to Erikson the young people:

> are working hard at defining their identity: one of the two boys wants to become a doctor and plays the atheistic rationalist, the other intends to be a minister and defends God's existence. Both, however, when driven to defense or offense, display a certain naive Cynicism, which is contrary to adolescent fidelity (Erikson, 1978, p. 10).

This essay by Erikson clearly indicates that he sees connections between the psychosocial development of individuals and their approach to religious dimensions of their lives.

The crisis of personal identity in young adulthood is closely connected with what Erikson calls the crisis of *intimacy*. When young adults become increasingly aware of their own personal identity, they also become responsive to the real nature of other persons and the uniqueness of the personality of others. A sign of this change is the shift in relationships with parents to a point where they can now be related to as friends or confidants, rather than merely as parents. In their relationships young adults become more and more selective, tending to concentrate in depth on a small number of relationships.

Related to the search for intimacy in young adulthood is the issue of *sexuality*. Sociological research has shown that there has been an increase in sexual activity among adolescents and young adults in our society (Kimmel, 1980, ch. 4). Thus young people face earlier the issue of how they will relate sexually with others. For Keniston, a psychoanalytic psychologist who continues the Erikson tradition, the sexual task of youth is to achieve "the gradual integration of sexual feelings with a real person" and to work through the fears and prohibitions against sexuality that originated in early childhood by developing a "capacity for genitality, that is, for mutually satisfying sexual relationships with another whom one loves (Keniston, 1970, p. 13)."

The unresolved intimacy crisis leads to isolation in personal relationships. The shying away from personal relationships may lead to promiscuity without intimacy, sex without love, or relationships without any real stability. Persons who have not established strong identities are most likely to experience the detachment and distancing in interpersonal relationships which leads to the "readiness to repudiate, isolate, and, if necessary, destroy those forces and people whose essence seems dangerous to one's own (Erikson, 1958, p. 13)."

The religious significance of the struggle for intimacy in young adulthood is clear. In religious traditions sexuality and intimate human friendship have a quasi-sacred character. Religious traditions resonate with the description Erikson gives to love, the virtue or power which must be developed in order to resolve adequately the crisis of intimacy. For Erikson, "love is the mutuality of devotion forever subduing the antagonisms inherent in divided functions (1968, p. 128)." Erikson takes a broad view of this love when he speaks of "young adulthood with its manifold playful intimacies which must mature into a quality of Intimacy—in friendship, in erotic life, and in work (1978, p. 8)." In identifying love with devotion, and seeing its expression in a number of forms, Erikson has forged a concept of intimacy that religious bodies can utilize in their ministry to young adults.

Before looking specifically at the religious or faith development of young adults, it may be helpful to examine developmental theories that have built upon and refined the Erikson theory of life cycles. Levinson and his associates (1978) have developed a theory of adult development based on the study of forty men from ages thirty-five to forty-five. These men came from four occupational groups: blue- and white-collar workers in industry, business executive, academic biologists, and novelists. His description of stages in young adulthood spans the ages from seventeen to thirty-three or forty.

In Levinson's theory the chief task of young adulthood is the building of a *life structure*, which he describes as the underlying pattern or design of a person's life at a given time. It includes occupation, love relationships, marriage and family, relations to self, use of solitude, roles in various social contexts, and all relationships with individuals, groups, and institutions that have significance for the person. This life structure evolves throughout the person's life.

Young adults typically pass through a number of stages. Between the ages of seventeen and twenty-two there is the early adult transition, in which young adults separate to a degree from their parents by moving out of the home to marry, attend college, enter the military, or begin an occupation. Levinson notes that in some cases a change in religious affiliation may take place at this time. During the ages from twenty-two to twenty-eight young adults build their first life structure in entering the adult world. In this time of relative stability provisional choices are tested, alternatives are searched out, and commitments are increased. Levinson found that a strong personal identity was not achieved until the late twenties. Around age thirty many of the men in the study experienced a crisis of transition. A questioning of the chosen life structure began, accompanied at times with great stress.

According to this research four major tasks arise during the early period of young adulthood. Young adults form and attempt to live out an exciting Dream of what they might become as adults. For men this Dream is associated with a special woman in their lives and with a mentor. The forging of the relationship with the mentor is the second task of young adulthood. A mentor is a sponsor, guide, examplar, counselor, or one who gives moral support. Hennig and Jardim (1976) present evidence that women also have mentors who aid them in their careers. The third task of early young adulthood is the formation of an occupation. Often a number of unsuccessful attempts precede the definitive assuming of an occupation. A final major task defined in the Levinson research is the forming of a marriage and family. This proves to be a difficult task for many young adults, especially those who are attempting to manage careers and raise families at the same time.

Levinson found that the second part of young adulthood, from years thirty-two to forty-one, was a time of settling down and building a second life structure. Five sequences are described for this period: advancement through a stable life structure, serious failure or decline within a stable life structure, attempts at forming a new life structure, advancement that produces a change in life structure, and an unstable life structure. This period ends with the beginning of the midlife crisis, which will be treated in the next section.

The stages of young adulthood reported in Gould's research (1978) in many ways parallel Levinson's work. However, since women were included in his sample, he does bring out a number of issues not found in Levinson's research. As a psychiatrist he is also sensitive to interpreting internal dynamics that occur in young adulthood. He points out the fears that young adults have in facing a life of independence from their parents. Young women especially experience this because society supports the idea that they must be protected throughout their lives. The tension young adults experience is between the need for freedom and separation from parents and the need for the stability and security that the parental family afforded.

The research of Levinson and Gould sheds light on development during young adulthood. However, it touches only lightly on religious or faith development. The research in this area is not extensive but what has been done can be integrated with developmental theory. Fowler (1977) describes the faith of young adults as *individuative-reflexive* which he describes as the attempt:

> to find or create identifications and affiliations with ideologically defined groups whose outlook is expressive of the self one is becoming and has become, and of the truth or truths which have come to provide one's fundamental orientations (1977, p. 199).

Faith at this period can be reflexive in the sense that it is not derivative of the faith of others.

Fowler's research on faith development in young adults can be related to what Simmons (1976) has reported. Simmons suggests that there is a new and distinctive type of faith that becomes possible and even necessary around the age of thirty, when a person enters a new phase of life. This new faith demands an affective autonomy by which young adults move beyond their own needs and have proper views of other persons. It demands a sense of social responsibility, and a commitment to bring about change in the social order. Finally, it demands a community sponsorship and support that present models of what it is to grow up with faith.

In the second half of young adulthood (after age thirty) a higher stage of faith becomes possible. Fowler describes this faith-stage as *paradoxical-consolidative*. This type of faith accepts the tensions between conflicting loyalties, for it accepts paradox as an essential characteristic of all truth. With this faith one can remain committed to a religious vision of life with the realization that it does not answer all questions, and with the awareness of one's own doubts and confusions (Fowler, 1981).

The research that Fowler has done on faith development appears to do justice to a faith that is highly intellectualized. It lacks, however, a grappling with the emotional and social realities that young adults experience in relationships to their religious faith and the religious bodies to which they have been connected. Manno (1979) reports on sociological research which classifies adults, and particularly young adults, with regard to their religious stances. He describes five typical stories of young adults who have distanced themselves from their religious bodies:

1) *alienation:* unites some type of religious association with low levels of religious practice;
2) *unchurchedness:* no religious affiliation or religious practice comprising less than yearly attendance;
3) *dissatisfaction:* unites religious association with displeasure in regard to the quality of the services offered in the local parish;
4) *disidentification:* departing from the religious denomination in which one is raised;
5) *voluntarism:* staying with a religious denomination but not accepting many aspects of its official teaching (1979, p. 210).

Manno's research on the alienation of young adults is supported by a study done by Murnion (1976) on alienation of young adults from the church in the Archdiocese of New York.

More research on the faith life of young adults could be reported, especially sociological studies of college-aged young adults. But from what has been reported a picture can be drawn of the faith life of young adults. Young adults will find faith meaningful only if they judge that it aids them in their search for personal identity and a satisfying intimacy. Many young adults have found meaningful faith outside the traditional religious bodies, precisely because other groups afford the identity support and the intimacy they seek. This fact has alerted religious leaders and educators to the religious needs of young adults that they have evolved in our time.

THE FAITH OF MIDDLE-AGED ADULTS

It was the psychologist Jung who first drew attention to the spiritual dimensions of the second half of life. He found in his psychoanalytic practice that the years after forty provided the opportunity to deepen spiritual and religious values through reflection on the meaning of life and death (Jung, 1933). Religion in his view aided persons to become individuated or integrated by providing a unifying philosophy of life. It functioned to integrate the various roles that persons played in life, the masculine and feminine dimensions of their personalities, and the dark elements of human existence such as sin, evil, guilt, and death.

Erikson followed the lead of Jung in seeing a potentially positive role for religion all through the life cycle, but especially in later life. He described the psychosocial crisis of midlife as the choice between *generativity or stagnation* or self-absorption (Erikson, 1978, p. 7). The crisis of generativity comes when persons, looking over their accomplishments, feel that these are meager and that their lives have stagnated. This crisis is resolved, according to Erikson, through loving care. Erikson defines this virtue of care as "the widening concern for what has been generated by love, accident; it overcomes the ambivalence arising from irreversible obligation (1964, p. 131)." This care is closely related to the religious virtue of love or charity and is an important virtue in all religious traditions. Erikson explictly refers to the religious care that celibates practice.

Though Erikson's description of midlife crisis has received general acceptance, a number of psychologists have added to his description. Peck (1955) presented four related crises in the middle years. In midlife adults must learn to value wisdom over the physical prowess they may have possessed in earlier life. In their human relationships they must come to see the value of all forms of social contact, thus moving beyond considering only the sexual as important in human relationships. Thirdly, they need to develop emotional flexibility which enables them to forge other relationships when their parents die and their children leave the home. The final task is the avoidance of mental rigidity by developing a mental flexibility that empowers persons to assimilate and accommodate new questions and answers.

Not all psychologists of midlife have accepted Erikson's theory of developmental stages. Neugarten (1964; 1968) has preferred to study the salient issues of adulthood. These she has enumerated: individuals' use of experience; their structuring of the social world in which they live; the ways in which they deal with work, love, time, and the death of others; changes in self concept and changes in identity as persons face the successive contingencies of marriage, parenthood, career advancement and decline, retirement, widowhood, illness, and their own deaths. Neugarten found that the fifties for most people represented an important turning point because of a restructuring of time (a person has more past than future); and the development of new perspective on self, time, and death. She also found in her studies important sex differences: men became more receptive to affiliative and nurturant promptness; women became more responsive toward and less guilty about aggressive and egocentric behavior.

The research of Neugarten and Peck does not explicitly treat the religious dimension of life, though what it reports certainly has implications for understanding religious development, as will be indicated later in this section. The same can be said for the more recent research of Levinson and his associates (1978). Levinson puts the midlife transition at forty years of age. Early adulthood is terminated at this time, and middle adulthood is embarked upon. Four tasks or polarities are encountered at this time which need resolution. The influence of Jung is clearly seen in the description of these polarities. Persons have to resolve the *Young/Old* polarity by neither clinging too tenaciously to youth nor becoming prematurely aged. The polarity between *Destruction and Creation* must be faced by accepting the dark side of personality: sin, death, suffering, destructiveness, and guilt. *Masculine* and *Feminine* must be integrated in individuals by an acceptance of toughness, achievement, ambition, power, thinking along with feeling, nurturance, softness, and cooperation. The final polarity is *Attachment/Separation*, which must be balanced throughout life, but most especially at this time. Levinson gives religion as an example of this polarity. Religion must become more personal for adults as they become detached from dependence on the religion in which they were socialized.

Levinson completes his treatment of midlife by pointing out how the life structure of individuals is modified at this time. Some modify the lofty Dream that they had in earlier adulthood to make it more realistic. Middle-aged adults become mentors to younger adults. Changes also take place at this time within marriage, especially middle-class marriages, with women becoming more free and assertive. This is also a crucial period in marriage, for the period of transition at times occasions for many couples a divorce and a remarriage.

The research in the area of midlife reported by Levinson is paralleled and also complemented in various ways by that of Gould (1978). According to his research women attempt at this time to break out on their own and attack the protector myth that society has foisted on them. Many return to school or work in midlife to develop careers outside the home. Gould found evidence that woman's liberation has influenced the lives of many middle-class women. It has affected the stability of marriage, the work world which has been previously male dominated, and the manner in which children, especially daughters, are being raised.

A more recent sociological study of midlife crisis among women (Rubin, 1979) has revealed a number of interesting findings. Rubin's results are based on her interviews with 160 women between the ages of thirty-five and fifty-four. Her sample appears biased towards women with a high degree of education, though a few have never finished high school. Rubin rejects the empty nest syndrome with her finding that generally husbands and not wives experience anguish over children leaving the home. The chief problem women experience is finding their elusive selves. They find themselves torn between the self that needs human relatedness and the self that needs to achieve in the larger world. They resent the fact that men most often do not have to make this choice. Interestingly, women who are highly successful in the world still tend to define themselves by their family roles. In midlife women experience a greater need for sexual expression. Most women who get divorced at this time are not shattered by the experience, once the initial shock of adjustment passes. Women who return to the work world are often exhilarated by the experience, even though they are aware of prejudicial attitudes towards them. Often, however, they experience some guilt over their work commitments, if these appear to put home and family in a subordinate role.

What the adult religious educator misses in the research on adult development is explicit attention to the religious dimensions of human development in midlife. Vaillant (1977) has given some attention to the religious dimension in his follow-up study of men who were healthy and promising undergraduates at an elite college between the years 1939 and 1942. The major focus of his study is an analysis of the various mechanisms these men have used in coping with the problems they have faced in life. In dependence on Erikson, Vaillant places generativity at the heart of the midlife crisis and terms it a second adolescence. The men in their fifties lived quieter lives as they saw a new generation taking over. Many men during their fifties developed a capacity to care for others that they did not previously believe possible.

As to religious development of the men studied, Vaillant found a modal pattern. The men had a relatively high involvement in religion during adolescence, experienced a decline in the decades between twenty and forty, and then gradually increased their interest and involvement in religion in the fifties. In their view of God these men replaced the God who binds moral conscience with a God who is an invisible trusted power behind the universe. True to his psychoanalytic orientation, Vaillant explains the reappearances of religion in the fifties as the rediscovery of internalized parents. His research parallels that of Rizzutto (1980) who elucidated the extraordinary congruence between an adult's felt and experienced image of God and the internalized parents. Vaillant accepts as an apt description of adult development the Christian metaphor of "pilgrim's progress." According to this metaphor adult religious development depends upon mysterious growth within the person, inspired by equally mysterious forces outside the person.

One possible explanation for the renewed interest in religion in the fifties is given by the fascinating research study of Jacques (1965). In this study the midlife crises of a number of extremely creative people are studied: Bach, Keats, Dante, Michelangelo, Shelley, and others. In midlife all of these artists became keenly aware of the inevitableness of eventual death and of the existence of hate and destructive forces inside each person. Jacques contended that the midlife crisis is a reaction that occurs not only in creative genius but in everyone. It is fundamentally the painful awareness that one will die that causes this crisis. In midlife the awareness that one's parents are aging, together with the maturing of one's children, contribute to the sense that it is one's turn next to grow old and die. Jacques attributes a number of reactions to the awareness of the crisis, including increasing religious concerns:

> The compulsive attempts, in many men and women reaching middle age, to remain young, the hypochondriacal concern over health and appearance, the emergence of sexual promiscuity in order to prove youth and potency, the hollowness and lack of genuine enjoyment of life, and the frequency of religious concern, are familiar patterns. They are attempts at a race against time (1965, p. 511).

It is clear that Jacques does not consider increased religious concerns in this period of life as healthy responses to midlife crises. But what he proposes as healthy responses—a life lived with conscious knowledge of eventual death, acceptance of death as an integral part of living, and deepened capacity for love and affection and human insight—can all be found in sound religious experience. It is also interesting that Jacques concluded his article with the religious vision of life found in the "Paradiso" section of Dante's *The Divine Comedy*.

> But now my desire and will, like a wheel that spins with even emotion, were revolved by the Love that moves the sun and other stars (Dante in Jacques, 1965, 513).

A more explicitly religious treatment of religious development in middle life is found in Fowler's theory of faith development. In his theory of faith development Fowler contends that adults are usually found at stage 4 (Individuative-Reflexive Faith), at stage 5 (Paradoxical Consolidative Faith), or at stage 6

(*Universalizing Faith*). Stages 4 and 5 have already been discussed in this chapter. Stage 6 is found rarely and Fowler gives Ghandi, Martin Luther King, Mother Theresa, Thomas Merton, and Abraham Heschel among his examples of this form of faith (Fowler, 1980, p. 235). Such persons are characterized by universalizing compassion and enlarged visions of the universal human community. Often they are engaged in struggles with their own communities because of their universalizing tendencies. Often these persons are considered subversives in society.

Fowler's description of this faith stage presents the highest ideals of religious life found in nearly all religious traditions. From an examination of Fowler's psychological research on faith development it cannot be clearly assessed whether or not universalizing faith is exclusive to a spiritual elite. If such is the case the question remains concerning its value in a general theory of faith development. What may be needed in the area of faith development research are more descriptive studies of faith stories and religious journeys of individuals, with a limited amount of philosophical and theological interpretations of faith development. It would appear that though cognitively oriented theories, such as Fowler's, shed some light on the dynamics of religious development, a preferable model for study would be theories of psychosocial development that treat a number of dimensions of human development.

A fruitful approach to the study of adult development in the middle years has been presented by the social psychologist, Paul Maves (1970). His approach to adult religious development is sensitive to the social and environmental forces that influence religious life. It is his contention that:

> Religion as a dimension of experience or behavior response is integrally related to the total structure of the personality, so that changes in religious belief, attitudes, or behavior are subject to the conditions which determine changes in any other area of life (1970, p. 783).

In this view great changes will occur in adults who live during times of social and cultural instability or rapid technological and social change. According to this theory changes will be less related to age than to factors in the environment.

Maves admits that studies concerning religious development in adulthood are at an early stage. He reports that in these studies religion seems correlated with other dimensions of personality as an integral part of the total picture of responses. The dominant impression is that there is generally stability during the adult years, except for an inward turning to spiritual concerns at the beginning of midlife. Maves's theory of the importance of environmental factors as determinative of changes in adult life is yet to be tested.

In concluding this section, it is interesting to report a number of hypotheses on the relationship between midlife and religion that were developed by Miller in the early sixties (Miller, 1962). In surveying the literature, Miller came up with these hypotheses: (1) the ability to state one's religious beliefs will correlate positively with achievement and satisfaction in one's career; (2) persons with a religious orientation in midlife will look forward to retirement with less apprehension than those without a religious orientation; (3) there is a relationship between a male's struggles with passivity and his neglect or irregularity in religious observance; (4) persons who score high on a hypochondriac scale will manifest an arrested religious life; (5) increasing conservatism in religious beliefs during midlife is a function of the person's striving for self-consistency; (6) persons reporting a grief and life-enhancing mystical experience will manifest a higher degree of self-insight than those for whom religion is a routine affair.

It is clear then that the study of religious development in middle adult years is a fruitful area for researchers. The insights of those who have worked with adults in these years are also of great value. The interest that adults in midlife have expressed in such religious movements as Marriage Encounter, Charismatic Renewal, Bible Prayer and Study Groups, and the Cursillo Movement indicates a spiritual interest and hunger that is attributable to both psychological and cultural factors. In most religious bodies it is midlife adults who are the most active members in worship, education, administration, and service programs. The faith development of this group is vital for healthy church life.

THE FAITH OF OLDER ADULTS

The first psychologist to direct attention to the advanced years of life was Jung (1933). He noted that deep-seated changes took place within the human psyche at this time. He suggested that in the advanced years of life individuals turn inward to find a meaning and a wholeness in life that would make it possible to accept death as the end of life. Jung wrote that:

> What youth found, and needed to find outside, man in the afternoon of life must seek within himself. . . . It is impossible to live through the evening of life in accordance with the program appropriate to the morning, since what had greatest importance then will have little now, and the truth of the morning will be the error of the evening (1933, p. 17).

In Jung's view older persons need future goals in order to age successfully. He suggested that this is the reason why all the great religions have offered hope in an afterlife, in order to enable older persons to cope with pain, suffering, and death.

The major crisis in old age in Erikson's treatment of the human life cycle is the struggle between *integrity* and despair or disgust. Integrity is possessed if persons can look over the past events of their lives with a feeling of satisfaction and actualization. Despair expresses itself when persons feel that the time left to them is too short and there is no possibility to take an alternative route. Despair is often accompanied by a fear of death and a sense of personal failure for a wasted life.

Erikson himself has explained the religious dimension of this crisis. He speaks of the childlikeness of older adults and relates this to the Gospel message about children in the Kingdom of God. He contends that it is the world religions at their best that have:

> striven to provide an all inclusive world view for the containment of such human extremes as self-seeking vanity and self abnegating humility, ruthless power-seeking and loving surrender, a search for beliefs worth dying and killing for, and a wish to empathize and understand (1978, p. 21).

For Erikson the virtue needed for successfully resolving this final life crisis is wisdom, which he defines as "the detached and yet active concern for life in the face of death itself, and maintaining and conveying the integrity of experience in spite of decline of bodily and mental processes (1964, p. 133)." Erikson recognized that wisdom appears an old-fashioned term and not technical enough for psychologists. But he used the term because it contains the elements of hope and faith that are crucial for all periods of life.

The psychologist Peck (1955) has expanded and refined the crisis of advanced age described by Erikson. Older persons experience the crisis of distinguishing their personal selves from their work and family roles. This will enable them to accept both retirement and diminishing family responsibilities. The second task is to transcend preoccupation with bodily ailments by finding more satisfaction in relations with others. The final task of old age is to transcend one's own personal life and accept inevitable death. Peck suggests transcendence through one's children, friendships, ideas, and accomplishments. Some religious faiths hold out the hope of a transcendence beyond this life where persons achieve an immortality in life with God.

Advanced age has not received the same degree of attention from developmental psychologists as have the first two stages of adulthood. The research of Levinson and Gould does not include stages of development into the latter years of life. This period of life has been studied by other types of psychologists and social scientists, as will become clear in this section and in the next chapter on adult learning. Developmental psychologists, however, even debate the propriety of using the word "development" of a period of life that is marked not by growth and maturation but by decline and disengagement (Maves, 1971, pp. 780-781). Now that the developmental model of psychology has been somewhat detached from its biological origins and broadened to include growth in personal and interpersonal terms, it can be expected that research on adult development will give more attention to adults of advanced age.

One focus of research on older adulthood concerns theories of successful aging. Kalish (1975, p. 60) presents a number of theories on successful aging. One view is that older persons age successfully when they adopt a way of life that is considered *socially desirable* for their age group. This description presumes that society knows best what is good for its older members. A second theory suggests that successful aging is related to the *maintenance of middle-age activities*. A third view is that persons age successfully if they have a sense of *satisfaction with their present status and activities*, e.g., health status, financial status, and so forth. The final view contends that successful aging comes from *a feeling of satisfaction with one's life.* In a study done by Neugarten, Havighurst, and Tobin (1961) five components of life satisfaction were enumerated: zest and enthusiasm for life, resolution and fortitude, relationships between desired goals and achieved goals, a healthy self-concept, and a mood that is optimistic, happy, and spontaneous. These components have formed the basis of a great deal of research on the elderly.

In a later study of successful aging Clark and Anderson (1967) developed six themes that produce high morale in the elderly: sufficient autonomy to permit the person to function with integrity; agreeable relationships with other people who are willing to help when needed; a reasonable amount of bodily and mental comfort in physical environment; adequate stimulation of mind and imagination; mobility to permit variety in surroundings; and some form of intense involvement with life, in order to avoid preoccupation with death.

Of particular interest to adult educators is the sociological research on religion and aging. Gray and Moberg (1977) have summarized this research, building on the doctoral dissertations that both researchers did in the area of the influence of religion on personal adjustment of the elderly. The research will be reported rather extensively because it affords us the best picture that social science can present in this area.

The religious practices or activities of the elderly that take place outside the home tend to diminish in old age. However, internal and personal religious activities that do not depend on health and mobility, apparently increase in those who have religious faith. Almost all studies show that the highest proportion of people who believe in God, as well as those who believe with absolute certainty, are older persons. A number of studies tend to establish a correlation between successful aging and church attendance and a religious philosophy of life. Moberg, however, contends that it is not church membership in itself that produces this effect but rather the motives that accompany church participation. Research on whether a religious faith enables a person to face death with equanimity is mixed. While some research shows that intensely religious people accept death more easily than others, if they are authentic in their internalized faith, other research shows that it is not religion but rather close association with others and the avoidance of isolation that are the important variables in determining how death is faced. It has been found that taking part actively in church activities by assuming positions of leadership contributes to good personal adjustment in old age, even after positions have been given up.

The research reported above is basically that of Moberg. Gray's contribution to the research study is based on his dissertation on the personal adjustment of older persons. Though this study was done in 1953, Gray contends that later research has confirmed his earlier findings. His major finding was that church members had better personal adjustment than the general population of older persons. He found no evidence of persons turning to church membership in old age; it was rather people who had been lifelong members of churches that found their needs met in old age. Gray found that older persons reported the following contributions that religious faith made to their lives: alleviated fear of death, provided companionship and friendship, welcomed them into activities, helped them adjust to bereavement, offered support during discouragement and crises, and came to them in need.

These positive contributions that Gray found must be balanced with a number of problems that older persons reported with regard to their churches. Some felt pushed aside by younger members with whom they considered themselves in conflict. Others said that they did not attend church because they could no longer contribute financially or dress properly. Many older members of churches have expressed dissatisfaction with changes in their religious bodies. In recent years religious bodies and other institutions of society have become more attuned to the religious needs of the elderly. It is hoped that some of these problems will be seriously addressed at this time.

Both psychological and sociological evidence points to the fact that religious faith can be a strong force in the latter part of life's journey. Religion will have meaning in old age to the degree to which it had meaning in the earlier stages of life. However, the religious faith of the elderly will have a different emphasis and perspective. At this time perspectives on faith are open to persons that were not available to them when they were younger. Older persons have the potential of seeing deeply into the fundamental truths of religious faith. They can come to an appreciation of the positive role of suffering as found in the book of Job. As persons become older, they become more aware of their dependence on others. This reality affords the opportunity for insight into the fundamental creatureliness that we have in our relationship with God. Also, it is only at the end of life's journey and in the face of suffering and death that persons come to a full realization of the central religious mystery of death and resurrection.

Social science research reports that those persons best face the inevitability of death who have religious faith and a community of persons to support them and care for them. A religious body can supply this care and support for individuals who do not have the support of a family or friendship group. It is easier for the elderly to experience the acceptance of God, if this is mediated through a loving community. In advanced age persons have the potential of coming to the maturest form of prayer which is acceptance of God and openness to God's love. The maturest prayer is found in the elderly person who says "Be it done to me according to Thy word."

One of the findings on successful aging is that continued activities contribute to happiness. In later life persons have many opportunities for activities that express the charity and love preached within all religious bodies. One of the dangers that older persons face is the disgust with life that Erikson contrasts with integrity. Advanced age is filled with small opportunities to show the courage and the love that dispell disgust and produce integrity. It is with courage and love that people are able to accept both the sufferings and the joys of old age.

CONCLUSION

This chapter has attempted a difficult task, the description of the faith journey of individuals from infancy to old age. Reliance has been mainly on the theories and research of the social sciences. The wisdom of religious traditions on this journey was presented in the first chapter. Social science often takes as its task the examination of conventional wisdom, including that of religious traditions. Though a great number of social scientists have examined human development without considering the religious dimension, an increasing number of researchers have begun to look explicitly at religious development as an integral part of human development.

The adult religious educator can benefit considerably from a knowledge of adult developmental studies. The number of books on adult development that have become best sellers in this country in recent years attests to the fact that adults are attempting to come to a deeper knowledge of what is happening in their lives. Adult education outside of religious bodies has become increasingly involved in probing the problems that adults experience at the various stages of life. Courses and educational experiences are held on human development, personal relationships, human sexuality, marriage and parenting, divorce and separation, the midlife crisis, career advancement, women in the work world, grief and bereavement, and death and dying.

The function of religious bodies should not be to duplicate what is being done in these programs of general adult education. Often these programs can be recommended to church members. The function of adult religious educators is to determine what areas of adult development need special treatment from a religious point of view. This can be done by an examination of the area under discussion and by a needs assessment of members of the religious body. In this chapter an attempt has been made to indicate those areas of adult development which are especially open to a faith dimension.

For too long adult religious education has proceeded from the starting point of the doctrines, moral laws, history, and ritual practices of the religion. What this chapter attempts to do is to establish another starting point, the developmental tasks and needs of adults at various stages of life. This approach to adult religious education programming will be fully presented in a later chapter. Certainly the religious teachings of religious bodies are not to be ignored. Yet these are not psychologically and educationally the best starting points or organizational principles around which to develop programs. The challenge is to begin where people experience themselves to be and to shed light on their problems and tasks both from religious sources and other sources.

What the psychological and social sciences tell us about individuals are relevant as useful generalizations. This knowledge can never supplant the firsthand knowledge to be gained from direct contact with people. Many people do not fit into the generalizations of the social sciences, no matter how subtle the gradations. But this is no reason for not beginning with these findings as heuristic starting points in our dealings with adults in educational settings.

Though a knowledge of adult development is essential for adult religious educators, this knowledge can be beneficially supplemented by an understanding of how adults learn. A significant body of literature has developed in the past few decades that provides useful generalizations for adult religious educators in determining the types of educational experiences that should be provided for different groups of adults. The next chapter will examine this literature and attempt to relate it both to adult developmental stages and adult religious education.

CHAPTER IV
LEARNING IN ADULTHOOD

To be human means to learn. To be fully human entails a lifelong effort in acquiring knowledge, attitudes, skills, and behaviors. The complexity of life and the constant changes that persons face increasingly demand that adults continue to learn throughout their lives. As adults successively take on the different roles of spouse, parent, worker, citizen, and friend, they are faced with learning how to function in these new roles. In passing through the various stages of adulthood adults learn about the tasks which face them. Though in all societies and cultures adults continued to learn throughout their lives, in modern industrial society this learning has increased because of greater interpersonal demands, the need for constant development in one's work skills, and the greater opportunities that are afforded through increased leisure time.

Many religious adults continue to learn about religion throughout their lives. Participation at worship is a powerful learning experience. Many adults take advantage of adult education opportunities offered by their religious bodies. Religious adults also often pursue religious learning through self-directed activities. Adult religious learning focuses upon such topics as marriage, parenthood, religious literature, the beliefs and doctrines of the church, prayer, and spiritual development. Also, religious learning is concerned with developing attitudes of coping with personal problems and crises such as sickness and bereavement.

Though adult religious learning is extensive in religious bodies, the task of the adult religious educator is to engage more adults in valuable religious learning experiences. A body of theory and research exists that sheds light on the possibilities for learning in adulthood. This chapter examines this body of knowledge in four sections: participation and motivation in adult learning; research on adult learning and adult religious education; theories of adult learning; and adult learning theory beyond andragogy.

PARTICIPATION AND MOTIVATION
IN ADULT LEARNING

Extensive studies have been done on *participation* in adult learning. If one views adult learning in the sense of self-directed learning—"sustained, highly deliberate efforts to learn a knowledge or a skill (Tough, 1979)," then all persons are involved in such activity. If adult learning is defined in terms or organized learning activities, then between 12 and 33 percent of the population is involved, according to which research reports are accepted (Cross, 1981, p. 51). A smaller group of adults pursue education for credit at colleges and universities.

Tough (1979) has done extensive research on *self-directed learners*. He has found that almost all persons are at some time involved in it: hobbies, recreation, how-to-do-it books, televised courses, and reading. All classes of persons participate in this form of learning. Armstrong (1971) in examining the personalities of self-directed learners has developed a profile of the "learning prone personality": reliable, tenacious, independent, with broad interests, high achievement motivation, and openness to new experiences.

Studies on participation in religious and ethical learning activities have not been common. In the Johnstone and Rivera study (1965, p. 4) it was reported that approximately 12 percent of respondents were involved in such activities. They estimated that there were approximately 3,820,000 adults involved in religious and ethical learning. Religious studies ranked third in the eight categories studied. Protestants made up 87 percent of the participants, and Catholics 6 percent. A more recent national study has not been done in the United States. Canadian studies indicate that adult participation in religious programs amounts to 39 percent of the total offering of adult education in the country Dickenson and Verner, 1979).

The only reported study on *self-directed learning in religion* was done by Wickett (1980). Fifty persons between the ages of thirty-five and fifty-five were interviewed on their learning activities for spiritual growth. The amount of time spent by those sampled in learning for spiritual growth was more than 50 percent of learning time. Examples of spiritual growth include prayer, meditation, participation in retreats and discussion groups, television viewing, and Bible study. The study reveals that the learning activities of many people are connected with a particular crisis in their lives, e.g., alcoholism, marriage breakdown, and death of significant persons. Many expressed a desire for the assistance of a director for their spiritual growth. Few people reported using materials developed by religious bodies.

Rather extended research has been done on the adults who participate in *organized learning activities*. One conclusive finding of such studies is that participants in adult education come from high socioeconomic classes. Those most underrepresented include "the elderly, blacks, those who failed to graduate from high school, and those with annual incomes of under $10,000 (Cross, 1981, pp. 53-54)." The strongest participation variable is education; the more education people have the more they want. The poorly educated do not usually accept the value of education. Surveys show that age is also a strong factor: interest and participation start declining in the early thirties, continue to decline through the forties, and drop rapidly for those over fifty-five (Anderson and Darkenwald, 1979). Many elderly persons feel that they are too old to learn. Women have as much interest in learning as do men. Places of residence and climate also appear to be influential variables (Cross, 1981, pp. 60-62).

A smaller number of adults participate in *adult learning for academic credit*. Adult students at colleges tend to be upwardly mobile, heavily career motivated, and desirous of structured programs. No studies have been done on adults participating in academic programs in religion. But a review of the number of year around and summer programs in religious studies listed in such an advertising source as *The National Catholic Reporter* indicates that many adults are pursuing religious studies for academic credit. Though many of these programs began for the education of the clergy, large numbers of lay persons now attend them.

When we pass from a study of who participates in adult education to *why people participate or do not participate*, we find extensive research: depth interviews, statistical analysis of motivational scales, survey questionnaires, and hypothesis testing. Houle (1961) utilized depth interviews in developing his famous classification of reasons: *goal-oriented learners* who want to achieve specific objectives; *activity-oriented learners* who are interested more in the activity than in learning a skill or subject matter; and *learning-oriented persons* who pursue learning for its own sake. Utilizing this typology Harvey (1972) found that the first group tends to be young and middle-income; the second group comes from all classes and levels; the third group tends to be older and in higher and professional classes. Tough (1979) has found that: almost every learner has more than one reason for engaging in learning; pragmatic reasons predominate; learning has certain patterns—awareness, puzzlement, and curiosity; extensive time is involved; and adult learners enjoy learning.

A more sophisticated approach to motivation studies is found in the work of Morstain and Smart (1974). Six factors, each with a number of examples, were isolated through statistical analysis: (1) external factors (e.g., meet new friends); (2) external expectations (e.g., carry out recommendation); (3) social welfare (e.g., prepare for service to the community); (4) professional advancement (e.g., gain higher status in job); (5) escape/stimulation (e.g., get relief from boredom); (6) cognitive interest (e.g., satisfy an inquiring mind).

Motivation study has also utilized *survey questionnaires.* Burgess (1971) used Houle's typology and identified seven interpretable factors for participation: (1) desire to know; (2) desire to reach a personal goal; (3) desire to reach a social goal; (4) desire to reach a religious goal; (5) desire to escape; (6) desire to take part in a social activity; (7) desire to comply with formal requirements. Carp, Peterson, and Roelfs (1974) added the factors of desire for personal fulfillment and desire for cultural knowledge. In the latter study 12 percent of those surveyed considered serving the church as very important and 19 percent considered the furthering of spiritual well-being as very important. In reviewing these surveys Cross (1981, p. 94) concluded that there is a steady increase in the proportion of persons taking courses for personal and recreational reasons—a category that includes preparation for community involvement, personal and family interests, and social and recreational interests.

A major hypothesis to explain adult participation has been presented by Aslanian and Brickell (1980). They contend that *transitions*—such as job changes, marriage, the arrival of children, and retirement—require adults to seek new learning. This hypothesis needs further testing since Tough (1979) found that only one-third of learning projects in his sample were the result of transitions or anticipations of them.

Research has been reported not only on why people participate but also on *why they do not participate* in adult learning. In their national survey Carp, Peterson, and Roelfs (1974) presented three types of barriers to participation: *situational* barriers which arise from one's situation in life at a particular time (time, cost, responsibilities); *institutional* barriers which include procedures and practices that exclude or discourage participation (scheduling, location, transportation, lack of information); and *dispositional* barriers which are related to attitudes and self-perceptions about oneself as a learner (fear of school, lack of interest, and lack of confidence).

Barriers to participation in adult religious education have been studied by McKenzie (1978, 1980). His studies were done in urban parishes in the Midwest. Seven dimensions of nonparticipation were found: (1) programmatic non-relevance was found among 14 percent of those not participating; (2) involvement in other activities ranked highest in the twenty to twenty-nine age group; (3) physical incapacity was highest among older persons; (4) alienation from church activities was found most frequently among young and middle-age adults with more than twelve years of schooling; (5) negative attitude towards education and resistance to change were found among many adults over fifty-four and at least one-fifth of the adults in the twenty-six to fifty-three age group; (6) estrangement or a feeling of not belonging was found among all age groups; (7) marginality or a non-joining life style was found in one-third of those sampled. In his follow-up study (1980) McKenzie replaced the barrier of physical incapacity with confusion, which was found most frequently among middle-age and older groups.

Till this point I have mainly described the research in the area of participation and nonparticipation. The implications for adult religious education will be drawn in a later section of this chapter after viewing attempts at understanding adult motivation and theories of adult learning. The research reported in the last section was purely descriptive. Little effort was made to develop explanatory models or theories of adult motivation for learning. It is thus important to move beyond these descriptions and examine models and theories.

Understanding adult participation demands attention to models or theories for understanding adult motivation. A number of attempts have been made in this area. Miller (1967) presented a *social class theory* that utilizes Maslow's hierarchy of needs (1954) and Lewin's field force theory (1951) to explain why there are differences between social classes in regard to participation in adult education. Lower-class persons are reported as uninterested in higher needs such as recognition (status), achievement, and self-actualization since they are concerned with meeting fundamental needs of survival, safety, and belonging. Miller also utilized various social factors described by Lewin—changing technology, action-excitement orientation of male culture, hostility to education among certain classes, weak family structures, limited access to organizations—to explain why lower classes are resistant to efforts in adult education. Clearly this theory makes use of both psychological and social factors to explain motivation.

Another model to explain motivation for adult education, an *expectancy-valence paradigm*, has been developed by Rubenson (Rubenson in Cross, 1981) which takes as its starting point theories of motivation that explain human behavior in terms of the interaction of individuals with the perceived environment. According to this theory people participate in education if they have an expectation of personal success and if they see this success as leading to positive consequences. Rubenson places the emphasis in motivation less on external factors and more on factors and perceptions within the individual.

A third theory to explain motivation for adult education is the *congruence model* developed by Boshier (1973). According to this model adult participation and dropout is explained by the amount of discrepancy between participants' self concept and key aspects (mostly people) in the educational environment. The more the incongruences between the individual and the environment, the less is the possibility that the person will be involved in adult education.

A fourth motivation theory places the emphasis on *anticipated benefits* (Tough and associates in Cross, 1981, pp. 120-122). This theory hypothesizes a movement from engaging in a learning activity to retaining knowledge or skill, applying the knowledge, gaining a material reward (promotion), or gaining a symbolic reward (credits, degree). Anticipated benefits include pleasure, self esteem, and approval from others.

A final theory to explain adult motivation for education is Cross's *Chain-of-Response Model* (1981). This model builds on the previous theories and is useful in organizing existing knowledge. This theory assumes that participation is the result of "a chain of responses, each based on an evaluation of the position of the individual in his or her environment (p. 125)." The Chain-of-Response moves from (A) self evaluation or self concept; to (B) attitudes toward education from one's own experience and from significant others; to (C) the perceived importance of goals and the expectation that participation will meet these goals; to (D) attention to life transitions and periods of change; to (E) meeting concrete opportunities and dealing with barriers; to (F) availability of information about existing programs; to (G) actual participation in programs of adult education. Cross's model has been developed from a review of present research and theory. She presents it as an aid for research in this area.

A number of *implications for adult religious education* can be drawn from this review of theory and research on participation and motivation. A fuller treatment of these implications is presented in the second part of this book where the practice of adult religious education gets full treatment.

Adult religious educators need to build up the confidence of members of religious communities about their capacity and need to continue to learn throughout life. Many persons still believe that religious education is only for children and that after a certain age, it is neither necessary nor possible to learn. Confidence is developed in persons by creating atmospheres that are non-threatening. Very often adults prefer to be involved in educational activities which are self-directing and in which there is a minimal amount of pressure placed on them to discuss and be evaluated.

It is important for those in leadership positions in religious bodies to promote positive attitudes toward education. Attitudes manifested by leaders and influential members of religious bodies about lifelong religious learning often shape the attitudes of the membership. If leaders are seriously involved in their own continuing education, they are in a strong position to promote the lifelong learning of members.

Participation will be fostered if the goals and expectations of learners are met. The assessment of needs and the clear description of goals are important for successful programs. People need to be exposed to quality educational experiences. Meeting people's goals is not necessarily utilizing the market approach to adult education, whereby programming is done exclusively by meeting the expressed interests of individuals. There is a place for priorities setting by educators, as will be developed in Chapter Eight.

The importance of adapting religious education to the life transitions and phases of adults is an important implication from the research on participation and motivation. These transitions include leaving the home, first job, marriage, children, increasing responsibility in the community, divorce, retirement, and so forth. These transitions are variously called "teachable moments," "marker events," or "trigger events." They are powerful motivating factors, times when persons are open to developments and decisions that may shape the future direction of their lives. A treatment of the religious dimensions of these events was presented in the preceding chapter. These events also form an integral part of the program planning process that will be developed in the second part of this book.

Adult religious educators need to create the opportunities for and remove the barriers to participation. Some good programs have been developed in response to consumer demands. Other programs have begun with the ideas of a religious leader or educator. The success of such adult education programs as Weekend and Evening Colleges, External Degrees, Elderhostel (college experiences for the elderly), televised courses, and so forth indicate what opportunities can open up when traditional barriers are removed.

Finally, adult educators should be responsible for providing accurate information about programs for potential learners. Often educational programs do not draw the participants for whom they are intended because information is poorly or inaccurately disseminated. Accurate information should address the goals, processes, and atmosphere of the educational experience.

RESEARCH ON ADULT LEARNING AND ADULT RELIGIOUS EDUCATION

From a consideration of adult motivation for participation in adult religious education it is now necessary to move to the research that has been done in the pasty fifty years on learning processes in adulthood. A number of good reviews of theory and research are available (Kidd, 1973; Knox, 1977; Kimmel, 1980; Cross, 1981). The purpose of this section is to select research findings that will be of particular importance to adult religious educators.

With increasing age, various changes take place that alter *physical and sensory capacity*. Vision and hearing loss begin to affect persons in the second half of life. Illumination becomes more important with age. Hearing is affected with regard to pitch, volume, and rate of response. Reaction time becomes slower with the passing of time. In general, it can be said that with increasing age it takes longer to learn something. Kidd (1973) gives a number of practical implications of findings in this area: the need for adequate illumination; the elimination of glare in rooms; the effective use of chalkboards, etc.; the positioning of people close to the speaker and to one another; the use of sharp color contrasts; and the use of speech that is slow, clear, distinct, and loud. It is important to recognize that physical difficulties translate into psychological barriers which may seriously impair the ability of aging adults to take part effectively in educational activities.

Rather extensive research has been reported on the development and arresting of *intellectual functioning* with increasing age. A difficulty in determining intellectual abilities in adults is the long-standing controversy over the suitability of the tests that are used to assess intelligence. Also, intelligence tests fail to take account of adult motivation and opportunity for learning.

Research reported on intellectual functioning shows a gradual slowing down or decline in intelligence. A great amount of this decline is connected with loss of speed in performing test functions.

Speed in intellectual functioning, however, is not usually an important factor in adult learning since in real life people are rarely confronted with items similar to those that appear on tests. Also, research has fairly well established that the decline of learning abilities has little practical difference until ages of sixty or seventy-five, depending on the particular research cited (Cross, 1981, p. 159).

It is important to be aware that while one type of intelligence—*fluid intelligence*—decreases in adulthood, another type of intelligence—*crystallized intelligence*—increases. The former type of intelligence consists in the ability to perceive complex relations, engage in short-term memory, form concepts, and engage in abstract reasoning. Crystallized intelligence entails the ability to perceive relations and utilize judgment and experience (Horn, 1970). This research confirms a common sense observation that while the young may be characterized as brilliant, those in advanced years increase in experience and wisdom. Different stages in life call for different learning abilities.

Though it may be considered a part of intelligence, *memory* has received a considerable amount of attention in the research. Minor deterioration in memory appears in older persons, but this may be a function of the quality of the initial learning. Research also suggests that older persons may have memory problems because they have accumulated large stores of information and scanning this information takes time (Cross, 1981, p. 164).

A number of practical implications flow from this research on intellectual functioning and memory. It is important that adult learning be self-paced and that care should be used in any evaluative process to allow adequate time for learners to absorb new ideas. Adult religious education should turn to areas where experience and wisdom-sharing take precedence over formal reasoning processes. Adult religious education should emphasize the integration, interpretation, and application of knowledge. In presenting new information to adults an effort should be made to ensure that information is meaningful, well organized, and carefully presented. The educational process should also make use of summaries to aid retention and recall. These are good norms for the education of all persons, but they have a particular importance in the education of adults because of the various changes that take place in adulthood.

Closely connected to intellectual functioning in adults is a consideration of differing *cognitive styles* that adult learners have. Knox (1977) describes nine contrasting styles but also reports that little research has been done on these in adulthood. From my own experience I have found these styles helpful in dealing with different groups of adult learners. The styles deal with the form and not the content of learning: (1) *tolerance versus intolerance* (Can one accept perceptions that differ from conventional experiences?); (2) *reflectiveness versus impulsiveness* (Are various possibilities considered before a decision?); (3) *constricted versus flexible control* (How susceptible is the person to distraction and interference?); (4) *focusing versus scanning* (How long and intense is one's attention span?); (5) *leveling versus sharpening* (Does memory blur or accentuate similar objects and events?); (6) *complexity versus simplicity* (Is the social world construed in a multidimensional and discriminating way?); (7) *conceptual differentiation versus description* (Are different categories used in classifying things and events?); (8) *analytic versus global* (Are objects considered discrete from their backgrounds and contexts?); (9) *breadth versus narrowness of categorizing* (Does one have a broad or narrow category range?).

Another important area that has received little attention is research in the *affective or emotional domain* in adulthood. Some of the participation and motivation research in the first part of this chapter includes affective dimensions. Kidd (1973) has also treated a number of important affective issues for adult learning. Adults may have come to associate schooling and education with unpleasantness because of unhappy prior experiences. A strong element of fear may be present in adults approaching learning. Adults often exhibit anxiety and tension, rigidity and inflexibility. Besides these negative emotions or barriers to learning, there are also positive emotions that adult educators can expect in adult learners. Many come with a love and curiosity for learning. Motivation to learn is often very intense. Adult learners are most interested in learning that appears to be immediately relevant.

The task of the adult religious educator is to maximize the positive attitudes and emotions of adult learners while minimizing the negative attitudes or barriers. The first step in this process is to become aware of the presence of both factors within each learning situation. The adult educator must be able to handle negative emotional expressions when they appear in the learning situation, or more often when anxious learners approach educators before and after classes and during breaks. Personal problems of individuals, however, should not get extensive attention in an educational setting. This may cause embarrassment and uneasiness for participants and detract from the goals of the program. Positive emotions and attitudes can be skillfully channeled into powerful learning incentives.

Emotional and affective factors are closely related to *personality changes* in adulthood. The major conclusion of research in this area is that there is remarkable consistency in personality throughout lives of individuals. People who were active and involved when they were young manifest the same tendencies in later life. Consistency, however, is accompanied by a number of significant changes in adulthood. Studies show a rise in self-concept and self-esteem as people enter their forties and fifties (Kuhlen, 1968; Neugarten, 1968). As persons age they turn more to internal satisfactions. Older adults manifest a general tendency toward accuracy and dependence upon solutions that they have arrived at in the past. Often older adults are less prone to take risks in learning and are more likely to report confusion in their learning experience.

Though adulthood is marked by consistency, it is the *change events* or transitions of adulthood that are of most interest to adult educators. The importance of these events was mentioned in the previous section. Knox (1977, p. 537) has analyzed these events into five stages: prestructure—the period of stability before the change event; anticipation—the awareness that a change event will take place; actual change event (e.g., marriage, moving, etc.); disorganization period—time between change event and reestablishment of a stable pattern of life; poststructure—a stability which reflects reorganization. Adults often respond to change events by developing strategies to deal with the events. For some adults, a strategy is to seek information or learning about how to cope with the situation.

Adult religious educators need to be especially attentive to change events in the lives of learners. These events affect family relations, occupation, religion, politics, and leisure activities. Though individuals are unique in their handling of these events, there are certain common features of the strategies developed by individuals that can be made the basis of learning experiences. As Knox notes, "when practitioners help adults adapt to change, the specific instances are unique but the process is generalizable (1977, p. 543)."

Research on adult learning has addressed itself to *what adults want to learn* and *how adults prefer to learn*. Tough's research (1979) indicates that in self-directed learning adults take almost any topic as an object of learning. Three-quarters of adults prefer to learn such practical things as business, home repairs, travel, etc. About 17 percent of adults in his studies desire to learn such intra-self topics as religion, philosophy, art, music, and psychology. Tough contends that most adults (73 percent) prefer to direct and plan their own learning. The remaining 27 percent utilize groups, professionals and friends, and nonhuman resources such as books (Tough, 1978). Penland (1979) agrees with Tough in the area of self-planned learning but differs in finding more dependence among adults on nonhuman resources and one-to-one helpers.

Penland has also extended Tough's research by examining the reasons why people prefer to learn on their own instead of taking a course. The most important factors are: desire to set one's own pace; desire to use one's own style of learning; desire to keep learning strategies flexible; desire to put structure into the learning project; not wanting to wait for a class to begin; and not knowing whether there was a class on the subject. It is clear that many prefer self-directed learning because of the freedom to determine what is learned and how the learning will take place.

One interesting feature of studies of self-directed learners concerns the *resources* they use. Better educated persons use books as important sources of information, whereas persons with less education rely more on electronic media as sources of information (Cross, 1981, p. 196). Coolican (1974) reports that the three preferred methods in self-directed learning are practice, reading, and discussion, in that order. Listening, observation, and instructors are used less frequently.

Another research source for *what adults learn* and how they prefer to learn is found in various surveys that were carried out in the 1970s. Boaz (1975) did a survey of subject matter trends between 1969 and 1975. Occupational training was at the top of the list with 48 percent. Ranking fourth and fifth on the list were personal and family living (14 percent) and community issues (10 percent). In both of these areas there have been modest increases in the past six years. Religion, however, went from 5.2 percent in 1969 to 4.7 percent in 1975. This trend has not been confirmed by other research.

Two general trends for religious education come from these survey studies. Those who are most likely to be interested in personal development and religion are those who are not interested in career advancement—retired people, spouses who are not employed, and well educated people who have achieved the career success for which their education prepared them. A second trend is that adults are very pragmatic in their learning interests. Thus adult religious education may have to take on an even more pragmatic focus if it is to increase its share of participants.

Survey studies also contain information about *preferred methods of teaching/learning* by adult learners. A consistent and interesting finding is that while 70 percent to 80 percent say that they prefer to learn by methods other than lectures, lectures usually rank first or second in popularity (Cross, 1981, p. 208). Carp, Peterson, and Roelfs (1974) present findings at variance to the findings of Tough and Penland reported earlier. They found that only 17 percent preferred to learn independently. The item testing this in their study was not clear, for it could have meant independently with an instructor. This study also shows a cool reception to media-based education by adult learners. Many who consider these modes appropriate ways of learning report that they do not make use of television, radio, or audio-cassettes for their learning projects. It is clear that the potential impact of the new media has not been felt in adult education.

Survey research also contains information on *preferred locations* and *preferred scheduling* which may be of interest to adult religious educators. Boaz (1978) reports that colleges, universities, and commercial buildings are the preferred locations. Few prefer place of work. Private homes are preferred by 6.7 percent while 4.9 percent prefer churches. Location is of critical importance to the physically handicapped, geographically isolated, aged, and others with restricted mobility. Research on scheduling shows that evening hours are preferred by about 40 to 60 percent of respondents. Morning hours are preferred by those not in the labor force, especially the young and the retired. Weekend scheduling appears rather unpopular. Though the research does not examine this, it would appear that weekends provide suitable scheduling for religious bodies when adult education activities are connected with regular church services or where a strong custom is in place.

I cannot conclude the second section of this chapter without stating the obvious. Almost no research has been done focusing exclusively on adult religious learning. Wickett's research (1980) was cited in the first section of this chapter. A study by Ryan (1972) of leadership personnel in Roman Catholic dioceses in the United States is now rather dated. The study listed the following as the most promising subject areas for adult religious education: parent education, the essential mission of the church, worship, clergy education, and marriage. Since the research reports of Stokes (1977) and Cohen (1977) are more appropriate to the history of adult religious education, they will be treated in the next chapter.

Religion is usually included as an item in the general research on adult learning. However, when findings about religion are included within the more extensive findings on occupational education, these findings get little attention because of the relatively small percentages involved. It is clear that what adult educators need are both surveys and in-depth interviews that make adult religious education a primary concern. Only with increased findings on adult learners of religion will leaders and programmers be able to develop adult education activities that truly meet the needs of adults.

THEORIES OF ADULT LEARNING

The last one hundred years have witnessed many efforts to arrive at a theoretical understanding of learning, including adult learning. In this section a brief exposition of learning theories and their implications for adult religious education is presented. Since the material in this areas is rather extensive, only essential elements of each theory will be presented.

One of the oldest approaches to understanding learning involves *behaviorist theories*. In these theories learning is explained through processes of association, connection, reinforcement, conditioning, and extinction. The focus is upon external behavior and environmental factors. Little attention is given in the theories to such internal states of the mind as habits, motives, ability, needs, and cognition. *Thorndike* (1932) explained learning as a process of association in which an organism, when presented with a stimulus, establishes a connection or bond through a response. Thorndike contended that learners acquire and remember those responses that lead to satisfying effects (law of effect); meaningful bonds strengthen learning (law of exercise); and a strong bond develops if the organism is prepared (law of readiness).

While Thorndike's work has been followed by a number of behaviorists, the most prominent exposition of this theory is found in the work of *B. F. Skinner* (1971). The emphasis in Skinner's behaviorism is on learning through reinforcement of favorable responses. Behavior is a learned response and thus can be modified if environments are structured in particular ways. Skinner's theories have been influential in all forms of education, including adult education. Programmed instruction, computer-assisted instruction, personalized systems of education, skills training, and competency-based education are only some of the forms of instruction that rely on the theoretical framework provided by behaviorist theories.

Behaviorist theories are useful in explaining some types of learning: basic cognitive facts and external behaviors. Since it is not clear, however, that all forms of human learning can be explained on the basis of behaviorist principles, other learning theories have been hypothesized and tested. One theory that has attempted to account for advanced forms of learning is *Gestalt psychology*. Major proponents of this theory include Koehler, Koffka, and Wertheimer. These researchers studied the environment, not in its parts as the behaviorists did, but in its entirety. Gestaltists contend that learning comes about through the development of understanding, insight, and problem solving abilities. Learning entails the reorganization of experiences into systematic and meaningful patterns (Hilgard, 1956).

Though Gestalt psychology is no longer a dominant learning

theory, it paved the way for *cognitivist theories* of learning. The major cognitivist theorist of our times was *Piaget* (1967). Though his work was almost exclusively with children, other researchers have extended his ideas into understanding adult learning. According to cognitive-development theory, learning comes about through a process of assimilation-accommodation. Significant changes in thinking abilities, capacities, and processes occur as a function of age, experience, and intellectual sophistication. Piaget's contribution to cognitive learning theory is the careful delineation of stages of intellectual development, starting from sensorimotor intelligence in infancy to prelogical thinking in early childhood, to concrete operational thinking in childhood and finally to formal, abstract thinking in adolescence and the adult years.

The cognitive theory of learning originated by Piaget has formed the basis for a number of other learning theories. *Kohlberg* (1977) has developed a theory of development in moral thinking in which there is a progression from dependence upon rewards and approbation of others, to acceptance of the conventions of society, to a moral thinking that is based upon universal moral principles. As in the case of Piaget, learning is explained through an interactionist perspective wherein changes in cognitive structures develop by interaction of the developing person with the environment. Thus thinking is both a function of maturation and interaction with the environment. According to Kohlberg it is only in adult years that persons are capable of functioning at the higher levels of moral reasoning. Though Kohlberg's theory and findings have been widely discussed for the past two decades, recently they have been the object of serious criticism. Some have accused the theory of a sexist bias (Gilligan, 1977); others find the evidence for the existence of stages tenuous (Wilson, 1980).

In the third chapter the work of *Fowler* (1981) on faith development was reviewed. This theory is also in the Piaget tradition, accepting as it does the basic premise that structures of thinking develop progressively through interactive processes. Fowler finds the same general development described by Kohlberg: from dependence on faith of others, to dependence upon conventional beliefs, to development of one's own faith which is reflective accepting of paradoxes, and transcending of particularist orientations. Fowler's work has been of keen interest to adult religious educators (Gilmour, 1976; Elias, 1979a) who find in it implications for the understanding of adult faith development and the practice of adult education. Some criticisms of Fowler's work from a psychodynamic or psychoanalytic perspective are found in Chapter Three.

One cognitive-developmentalist whose work is particularly relevant for understanding learning in the area of religion is *Goldman* (1964) whose work was cited in Chapter Three. Though Goldman's work followed Piaget in its exclusive attention to religious thinking in children and adolescents, it has some relevance for understanding adult learning. The relevant conclusion of Goldman is that while thinking in religion does not differ from thinking in other areas, religious thinking develops later than other forms of thinking since it is involved with metaphors, analogies, and symbols. This peculiar character of religious thinking needs appreciation when educators deal with persons who are otherwise advanced in thinking. Religious literature, symbols, rites, and stories demand more developed capacities than are needed in other areas of learning. The same is true of literary or artistic appreciation.

While behaviorism attends to behavior and cognitive theory focuses on interactive mental structures for explaining learning, *psychodynamic theory* prefers to postulate certain drives within the individual which are responsible for learning and development. It is clear that within this theory primary focus is upon learning in the broad sense of personality development that includes cognitive, affective, and behavioral elements. Much attention is given to the existence and influence of drives within individuals that impel them to certain behaviors and activities. This theory postulates that learning is deeply connected with unconscious factors and internal feelings. The primary processes described in learning include identification with others, internalization of the values of others, resolution of internal conflicts of a biological and psychosocial nature, and the learning of defense and coping mechanisms that enable persons to handle difficult emotional situations (Vaillant, 1977). However, while psychodynamic theory has been fruitfully used as a theory for understanding past learnings and developments in persons's lives, it has been rightly criticized for its lack of attention to conscious elements and the influence of environmental factors.

Some of the strong points of behaviorist, cognitive, and psychodynamic theories have been incorporated into a dominant theory of learning, *social learning theory* (Dollard and Miller, 1950; Bandura, 1977). One group of social learning theorists attempts to combine the constructs of psychodynamic theory with the proven facts of behaviorism. These psychodynamically oriented learning theorists utilize such constructs as identification with others, internalization of values and behaviors, learning of dependency-independency, and learning of aggression in order to explain how learning takes place throughout life. While it is true that the basic elements of the theory were developed in research with children, the constructs also appear to have applicability throughout the adult years.

The second type of social learning theory attempts to combine behaviorist principles with a number of principles drawn from cognitive theorists (Bandura, 1977). The key processes to explain learning in this view are modeling, observational learning, imitation, external reinforcement, vicarious reinforcement (observation of what happens to others), and self reinforcement (recollection of what has happened to oneself). In this form of social learning theory, learning is explained neither by inner forces alone nor by environmental stimuli alone. It is explained "in terms of continuous reciprocal interaction of personal and environmental determinants. Within this approach, symbolic, vicarious, and self regulatory processes assume a prominent role (Bandura, 1977, pp. 11-12)."

Both forms of social learning theory make no distinction between adult learning and learning in pre-adults. The same processes are explanatory of the child learning at school, the worker learning on the job, and the elderly person learning to anticipate retirement. Socializing factors play an important part in all these forms of education. There are differences among the learners in physical, psychological, and sociocultural dimensions, but the same basic processes are explanatory of the learning of new behaviors and the gaining of new insights. The research base of this position, however, rests largely on studies done on pre-adults.

Two major theories in religious education utilize research from behaviorist and social learning theorists. In his social-science approach to religious instruction Lee (1973) has incorporated to an extensive degree the findings of learning theorists. Lee carefully draws many implications for religious instruction from learning theorists of a behaviorist and social learning orientation. Nelson (1967), Westerhoff (1976), and Marthaler (1978) in their enculturation or socialization approaches to religious eduation draw to a lesser degree on this research. Their primary social science sources are sociological and anthropological research which are in some degree of continuity with the psychological research. None of these theorists treat explicitly adult learning as distinct for the learning of pre-adults. These theories will receive some attention in Chapter Six of this book.

One theory of learning that has directed the greatest amount of attention to adult learning is the *humanistic or personalistic theory of learning* of psychologists such as Rogers (1969) and Maslow (1954). Humanistic psychologists assume that there is a natural tendency for people to learn and that learning will flourish if proper conditions are provided. Two prominent adult educators who to a certain extent espouse humanist assumptions are Tough (1979) and Knowles (1980).

The basic assumptions of humanistic learning theory, which is called experiential learning, are presented by Rogers: (1) learning requires personal involvement of cognitive and affective aspects of persons; (2) learning should be self initiated; (3) learning should be pervasive—make an impact on the behavior, attitudes, or personality of the learner; (4) self-evaluation should take place to determine if needs are met; (5) the essence of learning is the meaning that is incorporated into the person's total experience. Rogers sees these principles as applicable not only in self-directed learning but also in learning in groups.

Maslow's contribution to humanistic learning theory is chiefly in his analysis of human needs and the final goal he sets for all human learning and education—the self-actualized person. Self-actualization is an adult achievement even though few adults reach this level of development. Maslow gives many characteristics of such persons: realistic orientation, acceptance of self and others, spontaneity in thinking and acting, problem-centeredness, need for privacy, autonomy, proneness towards "mystic" or "oceanic" experiences, identification with all of mankind, intimate relationships with a few persons, democratic character structure, highly developed sense of ethics, and resistance to total conformity to culture (Maslow, 1954, pp. 203-208). As examples of such persons Maslow offers Lincoln, Beethoven, and Schweitzer.

The processes humanists recommend for achieving self-actualization of "the fully functioning of self (Rogers)" are spontaneous learning, intrinsic motivation, development of positive self-concept, discovery, and perception. *Mesirow* (1978) has elaborated on this aspect of perception in his concept of perspective transformation. He contends that persons reach a point in development where new learning is not merely added to previous knowledge but results in bringing about a new perspective. Examples of this learning include what may happen in consciousness raising experiences where people come to perceive themselves and society in a new light.

This theory of perspective transformation bears similarities to *Freire's theory of conscientization.* Freire (1970; 1973) incorporates elements of humanistic theory within his explicitly sociopolitical theory of human knowing and learning. Freire, however, accuses humanistic educators of failing to move from concern with self-development to concern with changing social reality. Freire is here influenced by Marxist thought which draws attention to how our ideas are socially determined. In his view only the person who engages in praxis (action and critical reflection upon action) is capable of achieving knowledge about self and the social world. Learning for Freire is the process of moving from an uncritical consciousness of what are the forces at work in one's life and in society to a true critical awareness of the dominant elements in one's culture. Knowing and learning take place in ongoing cycles of action, reflection, critical action. The learning process is primarily one of dialogue. Freire's theory of knowing and learning is not without its critics (Elias, 1976; Elias and Merriam, 1980, Ch. 6). For example, it is not clear that he completely escapes the charge of assuming some transcendent view of reality which is available for people who are engaged in the conscientization process.

Humanistic theories of learning have had a great impact in adult religious education. The emphasis on freedom, discovery, dialogue, and changing of perceptions is most attractive. These principles are found in many programs developed for adults. Such popular programs as Genesis II, Romans VIII, RENEW, and Faith Explorations incorporate humanistic principles of learning. Coughlin (1972) emphasized the importance of humanistic principles in good program planning. I treated both Rogers and Allport in my study of psychology and religious education and drew implications from their theories for the practice of religious education (Elias, 1979a).

Freire's theory of conscientization has also received attention from religious educators (Warford, 1976; Elias, 1976; Monette, 1979b; Groome, 1980). As education for social justice and peace becomes a more important dimension of adult religious education, theories of adult learning that emphasize the close connection of reflection and action will become more prominent. A discussion of the implications of both humanistic psychology and theories of conscientization is given in the second part of this book.

This section has reviewed a number of theoretical approaches to adult learning. It has examined some of the principal ideas coming from behaviorism, cognitive-developmentalism, psychodynamics, social learning theory, humanistic psychology, and conscientization. Though some continuities exist among these theories, it appears impossible at this time to synthesize adequately the various findings into an integrated theory. Given this situation, the next section takes a critical view of the Knowles's andragogy and attempts to move adult education beyond these theories.

BEYOND ANDRAGOGY IN ADULT LEARNING THEORY

Malcolm Knowles is the most prominent proponent of andragogy, the art and science of helping adults learn. He distinguishes andragogy from pedagogy, the art and science of helping children learn. In earlier writings Knowles stated that andragogy was a comprehensive theory of adult learning. In a more recent article he appears to consider andragogy a mode of instruction which is suitable both for children and adults (1979). He continues to maintain that andragogy has usefulness as a learning theory. McKenzie (1979) has attempted a philosophical defense of andragogy from a phenomenological perspective. Carlson (1979) sees the issue of andragogy as one of defining the political and legal reality in societies where dichotomies are made between children and adults. My position in the spirited debate is that andragogy is based on a set of assumptions that have little or no research support. My other concern is that notwithstanding some benefits that the theory may have had in mobilizing some parts of a profession, andragogy brought into adult education an artificial jargon that served to cut adult educators off from educators in general (Elias, 1979b).

The assumptions behind andragogy are well known: adults are more self-directing and independent than children in learning; adults have a great reservoir for learning in the vast experience they have accumulated; adults' readiness to learn becomes increasingly oriented to developmental tasks of social roles; the time perspective of adults is present-oriented while that of children is future-oriented; and the orientation of adults is towards problem solving while that of children is subject oriented (Knowles, 1980). One of the values of andragogy is that it does focus attention on a number of characteristics of adults (and children) that deserve attention. But these characteristics do not constitute a distinct adult learning theory because children also possess each of the characteristics in some degree: independence and self-direction, experience, developmental tasks, multiple-time perspectives, and problem-centered orientation.

Another serious problem with andragogical theory is that it takes little account of adults in advanced years. The assumptions do not take account of research findings in gerontology: older persons often become more dependent in their self-concept; past experience often is a block to new learning; there is often a disengagement from social roles; time perspective often shifts to the past in life reviews and to the future (Kimmel, 1980). The ideal of adulthood implied in andragogy is that adults become independent, self-directing, rational, objective, and present-oriented. Developments in later life often belie these assumptions. Development is not the linear process andragogy seems to assume it is.

The point in opposing andragogy as a learning theory is not to assert that children and adults are the same. There are obvious differences between children and adults which need to be attended to in learning situations. Cross (1981) describes how personal characteristics (physiological aging processes; sociocultural life phases, and psychological developmental stages) exist on a continuum throughout life. Certain situational characteristics, she contends, exist in opposition: adult learning is usually part-time and voluntary while learning for children is full-time and compulsory. Cross sees an opposition here, because in this instance she almost equates learning with schooling. If one takes a broader view of learning to include learning through play and work experiences, such a dichotomy no longer exists.

Though some differences between the learning of children and adults must be recognized, adult learning must always be viewed within the perspective of lifelong learning. For too long researchers have looked either at child learning and development or adult learning and development. What this approach misses is the continuity that exists from the beginning of life to its end and the similarities between people at the beginning and end of the life span. Though continuity is primary, within it there is room for particular emphases and phases throughout life. We need to be reminded that complexity and variety exist within the lives of both adults and children. Nothing is gained by developing a theory of adult learning that does not take account of the continuity, variety, and complexity of all human lives, both of adults, and children (Moran, 1979, p. 106).

A more fruitful way of viewing adult learning is to view it within the concept of lifelong learning. This entails going beyond andragogy. Going beyond andragogy does not mean going back to pedagogy as it has been caricatured among some adult educators; however, not so by Freire who did not hesitate to call his education of adults a "pedogogy of the oppressed." Going beyond andragogy entails recovering a sense of the unity of learning and education in human life.

CONCLUSON: LIFELONG LEARNING
IN RELIGION

Adult religious educators should be particularly sensitive to maintaining the unity of human learning. Religious bodies have customarily divided learners into different age groups for certain educational activites. There is some justification for this insofar as there are certain problems and issues that are of special concern to a particular group—children, youth, young adults, adults in midlife, and adults of advanced age. There is little justification for this if it is based on assumptions that these groups learn differently from one another and cannot learn from one another. If one examines the contexts of religious learning, it is clear that the natural and preferred practice for learning religion may be situations where more than one generation is involved in the learning process.

Religious learning takes place primarily within the family. Families are by definition multi-generational. Children, parents, grandparents, and others connected with families participate together in many religious experiences which are truly learning experiences: prayer, worship, service, suffering, death, joy, religious celebrations and festivals, sharing, dialogue, etc. All members of a family bring insights to all these events and experiences. Our deepest learning experiences are those which we have shared with our children and parents and with friends, both older and younger. The renewed emphasis on family education and intergenerational education within many religious bodies attests to the realization that a continuity in human learning exists and that we are diminished if we view religious learning solely in an age-differentiated mode.

While the primary goal of worship services is not learning as such, learning is an important part of such activities. While liturgies for particular age groups have their place, the most natural type of service is one in which participants cross generational lines. The readings, symbols, homilies, and gestures have meanings at various levels. All learn at these events because the basic learning processes of identification, assimilation, reflection, insight, and modeling involve children and adults according to their differing capacities.

Part of the difficulty with rites of religious bodies is that they have so developed that certain rites are deemed appropriate only for childhood and youth: baptism, confirmation, and bar and bas mitzvahs. In many religious bodies the greatest educational efforts are concerned with preparing the young for these rites. Often this is done to the detriment of the practice of lifelong learning that would be of great value to a religious body.

A theory of learning that sees continuity between childhood and adulthood would seek ways to develop more intergenerational forms of learning. Religious bodies are in a unique position to break down the dichotomy that exists in society between the worlds of home, school, and work. Lasch (1977) has pointed out many of the problems that result from separating the family from the functioning of other institutions. Coleman's research (1972) indicates the harmful effects of segregating youth into school groups and isolating them from the world of work. His study proposes more utilization of work study programs. The point here is not directly to discuss the reorganization of societal institutions to allow more interaction among groups and among institutional settings. It is rather to suggest that religious bodies should be careful not to imitate some of the harmful segregating social arrangements that have developed. Religious bodies have the potential of emphasizing the continuity of learning that exists from youth to old age.

CHAPTER V
HISTORICAL PERSPECTIVES ON ADULT RELIGIOUS EDUCATION

Recent years have witnessed an increase in interest and activity in adult religious education. All religious bodies have begun to allocate more of their resources to provide for the educational needs of their adult members. Though adult religious education has received new emphasis in our time, religious bodies have always engaged in various forms of adult education and formation. To understand the present situation, it is helpful to look at the historical development of adult religious education in religious bodies. In this chapter this history is sketched, with particular emphasis on the Christian and Jewish traditions. Earlier periods of historical development are treated briefly. Emphasis is placed on the adult religious education movement as it has progressed in the United States.

To treat adequately adult religious education in an historical context, it is first necessary to clarify the meaning of the term education. Cremin's broad definition, which comes closer to a definition of socialization or enculturation is utilized in this work. Cremin defines education as:

> the deliberate, systematic, sustained effort to transmit, evolve, or acquire knowledge, attitudes, values, skills, or sensibilities, as well as any outcomes of that effort (1977, p. viii).

According to this inclusive definition of education, Cremin is able to treat historically not only the work of schools and colleges, but also efforts of families, churches, the media, and communities. While there is certainly legitimacy to histories of education that focus exclusively on the institutions of schooling (Tyack, 1974), Cremin's broader view provides a fuller picture.

BIBLICAL TIMES

In *Judaism* the three centers of worship and education were the home, the Temple, and the synagogue. The *home* has had an importance in education in Judaism, much greater than in other religions. Circumcision of the male children took place there. The weekly Sabbaths were celebrated by the father or presiding person amidst great joy. Parents had the duty of instructing their children in the rituals, laws, and teachings of the religion. The *Temple* in Jerusalem was where devout Jews came in the years before the Exile for sacrificial worship and for the great festivals. Through the temple rites people were more closely associated with the principle religious teachings and attitudes. In Post-Exilic Judaism the *synagogue* became the local center of worship and instruction where the Jewish community learned the Torah and its application to practical life. The readings from the law and the prophets made up the core of the synagogue service and were surrounded with acts of praise and thanksgiving. In later years the rabbis attached to the synagogues schools where boys were taught the Hebrew language, the oral tradition, and the distinctive Jewish way of life.

The ministry of Jesus must be seen in the light of the Judaism in which he was raised and within which he functioned. He was initiated into Judaism within the home, though his circumcision took place in the Temple. He celebrated the Sabbath in homes. His last supper was a ritual meal within a home. Though Jesus was highly critical of what often took place in the sacred Temple, he still referred to it as his Father's house, and wept over its iminent destruction. Jesus was also a teacher on a number of occasions at synagogues, though his reception there was not always friendly.

The *ministry of Jesus* and his immediate followers was a ministry to adults. The Gospel accounts of Jesus's preaching and teaching present him as dealing almost primarily with adult groups. Recent studies of the parables of Jesus show how Jesus challenged the adult faith and intelligence of his audiences. He put difficult problems before his listeners. He challenged them to conversion. His examples were drawn from various aspects of adult life (Crossan, 1975). In only one instance are children mentioned as coming into direct contact with Jesus. He took the occasion to point out those characteristics of childhood which would enhance adult maturity.

The letters of Paul, other letters of the New Testament, and the description of the Apostolic Church in the Acts of the Apostles clearly indicate the centrality of the teaching ministry to adults. Some members of the community learned about Christian faith in family settings (Timothy), others needed some instruction before they were admitted into the community (the Ethiopian eunuch), and still others came to the faith after being educated in Jewish or Greek schools (Paul). But at this period it is clear that the way of life of a Christian, a follower of Jesus, demanded an adult decision to live a life that was different in many ways from the lives of those outside the group.

In later New Testament writings there is mention of persons within the community who had the charism or gift of teaching. These teachers instructed members in the doctrines of the community. Presumably they did this in a less "enthusiastic" or inspired manner than the prophets. Paul refers to himself as a teacher of the Gentiles (1 Timothy 1, 11). Summaries of doctrines appear in the later books of the New Testament and apparently reflect the preaching and teaching that took place in the communities. The Catholic Epistles, especially the letters of Peter and of John, emphasize the importance for members of the community to adhere strictly to the doctrines they were taught.

EARLY CHRISTIAN TIMES

One of the first problems the early Christian communities faced was that of training for membership. What developed to provide for this was the institution of the catechumenate. Potential members were expected to remain in the catechumenate for long periods of time, from three months to three years. Only those who went through training in this institution were admitted to membership through the sacraments or mysteries of the faith. The catechumenate was an educational, emotional, affective, practical, and strenuous testing of the faith and character of potential members. Throughout this process potential converts received strong support from members of the community (Marrou, 1956, p. 42). It is of some note that the Roman Catholic Church has issued a document calling for the restoration of the catechumenate at the local churches. At a time when membership in the Christian churches takes place almost automatically at birth, the document presents as a norm of Christian initiation and membership a more strenuous education in the faith.

Education in the early Christian period was part of the total life of Christians and reached its high point in the liturgical celebrations. Home, worship services in church, and community were the instruments of this education. In writings of the fathers of the church the home was referred to as the "domestic church" where religious faith was lived, learned, and celebrated. The worship services included homilies and sermons which provided a deepening of understanding of doctrines, rituals, and moral norms. The entire community supported the distinctive way of life since it was a community which defined itself in opposition to the life lived in the Greek, Roman, and other communities. For the first three centuries of its existence this community existed as a sect in opposition to established religious cultures.

An educational need of the early Christian communities was for educated apologists who could defend this new way of life and interpret it for educated persons who were interested in knowing about the religious teachings and practices. To provide the community with apologists for its way of life, church leaders established catechetical centers, or schools of theology. The catechetical school of Alexandria had as its foremost teachers Clement and Origen. Another famous school was established at Antioch. Founded in the middle of the second century, these schools were influential in producing both teachers for members of the community and apologists to the broader community.

It is interesting to note that there was no formal or special education in religion for children at this early period. The education of the young was through family and church. Good example and admonition were to be given to children. This is not unusual, given the Jewish origins of early Christianity. The children of Christians went to the Greek and Roman schools and received the same education as other young people. In reading the fathers of the Christian Church it is clear that they were trained in the philosophies and disciplines of classic Hellenistic culture. Some church fathers were fearful of the effects of this "pagan" learning.

Others believed that this learning was essential to develop Christian faith in contemporary culture. This tension between the religious tradition and the culture in which it attempts to exist faces all religious bodies especially those which perdure during changing cultural periods or which attempt to move from one cultural situation to another.

In summary, by the end of the fifth century religious education in Christian communities was primarily through family, church, and community. No specific Christian schools existed. The catechumenate died out gradually as the number of adult converts to the faith decreased and infant baptism prevailed as the normative initiation into the community. There is no evidence in the writings of this time of any direct religious education of children after baptism. The focus was still on adult religious formation.

THE MIDDLE AGES

Once Christianity was established in the Roman Empire under Constantine, the educational situation changed drastically. Large numbers of persons began to become members of the church at infancy. The need now arose for education that would provide a basic knowledge of religion. Christians, however, were inadequately educated in their faith in the early Middle Ages. This lack of religious education was part of a general decline in learning in society. Whatever learning took place in the church became simpler and more authoritative. Kennedy describes the religious education of this period:

> It was communicated through drama and sacraments, through architecture, through pictures of mosaic and stained glass, and through the confessional where sacramental developments led believers to seek guidance. Thus in the absence of formal schooling and literate culture, liturgy, drama, and architecture became more important educative instruments (1966, p. 23).

These educative instruments were adequate to keep Christianity alive in a weakened form among the ordinary members. But a vibrant Christianity needed educational efforts that interpreted and explained the faith in a more sophisticated manner. Liturgy, drama, and architecture of themselves could not give Christians the intellectual depth faith needed for survival. These forms had to be supplemented by more formal educational instruments.

Educational institutions began in Christianity in conjunction with monasticism. Education of young monks took place in monastic schools under the direction of the abbot or spiritual father. In these schools the Scriptures were meditated upon. The writings of significant fathers of the church were later added as books for meditation. The monastic movement in the eastern part of the Roman Empire generally remained negative to classical learning. Marrou comments that these monasteries became centers of asceticism and "instead of trying to influence the world, they tried to get away from it (1956, p. 443)." The monastic schools in the West gradually became genuine centers of culture. A great emphasis was placed on literacy. The rule of St. Benedict set down in detail how members of the community were to be educated. The monastic schools in the West in time began to educate other persons when they instructed young people who had no intention of becoming monks or nuns.

Besides the monastic schools of the early Middle Ages other schools were established to train young men for the priesthood: episcopal schools under the direction of a bishop and presbyterial schools under the direction of a priest in a rural area. These schools included education in literacy and some classical learning as the secular schools began to decline. In fact, it was through the religious schools of the early Middle Ages that the classical learning of antiquity was preserved.

While it is true that all of these schools were intended primarily for monks, nuns, and priests, an educational ideal was fashioned in these institutions which made Christianity both a religion for the masses and an intellectual religion. A distinctive ideal for the Christian teacher emerged at this time: a person who taught not only doctrines to an elite but who also taught the masses a way of life. Marrou compared this ideal of the teacher to the teacher in classical antiquity and judged this synthesis of teacher and spiritual father in the person of the school teacher as the essence of medieval and Christian education (1954, p. 451).

From the eleventh to the thirteenth centuries with the development of towns, great universities began to take form in places like Paris, Bologna, and Oxford. In these schools religious learning was closely connected with the classical learning of Greece and Rome. The University of Paris originated as a school of theology that trained clergy to teach religion in the monastic, episcopal, and presbyterial schools. In these universities the leaders of the Christian churches were educated. The great majority of Christians, however, learned through participation in the life and worship of the church.

In the latter part of the Middle Ages no new patterns for the education of adults were introduced. With the rapid increase in membership at this time, the old informal forms of education of clergy and laity proved to be inadequate. Church synods of the period direct that education in the faith or catechesis be given to adults. Jungmann in describing this period says that in some places parents attended catechesis with their children and it was their responsibility to give a fuller explanation to children in the home. The preparation of children for sacraments was also in the hands of the parents (1959, p. 14). However, formal religious instruction for adults was rare and socialization in faith took place through family, the parish liturgy, festivals, the Christian environment, the liturgy celebrated in the cathedrals (catechisms of stone), and the mystery and morality plays. The inadequacy of these forms of education in the faith began to come under criticism by reformers within the Christian communities.

THE REFORMATION PERIOD

The low level of religious understanding and the widespread existence of superstitious beliefs and practices became rallying cries for reformers such as Hus, Luther, Zwingli, Knox, and Calvin. The Protestant movement developed distinctive patterns to nurture faith. The educational sermon became central in worship, and dramatic liturgical activity was minimized. A major form of religious nurture the reformers recommended was private meditative reading of the Bible. To make this possible, schools for educating in literacy were established. Once literate, persons could read the Scriptures and study the catechisms. Luther's first catechism was for the education of priests and teachers. Later he wrote a catechism for children. This combination of religious zeal and humanistic concern encouraged what was to become universal compulsory education.

During this period changes also took place in Roman Catholicism. To the traditional educational forms of home training, worship, pastoral teaching, and guidance in the confessional were added more formal educational efforts. The Council of Trent developed a catechism designed for pastors to use in instructing adults and children. The main form of catechesis was to be for adults and it was to be given on Sunday afternoons in the church. It was only in the sixteenth and seventeenth centuries that a catechesis especially for children began to fit within the framework of ordinary parish life.

A number of religious orders founded in the Roman Catholic Church in the years after the Council of Trent dedicated themselves to the task of preaching and teaching among adult members, especially the poor. Jesuits, Brothers of the Christian Schools, Sulpicians, and other groups attempted to raise the educational level of Roman Catholics. These groups eventually established schools to train candidates for their orders and also other young persons. In time the education of the young took precedence in their work.

Within Protestantism in Europe, educational efforts were intensified in certain groups such as the Puritans and Moravians. Their efforts were directed both at forming a community of faith and at individual development. These efforts were intensified as the influence of the churches over all formal learning began to decline. In England the merchant class and in Germany the state began to exercise more influence over formal education. Society could no longer depend on the informal patterns of family, church, work, and community to produce the types of citizens that were needed in the new urbanized and industrial society. These changes are seen in educational developments in the United States, where such groups as Puritans and Moravians exercised great influence.

COLONIAL AMERICA

Among the arguments in England and Holland for settling colonies in the New World was the opportunity to expand Protestanism. The Puritans in New England, the Dutch Reformed in

New Netherland, and the Episcopalians in Virginia were determined to implant an active religious life into the colonies. Cremin (1970, pp. 31-108) has detailed how the colonists brought with them ideals of piety, civility, and learning. These ideals permeated all the institutions that the colonists brought from Europe and adapted for life in the New World.

The educational institutions that the colonists established had as their ultimate goals the practice of true piety through Bible reading and reading of other devotional literature. Households were responsible for teaching both literacy and the catechism. The colonial churches' educational efforts were mainly preaching and catechizing. They took responsibility for teaching both literacy and the catechism. The colonial schools trained the young in piety and put great emphasis on languages, especially the Biblical languages, Latin, Greek, and Hebrew. The colonial colleges trained young men to be ministers to congregations. Though the ethos of the colonial communities was primarily practical, religion and piety were reinforced through laws, customs, books, and forms of popular culture.

The colonial period produced a number of innovative approaches to adult education. Cotton Mather in his *Essays to Do Good*, written in 1710, advocated that households organize themselves into societies of associated families committed to religious activities. For these families he advocated religious discussion groups. A minister should be present to lead prayer. Mather proposed discussion questions about public disorders, disorderly persons who needed charitable admonitions, services the ministers should be engaged in, means of educating people in piety, recommendations to legislators, and ways of aiding persons who suffered afflictions (Grattan, 1959, p. 16, 17). Mather's discussion group was later adapted by Benjamin Franklin when he formed his Junto, a group committed to the discussion of issues in morals, politics, or natural philosophy (Franklin, 1964 edition, pp. 116-117).

Another form of adult education in colonial America was the Quaker "guarded education." This education of adults and children was based on an indoctrination into the history and beliefs of the Society of Friends and constituted a protection from the corrupting influences of society. Simplicity in doctrine and a contempt for learned theologizing characterized this form of adult education. Quakers also made strenuous efforts in the education of Indians and blacks.

In the 1730s and 1740s religious efforts to reach adults more and more took the form of "the religious revival." In this period of the Great Awakening a radically new preaching responded to what appeared to be moral and religious decline and theological uncertainty. The new preaching emphasized the terrors of hell and called sinners to repentence. This evangelistic movement inspired the establishment of a number of colleges, including Dartmouth, Brown, and Queens (later called Rutgers). The purpose of these colleges was to train ministers for the new evangelical piety.

A strong educational effort in colonial America was directed at the Indians who inhabited the country before the colonists. Indians were taught to read and write so that they could read the Bible and the catechism. Efforts were made by some to convert the black slaves to Christianity. Others, however, did not foster the education of blacks because such education might imply duties in charity and eventually emancipation. Missionary efforts were not greatly successful in colonial times with either group.

By the end of this period a number of changes had taken place in education in the colonies. With the growth of schools and churches families became less involved in education of children. The educational influence of the churches continued but in different forms. A diversity of educational styles developed in different churches—practical sermons, exhortations, evangelistic preaching, and elegant styles. Religious pluralism brought about a certain amount of toleration of different approaches. While the schools and colleges still trained in piety, they had added many other subjects to their curriculum.

By the end of the colonial period there had also emerged numerous voluntary associations of informal education where Americans gathered information and exchanged ideas. Cremin (1970) lists these associations:

> the young people's societies organized by New England preachers; the neighborhood groups that gathered around

the coffeehouses, taverns, and inns of the towns and cities; the salons of Boston and Charleston; the innumerable ministers' associations, merchant associations, professional societies, Masonic Lodges, and Committees of Correspondence (1970, p. 520).

While some of these forms are religious in nature, the others show the secular direction that education began to take at the time of the Revolution. All of these new educational institutions, together with the more established ones, were committed to the ideals that education could be a force for achieving moral and intellectual growth. Religion still remained a part of this educational effort but it now stood with many other areas of life.

THE NATIONAL EXPERIENCE (1783-1876)

The period immediately following the Revolution was marked by a great amount of discussion about the role of education in forming the new republic. Influential persons such as Thomas Jefferson and Benjamin Rush proposed plans for state or federally controlled education. These efforts failed because of differences of opinion about the nature of this state-controlled education, the vested interests of churches and other groups, and the fear of state control. Most of these plans concerned only the education of children and youth.

During this period the churches began to establish what Cremin calls "new institutions of deliberate nurture (1977, p. 48)." The evangelistic revival spirit prevailed in Protestant groups, especially among the Methodists and Baptists. Churches created new agencies like the camp meeting and the Sunday School to provide religious nurture. They also attempted to infuse their ideas into families, schools, colleges, the press, and the voluntary associations (Cremin, 1977, p. 49). These institutions taught the ideals of religious revival long after the actual revival had ended. The churches were also able at this time to infuse society with a type of Protestant learning that has become deeply imbedded in the American spirit.

While the churches remained an influential force in education during this period by their own internal activity and their cooperative work with other institutions of society, their influence lessened as the influence of schools and colleges for young people and the influence of the work world for adults assumed greater educative power in peoples' lives. The churches were influential in taming the frontier, but once tamed, the frontier was more open to influences from other forces in society.

During the national period a number of adult education institutions came into existence, some of a secular nature and others of a more religious nature. Mechanics institutes were set up in many cities for the education of tradesmen. The lyceum movement was imported from England and became in this country a national network of local study groups that sponsored many distinguished lecturers throughout the country. The movement introduced countless adults to the liberal ideas of Emerson, Thoreau, Holmes, and others. Strong between the years of 1820 and 1840, the lyceum movement eventually died out after directing its strongest efforts toward the promotion of the public school movement (Knowles, 1977, pp. 16-17).

To examine more carefully the adult religious activities of the religious bodies of this time, it was necessary to separate Protestant efforts from Catholic and Jewish efforts. Lynn (1976) has described the ecology of Protestant educational institutions in this period. American Protestantism viewed itself as a special missionary force to Christianize first the United States and then the world. The foremost educational institution was the revival, the great school of the Protestant public. The revival attempted to set up a community and give it an identity. The revivalism of the 1830s and 1840s was so strong that the period has been termed the Second Great Awakening.

An allied institution to the revival was the Sunday School which provided the context for the conversion experiences of the next generation. The American Society, established in 1816, and the American Tract Society, established in 1824, were influential forms of adult religious education in Protestantism (Knowles, 1977, pp. 22, 23). Other educational institutions that aided the revivalistic movement included denominational colleges and seminaries, Protestant benevolent societies, and in a limited manner the public school since it still retained elements of Protestant faith—e.g., reading from the King James version of the Bible and recitation of the Lord's Prayer.

Lynn judged this educational environment a powerful one in its influence on Protestants and the general public. In his view this powerful ecology came into existence not according to some plan but rather through particular responses to particular problems. Though separate as educational insitutions, these forms of spreading Protestantism were held together by:

> the evangelistic spirit, a spirit aroused and enlivened by the conviction that at last in America Christians were on the verge of entering God's future. For here they were planting the seed of the posterity of a new Adam in the virgin soil of Eden, warmed by the Sun of righteousness (Lynn, 1976, p. 11).

The educational efforts of the Roman Catholic Church in this country at this time must be seen as part of the history of an immigrant church that existed in a generally hostile environment. During this period the Roman Catholic Church remained outside the principal cultural and political forces (McCluskey, 1966, p. 366). The leaders of the church were engaged in struggle for survival. McCluskey estimates that in the colonial period alone two hundred thousand Catholics lost their religious identity (1976, p. 11). Catholic educational efforts were almost exclusively directed toward the education of children. At first Catholics attempted to get the public schools "deprotestanized," and when this failed, strenuous attempts were made to gain public financial support for Catholic schools. When these efforts also failed, many leaders in the Church decided to establish a system of Catholic schools outside the public school system.

Adult Catholics of this time learned their faith through contact with the preaching at worship and guidance in the confessional. The earliest forms of separate adult educational efforts were in the reading circles founded in connection with parish libraries. In 1854 the New York City Catholic Library Association was established to disseminate Catholic truth and advance the intellectual level of its members. By 1860 this association had added groups interested in history, debating, and science. Catholic young men's societies were also formed to promote serious reading among alumni of Catholic colleges (Knowles, 1977, p. 23).

Little information has been documented on the adult educational efforts within the Jewish community during this period.

Knowles considers the development of the movement for Reformed Judaism as the most significant adult education development within the Jewish community at this time. This movement was considered a great force in enabling Jews to integrate themselves within the culture. Educational efforts in Judaism became stronger with the influx of larger numbers of Jews during the latter part of the nineteenth century (Knowles, 1977, p. 23).

In concluding this section on the period of the national experience, it should be noted that many of those who had great interest in adult education were motivated by religious ideals. Josiah Holbrook, the founder of the lyceum movement in this country, saw this movement as providing useful instruction for the "150,000 to 200,000 teachers of Sabbath schools, . . . engaged in forming the character of the rising generation and moulding the destiny of our nation (Holbrook in Grattan, 1959, p. 32)." John Lowell, the founder of the Lowell Institute in Boston, wanted lectures to be given in his institute on "the historical and internal evidences of Christianity (Lowell in Grattan, 1951, p. 38)." Peter Cooper, the founder of Cooper Union in New York City, was religiously motivated in desiring that those who came to his institute would "see the beauties of creation, enjoy its blessings, and learn to love the Being from whom cometh every good and perfect gift (Cooper in Grattan, 1959, p. 49)." Cooper showed uncommon tolerance for his time when he forbade any religious test for admission to his institute.

EARLY METROPOLITAN AMERICA (1876-1920)

With the marking of its first centennial the United States was on its way to becoming a nation of cities and was also exporting to other nations its culture and civilization. Becoming a nation of cities also meant becoming an industrial society. This changed situation placed new burdens on all educational institutions. The existing institutions greatly expanded and new institutions were developed to meet new needs in the nation. Schools were greatly transformed with the development of the public high school and the introduction of vocational training. Colleges and universities greatly expanded in numbers and in curriculum offerings. Graduate and professional schools were added to many colleges and universities. New types of households began to form with the great influx of immigrants from Europe. Profound changes took place in the world of work with the development of factories, coal mines, and unions. This period also saw the beginning of the rise of the mass media of communication, especially newspapers, as a stronger educative force.

Though the adult education movement was not an identifiable entity at this time, many institutions were established for the education and training of adults. Knowles lists the more important institutions: correspondence courses begun at the University of Chicago, farmers' institutes, colleges for laborers, university extension programs, libraries, evening schools for adults—especially immigrants—at the public schools, numerous voluntary associations—Womens' Clubs, youth organizations such as the YMCA, Settlement Houses, fraternal organizations, and professional societies (Knowles, 1977, ch. 3).

Religious bodies in the United States were also involved in developing institutions and associations committed to adult religious education. Within Protestantism a great deal of effort was expended for preparing teachers for the Sunday Schools. William R. Harper founded the American Institute of Sacred Literature in 1889 in order to communicate to adults Biblical scholarship. To do this the Institute used popular Bible study, summer schools, extension courses, and weekly institutes (Knowles, 1977, p. 73). Other organizations were established: the Religious Education Association in 1903, the World Sunday School Association in 1907, and the International Council of Religious Education in 1922. The existence of these institutions indicates the strength of Protestant efforts to provide religious education beyond what was given in public schools and in worship services.

In Protestantism the most famous institution for adult religious education developed during this period was the Chautauqua movement, based in western New York. This program which entailed the careful, systematic, and guided reading of books and other materials, mixed a strong religious orientation with liberal education. The movement was founded by John Vincent, a minister, and Lewis Miller, a businessman and church layman. Vincent outlined the basic philosophy of the movement: all of life is educational but the true basis of education is Christian faith; all knowledge becomes sacred by its relationship to God; those who receive no cultural education in early life desire it more avidly in later life; the intellect is to be developed through reading, reflection, and production (Vincent in Grattan, 1959, pp. 72-74).

When the Chautauqua movement began in 1874 it was connected with the Methodist-Episcopal Church. By 1886 it had become a movement embracing many Protestant denominations. The type of religious faith fostered by Chautauqua was not the revivalist faith that had predominated in Protestant religions of this time. Vincent opposed the superficiality and spasmodic efforts of revivalistic religion. He favored the continuance of religious education through one's entire life. In holding that all knowledge was sacred, Vincent laid the foundation for a theology of culture in which all of creation was religious and open to study. This provided the basis for Chautauqua becoming not only a religious center but also a center for the study of science, literature, languages, liberal arts, and the performing arts (Stubblefield, 1980, p. 4).

Though the Chautauqua movement is not a dominant religious movement in Protestantism today—the curriculum has become greatly secularized—the movement has left a powerful legacy for adult religious education. Vincent considered religious education, and all education, as a right and a duty. Secondly, Vincent believed that the adult years were uniquely suited for learning because adults bring to the learning process valuable experience from life. The third, and perhaps most important part of the legacy of Chautauqua, was the belief that education, including religious education, should face the challenges of contemporary society. The Chautauqua leaders:

> wanted a relevant Protestantism. That could only be brought about by confronting directly the scientific challenges to faith and by addressing the social and human problems associated with industrialization and urbanization. Chautauqua, though located in rural America, addressed the problems of urban America (Stubblefield, 1980, p. 9).

Some of the issues which Chautauqua faced were temperance, Sabbath observance, women's suffrage, labor, trade, and property. Advocates of the Social Gospel and progressives were welcomed at Chautauqua. The Chautauqua leaders challenged the members of the movement to take Christian responsibility for social problems facing the country. They advocated prohibition as a solution to the poverty problem. For the immigrants they advocated education for acculturation in American society. They worked for an end to child labor and supported suitable protection for women in industry. They were critical of the excesses of capitalism but did not move in the direction of socialism (Utlaut, 1972, p. 178).

In Roman Catholicism no institution comparable to Chautauqua was established at this time. The chief forms of education for adults continued to be the pulpit, the liturgy, and the confessional. However, from 1885 to 1900, reading circles developed in Catholic parishes. In 1889 the Reading Study Union was founded with the following objectives:

> to encourage the diffusion of sound literature and to instill a love of good reading into the hearts and minds of the Catholic masses; to give those who pursue their studies after leaving school an available opportunity to follow prescribed courses of the most approved reading, . . . and, particularly, to encourage individual home study in systematic Catholic lines . . . (MacLellan in Knowles, 1977, p. 72).

A second form of Catholic adult religious education developed during this period of history was the Catholic Summer School of America established in 1882 at Catholic University. The purpose of the Summer School was to provide educational opportunities for adults who could not attend the regular university courses. In time other Catholic colleges and universities established similar programs. The majority of those who attended such programs were members of religious orders of women who increasingly took on the task of administering and teaching in the parochial schools (Bryce, 1978).

The most significant educational effort of the Catholic Church of this period was the expansion of Catholic elementary schools. The Third Plenary Council of Baltimore in 1882 mandated that every parish should have an elementary school. It also enjoined Catholic parents to send their children to Catholic schools. Catholic school enrollments rose to nearly two million students by 1920. By the mid 1960s this figures was 5.6 million. This achievement was remarkable but it was not without a price, as will be seen in the next section of this chapter. Part of the price concerns a lack of commitment to adult religious education.

Adult religious education in Judaism developed in synagogues and temples in the latter part of the nineteenth and early twentieth centuries. Almost two and a half million Jews came to this country, mainly from southern and eastern Europe. It was only in this period that communal Jewish life began, since before this time only a few hundred thousand Jews lived in this country (Beckerman, 1973, p. 87). The efforts at adult religious education took the traditional forms of lectures on and study of the Bible and Talmudic writings. One exception was the program at the Sinai Temple in Chicago which "launched its first series of lectures in the fall of 1914 and rapidly gained a national reputation as a champion of free speech in the Chicago area (Knowles, 1977, p. 73)."

LATE METROPOLITAN AMERICA (1920-1981)

The adult education movement in the United States developed considerable strength after the First World War. The movement grew in response to a number of changes in American life. The population grew somewhat older. The large number of immigrants who lived in large cities were in need of Americanization education. The labor force became more skilled. The power of labor unions brought about a shorter workday for many workers. Government began to take a more active role in people's lives, especially in the 1930s. The arts began to flourish and the mass media of newspapers, magazines, and radio began to influence larger numbers of people.

Various institutional developments took place in adult education. Companies began to provide training for their employees. Colleges and universities expanded their educational extension services. Government agencies and voluntary health and welfare agencies entered into the area of education. Expansion was also found in labor education, residential centers for adult learning, library educational programs, and public school evening programs. Agencies developed to coordinate the efforts of these groups. All of these agenices have continued to develop until the present time. More recent efforts in adult education have been launched by community colleges, proprietary schools, foundations (Ford and Carnegie), government agencies (Adult Education Act of 1966 and Lifelong Learning Act of 1978), and educational television. The rapid growth of adult education between the World Wars led to successful efforts to establish national organizations of adult educators. In 1925 the American Association for Adult Education was established. This organization dissolved in 1951. A new organization was established, The Adult Education of the U.S.A. This organization exists today as an umbrella organization which includes adult educators from all sectors of society, including adult religious educators.

In the first part of this period, between the years 1920 and 1960, religious bodies lagged behind other institutions in the expansion and diversification of adult education programs (Knowles, 1977, p. 145). After 1960, however, adult education began to grow rapidly in all religious bodies. This growth is attributed to the response of church leaders to the drop in religious activity among adult church members (Stokes, 1970, p. 354).

Adult religious education in *Protestant churches* has expanded in a number of ways. Large churches have hired directors of adult education or adult ministries. In 1930 the United Christian Adult Movement under the auspices of the International Council of Religious Education established a number of objectives for adult religious education in the areas of Bible, personal faith, family life, church outreach to others, community issues, major social problems, and world relations. The work of this group was assumed under the National Council of Churches in 1950.

Protestant adult education has witnessed the introduction of various methods of education. While Bible study remains predominant, a large variety of methods are being utilized. In the 1950s and 1960s group dynamics became a popular methodology, as it did in all of adult education. With the introduction of these new methods, leadership training in adult education began to be provided by various denominations. Specific courses on the religious education of adults are provided in institutions such as Princeton Theological Seminary. A number of publications have focused specifically on adult religious education: the *Adult Teacher*, published by the Methodist Church, and *Westminster Adult Leader*, published by the Presbyterian Church.

A significant development in Protestant adult religious education was the publication in 1958 of the Indiana Plan (Bergevin and McKinley, 1958). This plan resulted from experiments in fifteen local churches. The genius of the program is that adults participate in planning and conducting their own religious education. This plan and other publications of Indiana University's Department of Adult Education, have made significant contributions to the theory and practice of adult religious education.

By the year 1961 it is estimated that over fourteen million Protestants were enrolled in church sponsored programs in religious education (Knowles, 1977, p. 148). In 1958 and 1961 the School of Education at Pittsburgh sponsored workshops to examine the assumptions upon which various denominations based adult religious education and to propose solutions for improving services in this areas. Little (1962) reported the findings of these workshops. The participants called for allocation of more resources for adult religious education and the utilization of such methods as group dynamics to meet the real needs of adults.

Around the time that the workshops were held some critical voices were raised about the whole enterprise of Protestant adult religious education. Reinhart (1961) contended that the churches played only a marginal role in society and that adult education was only of marginal concern to the churches. Fry came close to despair when he contended that:

> The Church will not be reformed or transformed by adult education no matter what its exponents claim or expect. The church is not open to its future of grace. . . . It is oriented to its past; its present is filled with the contents furnished by tradition. That is the problem (1961, p. 5).

Essert a few years later contended that the problem with adult education in the churches was that it was too often "directed inward toward reinforcement and support of church doctrine rather than outward toward the problems of Christian living in modern society (1965, p. 9)." All of these critics challenged the churches to a form of adult education that would not only provide religious nurture for its members but would also be a force for social, economic, and political changes in society.

Some recent developments in Protestantism have been in

response to these challenges. Curricular materials published by various denominations have focused on the relevance of religion to life in society. Progressive congregations in the 1960s and early 1970s began to use in their adult programs such books as Robinson's *Honest to God* and Cox's *The Secular City*. The ecumenical movement gave rise to Living Room Dialogues in which Protestants discussed with Catholics issues pertaining to faith and society. This was a time for activism for many Protestant denominations as issues such as civil rights and war in Vietnam dominated public discussions.

The present situation of Protestant adult religious education has been described by Stokes (1977). From his research data he has identified eight major trends: (1) Denominations have different understandings of adult education: social action, personal development, and basic doctrinal instruction. (2) All denominations are concerned with faith crisis. There is a sense that people do not have a clear understanding of fundamentals of faith. A program of "Faith Explorations" has been developed by the United Church of Christ. (3) The concept of education is under question. While for some education means indoctrination in beliefs, for others it refers to the entire ministry of the church, including worship and the action/reflection model of education. (4) Interest in the entire life span has increased among denominations. There is an awareness that adults at different stages of life have special needs: young adults, middle-aged adults, and older adults. (5) Adult education programming is more and more taking place at the local and not the denominational level. (6) A variety of models of adult religious education are found. A program used in many denominations is *Christian Education: Shared Approaches*. Within the four approaches (knowing, interpreting, living, and doing the Word), there are six models of adult education available. (7) There is a recognition that adult education programs must speak to special needs: singles, women, single parents, parents, divorced people, childless couples, homosexuals, and the physically and mentally handicapped. (8) A cross-generational emphasis is found in adult education. Besides the renewed interest in family life, there is also an emphasis on intergenerational learning where children, youth, and adults together participate in an educational experience.

While Stokes's study came from a survey of Protestant churches, it is safe to say that a study of Catholic and Jewish religious groups would reveal similar findings. The relationships and contacts between religious bodies have become such in the past two decades that many similarities are to be found in educational efforts and other forms of church activity.

Developments in adult religious education in *Roman Catholicism* during this period have shown a steady growth. The establishment of the National Catholic Welfare Conference (NCWC) in 1919 served to promote broad religious, educational, and social interests of Catholics. The conference has been active in publications and in sponsoring such lay organizations as the National Conference of Catholic Men and the National Conference of Catholic Women. The Social Action Department of the Council has had a long history of involvement in labor education, social action education, and education in international relations.

Two pioneers in the development of adult religious education were Virgil Michel, a Benedictine priest, and Edwin O'Hara, the Bishop of Great Falls, Montana. Michel was deeply interested in the relationship between liturgy and religious education. In 1929 he established a liturgical summer school at St. John's Abbey, Collegeville, Minnesota. Classes in liturgy, pedagogy, religious music, and Christian art and symbolism attracted many religious sisters who staffed parochial schools. In 1926 he began publishing a journal, *Orate Fratres* (now called *Worship*) which has been a powerful instrument for both liturgical studies and religious education (Bryce, 1978, pp. 47-49).

Michel's interest in liturgical education was paralleled by O'Hara's interest in religious education, especially in rural areas. In 1929 O'Hara established the National Catholic Rural Life Conference (NCRLC) to develop rural religious leaders to further adult religious education and to provide educational opportunities for the religious education of children in areas where there were no parochial schools. While conducting his work in religious education O'Hara recognized the need for the establishment of a strong religious education organization such as the Confraternity of Christian Doctrine (CCD), an association which had its origins in sixteenth century Italy. By 1934 the American bishops formally approved the CCD with O'Hara as its chairman. O'Hara gave great prominence to adult religious education as "he proceeded to organize study clubs, correspondence courses, and even street preaching (Bryce, 1978, p. S-54)." A special concern for O'Hara was the training of lay catechists. He attempted to provide for their needs with congresses, courses, and Bible study groups. His deep interest in Bible study convinced him of the need for a more contemporary translation of the Bible. Such a translation was done by American Catholic scholars under the auspices of the CCD.

In the 1940s and 1950s the Chicago area was the scene of a number of innovative efforts in adult religious education. Bishop Sheil established a School of Social Studies which operated for a number of years after the Second World War. Walter Imbiorski, a Chicago priest deeply interested in marriage education, founded Pre-Cana conferences for couples preparing for marriage and Cana Conferences for married couples. Both of these movements spread nationally, together with the Christian Family Movement, a prayer-discussion-action group, which was also founded in Chicago.

Perhaps the most significant adult religious education experiment started in the 1950s was the Chicago Adult Education Centers (CAEC) founded by Cardinal Stritch, the Archbishop of Chicago. A center involved a "facility central to perhaps a dozen Catholic parishes, staffed by a full-time coordinator skilled in adult religious education approaches and techniques who serves the adults of several parishes (Schaefer, 1978, p. 139)." Such centers are concerned with continuing theological education for adults. The centers in Chicago grew from five in 1955 to twelve in 1969. The Chicago centers ceased to exist by 1969 when their activities were absorbed by other agencies (Ryan, 1972, p. 7). The enduring value of this experiment is that it provided models for other Roman Catholic dioceses such as Kansas City, Detroit, and Manchester, New Hampshire. The need for such centers has become less today since adult religious education has developed extensively as a function of the local parishes.

By 1958 a need was felt in the Catholic Church for a national association besides the CCD to promote and coordinate adult religious education. A group that previously met in conjunction with the National Catholic Education Association (NCEA) formed the National Catholic Adult Education Commission (CAEC). The Executive Director during the first years was Vaile Scott. The commission served to improve communications among and upgrade the skills of adult educators. Summer workshops and leadership training schools were set up to accomplish this task (Knowles, 1977, p. 149). This commission did not receive great support or recognition from the NCEA and in 1972 in ceased to exist as a commission and became a department of the NCEA (Ryan, 1972, p. 53).

The greatest impetus to adult religious education in the Catholic Church came with the Second Vatican Council (1962-65). The renewal that Pope John XXIII promised was written into the documents of the Council. This renewal demanded a more concerted effort at adult religious education in order to bring about reforms in worship, promote ecumenical dialogue, raise the status of the laity, and make the church more relevant to the lives of its members and to society in general. These documents have had great importance in setting ideals for adult religious education in the past decade and a half.

The year 1970 has been identified as the "beginning of a new era in Catholic adult education (Ryan, 1972, p. 8)." This was the year that a Division of Adult Education was established in the United States Catholic Conference (USCC) with Dr. Lawrence Losoncy as Director. That year also witnessed the increase of directors of adult education for Roman Catholic dioceses. Also at this time, parish directors or coordinators of religious education (DRE's or CRE's) began to direct more attention to parish adult religious education.

Another powerful force for the advancement of adult education has come from the writings of Roman Catholic religious educators. Mary Perkins Ryan (1964) created a storm in church circles when she argued that the Catholic school system was not the answer to the educational needs of Catholics. Her proposal was for more family-centered religious education. Gabriel Moran (1968) challenged the church to develop a more adult-centered religious education. In later works Moran (1970, 1974, 1979) has more fully described his adult-centered ecumenical religious education. A sophisticated analysis of programming planning for Christian adult education has been developed by Schaefer (1972). Other important writings in the field have come from Agnew (1976), Coughlin (1976), Girzaitis (1977), and Downs (1979).

Documents emanating from Rome and from the American bishops have expressed a strong commitment to adult religious education. The General Catechetical Directory issued from Rome in 1971 asserted that:

> catechesis for adults, since it deals with persons who are capable of an adherence that is fully responsible, must be considered the chief form of catechesis. All the other forms, which are indeed always necessary, are in some way related to it (Marthaler, 1973, p. 50).

The pastoral letter of the American bishops, *To Teach as Jesus Did* (United States Catholic Conference, 1972) stated that adult religious education was to be situated "not at the periphery of the Church's educational mission but at its center (Art. 44)." The document also spelled out the practical consequences of this principle:

> Formal programs of adult education at the parish and diocesan levels deserve adequate attention and support, including professional staffing and realistic funding. Adult education should also have a recognized place in the structure of Church-sponsored education at all levels: parish, diocesan, and national (Art. 46).

An extensive treatment of adult religious education is found in *Sharing The Light Of Faith* (United States Catholic Conference, 1979), a national catechetical directory for Catholics in the United States. After reviewing stages of adult development, the document gives a number of guidelines for the catechesis/religious education of adults at various stages of development. The document concludes its treatment of adult catechesis with this statement:

> Because of its importance and because all other forms of catechesis are oriented in some way to it, the catechesis of adults must have high priority at all levels of the Church. The success of programs for children and youth depends to a significant degree upon the words, attitudes, and actions of the adult community, especially parents, family, and guardians (Art. 188).

In this document an extremely broad view is taken of religious education. It includes education in the teachings of the Church, education for worship, education for social ministry, and education towards maturity in faith.

Though there has been strong support for adult religious education at the highest levels of the Catholic Church, the actual practice of adult education is beset with a number of problems that practitioners have grappled with for the past decade. A task force of adult religious educators has described the chief problems and challenges in this field (Department of Education, 1977): how to motivate adults for religious education; how to provide a conducive environment for adult education; how to develop leadership for the field; how to reconcile the tension between church authority and self-directed learning; and how to understand the dynamics of spiritual maturity. At the present time subgroups within the task force are working on clarifying these issues, setting realistic goals, and deciding upon actions to meet these challenges. It is expected that the task force will issue reports on a number of areas that have been isolated for further study.

Adult religious education has become a vibrant force in *Judaism* since the 1920s. Some agreement was reached between the years 1920 and 1960 on the goals of Jewish adult education: to establish Jewish identity; to foster a loyalty to the Jewish community; to restore the traditional Jewish ideal of liberal learning; and to draw adults to the synagogues to make prayer and worship important in their lives (Knowles, 1977, p. 149). Some differences existed among the major Jewish groups about priorities among these aims. The Orthodox emphasized the full observance of traditional laws and customs. Reform synagogues were more concerned with cultural issues such as problems of ethics and relationships with non-Jews. Conservative Jews attempted to balance both of these aims (Leon Feldman in Knowles, 1977, pp. 150-151). Differences have also existed among the groups in their manner of programming. Orthodox emphasized the careful study of texts. Reform temples utilized such forms as large meetings, debates, and lectures. A pattern widely adopted by Reform and Conservative synagogues is the Congregational Institute of Jewish Studies. Members meet at local synagogues one evening a week to study Hebrew, Bible, Jewish history, and other subjects. Lectures are also offered (Knowles, 1977, p. 150).

In the 1950s a number of cirticisms appeared of adult education in synagogues. Lily Feldman lamented the marginal status of the work: small budget, lack of adult education committees, lack of trained directors, and the unpreparedness of rabbis for this work (Lily Feldman in Knowles, 1977, p. 150). Leon Feldman criticized Jewish adult education as too indoctrinative, too promotive of specific Jewish causes, and irrelevant for contemporary society. Rabbi Feldman, however, sounded a note of optimism when he judged that Jews "were in the midst of transitional years which will lay the groundwork for a vigorous, healthy program of congregational adult Jewish education (Leon Feldman in Knowles, 1977, p. 151).

The turning point in Jewish education in this country was the Holocaust and the establishment of the State of Israel. Jews in America strengthened their ties with synagogues and sought guidance in their faith. At this time interest in adult education increased and with this the field became more professionalized (Beckerman, 1973, p. 88). Many Jewish organizations became involved in programs of adult religious education: American Jewish Committee, American Jewish Congress, B'nai B'rith, and Hassadah. Programs in adult education were established at Hebrew Union College, Jewish Theological Seminary, and Yeshiva University. What resulted from these efforts was "discussion and study guides: pamphlets, books, and magazines; courses, lectures, workshops, and retreats; concerts and exhibits. Topics vary from theology to cooking to civil rights (Beckerman, 1973, 89)."

The first major study of the status of Jewish adult education in this country was conducted in 1964 by the American Association for Jewish Education. The survey focused on educational objectives, curriculum, methodology, and activity format (Cohen, 1964). Of the thirty-nine congregations that formed the sample for the study, most reported having adult programs on the basic tenets of Jewish faith. However, little emphasis was placed on contemporary problems and issues, although the majority of the congregations reporting were concerned with instilling intellectual awareness and knowledge of Judaism (Cohen, 1964, p. 287). The survey did not include classes on the Torah and parent education programs.

A more recent report on the status of Jewish adult education (Cohen, 1977) concluded that adult education has become an an important field of American Jewish education. All of the 3000 synagogues in the country reported some form of adult education. The thirty-five acknowledged Jewish organizations promoted forms of Jewish adult education. Local Jewish community centers and YMHAs engage in adult education. Cohen estimated that over 600,000 Jews participate in adult education sponsored by Jewish organizations.

A second point Cohen made in his report was that the synagogue is no longer the central agency for adult Jewish education. Jewish organizations such as community centers or Hassadah now loom as central agencies for Jewish adult education. In fact Cohen pointed to an emerging tension between the synagogue leadership and the leadership of the local Jewish community for the control over adult Jewish education (p. 151). Members of the Jewish community have a variety of opportunities for pursuing education in Judaism.

Cohen's third point is that "theological, philosophical and ideological differences between the various adult Jewish education programs are becoming increasingly blurred (p. 152)." He suggests that while the synagogue is becoming more secularized in its religious programs, community programs are becoming more "regionalized." Cohen sees no differences between the major adult Jewish programs he has examined.

The lag between adult education, especially in synagogues, and general adult education constituted Cohen's fourth point. This lag exists in eight areas: crystallization and clarification of educational objectives; understanding of needs and interests of participants; involvement of more lay personnel in program development; development and use of more sophisticated instructional material; recruitment and training of more qualified teachers; more effective recruitment and promotion; adequate financing; and serious evaluation of programs (Cohen, 1977, pp. 152, 153). These findings can be generalized with a great deal of confidence to other religious bodies.

In concluding his excellent review Cohen identified four significant trends within the field of adult Jewish education. First, there is a trend toward recognizing the need for more professionalization in the field. Secondly, intergenerational cooperation has developed for reasons of economy and avoidance of unnecessary duplication. Thirdly, adult Jewish education has become increasingly concerned with the issue of Jewish identity. Fourthly, there is great concern for Jewish public issues and Jewish public affairs, such as the Holocaust, the State of Israel, and American foreign policy toward Israel. Cohen surmises that perhaps the reason why articles are no longer published about the vanishing American Jew is the "emergence of a widespread ongoing network of adult Jewish education programs in virtually every Jewish community in the United States (p. 155)."

In reviewing the history of Jewish adult education in America it is clear that this education deals more with secular issues than adult religious education in Protestantism or Catholicism. The political realities of Jewish life and the deep concern of American Jews for the state of Israel have no doubt been extremely influential in bringing about this situation. Some Jewish educators, however, have become concerned that the secularization of Jewish adult education might result in the abandonment of the centuries old Jewish tradition of lifelong study of the Torah. Greenberg (1973) has described and argued for a return to this older tradition because of his belief that:

> Only that is worthy of lifetime study which is relevant to the building of the religious or spiritual personality, and I know of no subject matter more suitable to that purpose than the Torah (p. 346).

Greenberg is not opposed to educational programs that focus on politics, literature, and art. He considers these good programs and says he would greet them more enthusiastically if they were "in addition to and not as a substitute for the lifetime study of the Torah (p. 346)." He considers such study indispensable for spiritual and intellectual growth and urges educators to develop materials for the relevant study of the Jewish tradition.

CONCLUSION

This brief history of adult religious education has only attempted to point out the leading developments that have shaped the present situation of the religious bodies in the United States. The present situation is one of optimism in all three religious bodies treated in this chapter. There is no immediate hope that adult religious education will become the central focus in the educational activity of these religious bodies. But there is reasonable hope that the future will be much better than the past. Progress has been slow but it has been steady. Schaeffer passed on sage advice when he commented that "Adult Religious Education is a matter of decades rather than years (1977, p. 143)." This historical survey has borne out the truth of this remark.

PART II
THE PRACTICE OF ADULT
RELIGIOUS EDUCATION

CHAPTER VI

THEORETICAL APPROACHES TO ADULT RELIGIOUS EDUCATION

Chapter Six serves as the bridge between the first part of the book, The Foundations of Adult Religious Education, and the second part, the Practice of Adult Religious Education. It serves as a bridge between the two parts because it presents the various theoretical approaches that attempt to connect foundations with practice in adult religious education. Ideally, each theoretical approach would presuppose some foundational position on understanding adulthood, an understanding of the influence of social contexts on adult development, an explanation of psychological and religious development, and a theory of how adults learn. In fact each theory directs itself usually to one or more of these foundational issues. The theoretical approaches treated are also part of the history of adult religious education, having developed at particular historical times. These theories bridge over into the practice of adult religious education since they attempt to describe and explain what is happening in adult religious education or to argue for ideals that should be achieved in adult educational activity: how it should be organized; what its objectives are; how to determine needs of adults; how to plan, design, manage, and evaluate adult religious education programs.

In an earlier work (Elias and Merriam, 1980) I developed six theoretical approaches to adult education. This chapter attempts to extend that work more specifically into the area of adult religious education. Six philosophies or theoretical approaches were found to be present in adult education: adult liberal education, progressive adult education, behaviorist adult education, humanistic adult education, radical adult education (a better term might be reconstructionist adult education), and analytic philosophy of adult education. With some modifications I believe that this same typology can be used to understand adult religious education theories. Writers chosen to illustrate these approaches are primarily

151

those who have addressed themselves explicitly to *adult* religious education. A number of other theorists will be included whose work, it appears, can be easily extended to adult religious education.

THEORY IN ADULT RELIGIOUS EDUCATION

Theoretical work in adult religious education has been on the increase in the past decade. A search of theory or models of understanding usually follows a time of increased practical activity. Practical activity, with its successes and failures, leads to a questioning of assumptions, an awareness of limitations in present theories and models, and a search for new theories and models. Though religious education (like education in general) has a built-in bias toward the practical, this has not meant that the field has been without highly developed theoretical approaches.

At the outset a distinction must be made between two meanings of the term theory. Philosophy or theory in a *professional sense* utilizes strictly the tools of philosophical inquiry: description, analysis (both descriptive and interpretative), logic, establishment of principles and laws, evaluation through norms of validation, correspondence, coherence, and constructive synthesis (Kaplan, 1964; Kaufman, 1975). Philosophy or theory in the *public sense* is less rigorous and systematic in its use of these tools. The former type of theory has the profession of academics as its audience; the latter form addresses itself to the general public. Thus when adult religious education (and religious education in general) is said to be weak in theory, theory is usually taken in the professional sense. The field has ample theoretical writings in the public sense. This chapter includes both forms of theory, though theory in the public sense will receive more attention simply because more of it exists.

The purposes of theory are well-known. Theory attempts to describe and classify, understand and explain, predict, and at times control. An educational theory attempts to do this for the practice of education, as theories of law, art, science, and medicine attempt to accomplish the same tasks for their respective fields. An adequate educational theory attempts to direct itself to the major elements of the educational enterprise: social contexts and institutions, aims and objectives, content and methods, persons and relationships, and evaluation of these elements.

In educational enterprises and activities, in persons involved in education, and in educational organizations there is at least an implicit philosophy of education or educational theory. An educational theory is clarified by responses to such basic questions as: why educate adults in their religion? what are the proper goals and objectives of adult religious education? why is a certain content or a certain method preferable to others? how is adult education related to broad social goals? why should evaluation be part of the educational process?

Though educational theories are at least implicitly present in the educational enterprise, more attention must be given to making theories more explicit. Often what educators think they are doing is not what they are doing. Organizational structures may be at variance with the stated goals of an organization and their members. Methods may be disconsonant with content. Methods of evaluation may result in achieving undesirable results. Persons within an organization may be working at cross-purposes with one another. People may use the same language to express different realities, attitudes, and purposes. Though some persons in education see little value in the careful analysis of goals and objectives, especially when these have to be put into writing, this painful process is invaluable as an exercise in theory development for individuals and organizations.

In presenting various theories of adult religious education, it it not my purpose to arrive at one adequate theory. It is clear from earlier chapters that this is currently an impossibility in many, if not all, areas of study. My purpose is rather to show the richness of the different approaches that have developed over the years. A major advantage from knowledge of theories is that such knowledge is the mark of a professional in a field. A knowledge of theories is often at the basis of the distinction between the professional and the paraprofessional. The practices of a profession are guided by and critiqued by its theories. The theories of a profession are tested, modified, and revised through implementation in practice.

ANALYSIS OF LANGUAGE AND CONCEPTS

The most widely practiced philosophy of education in the English-speaking world is analytic philosophy of education. This philosophical approach takes as its primary data the ordinary language and concepts which we use. In adult education this leads to an examination of our language about adulthood, adult education, needs assessment, rights of adults to education, and other issues. Imitating the rigor of science, this theoretical approach utilizes the techniques of traditional logic and contemporary semantics to clarify the meaning of educational language. Two recent works (Lawson, 1975; Paterson, 1979) have applied such techniques to the general field of adult education.

In religious education Williamson's (1970) work is the most rigorous example of this type of philosophy. Williamson examined such concepts as educational objectives, the needs curriculum, concepts of teaching and learning. He found much confusion in the use of language in the field of religious education. Melchert (1974; 1977) utilized the methods of analytic philosophy to provide helpful analyses of the concepts of "education," "religion" and "religious education." In expressing his concern "to arrive at a clear understanding of the nature and the task of religious education (1977, p. 354)" and by utilizing methods of language analysis, Melchert has moved beyond the rather negative conclusions that Williamson arrived at.

Neither Williamson nor Melchert focused upon *adult* religious education, though their analyses are as relevant for this field as they are for religious education. The field of adult religious education, however, has received careful analysis from Moran (1974; 1979) and Monette (1978; 1979b). Moran's work in language clarification is not situated within the school of analytic philosophy, though there are similarities between this school and Moran's methods. Beginning with *The Religious Body* (1974) Moran has become increasingly interested in clarifying language and in advocating precise meanings for words. He recognizes that "a precise use of language does not exclude all ambiguity (1974, p. 20)." He is more interested in fighting for the meaning of old words by recreating them in life. He wants language to have both precision and universal quality. Moran goes beyond most analysts in being keenly interested in the control of language by institutions. An example he gives is blurring of language, as when words like "community," "religion," and "education" are given many different meanings (1974, p. 38).

Some of the concerns about language that Moran raised in *The Religious Body* were raised again in his *Education Toward Adulthood* (1979), a theoretical treatment of key issues in religious lifelong learning. Moran uses theory in the sense of reflecting upon what is already in practice. He contends that if people engage in this type of theorizing they will see possibilities they have missed and "as they better describe their experience, the world is transformed beyond what any theory makers could envision (1979, p. 20)." Though this overstates the case for theory, Moran has pinpointed the high potential for theory in adult religious education.

One of Moran's analyses, that of adulthood and religious maturity, has been presented in Chapter One. Moran also makes important distinctions among adult education, the education of adults, and education toward adulthood. He contends that these distinctions reflect important philosophical choices (1979, p. 1). Moran is uncomfortable with the first two expressions because they imply that an educational theory can be developed which does not include the education of children. He further contends that for a proper education toward adulthood, religion must be an essential component. Moran's uneasiness with such terms as "adult religious education" is that they seem to imply that this is the province of the churches.

Education Toward Adulthood provides a number of other linguistic analyses. Moran makes an important distinction between a concept of adulthood that focuses on rationality, objectivity, and productivity, and a concept that attempts to integrate rationality with non-rationality, dependence with independence, and life with death (1979, ch. 2). In developing a model of education Moran makes careful distinctions between schooling, laboratory, work, family, retreat, and community (ch. 3).

This sampling of language analyses done in adult religious education by Moran gives some indication of the range of his interests. However, his concerns do not begin and end with language. To the contrary, as we will see later in this chapter, Moran uses analyses as a useful tool in developing a multifaceted theory of adult religious education.

Another religious educator who has joined Moran in his concern for language clarification is Monette. In a number of clearly and carefully written articles Monette has analyzed the use of the term "needs" in adult education and adult religious education. This term was the focus of analytic philosophers in this country in the 1950s and 1960s when the "needs curriculum" was promoted in public schooling (Archambault, 1957; Komisar, 1960). Adult educators have since that time advocated "needs meeting" as a primary element of programming in adult education.

In Monette's articles various meanings and uses of the "needs language" are analyzed: need, prescriptive need, motivational needs, and basic human needs (1978; 1979b). He also examines relationships between needs and policy making, the political dimension of needs, and the connections between needs and freedom/authority. A major point of Monette's analysis is that needs setting demands value judgments and a values framework. Meeting people's needs is not simply a matter of adopting a market approach to adult religious education. Monette offers a number of suggestions for the practice of adult education based on this analysis of needs. These suggestions will be examined in Chapter Eight.

Monette is similar to Moran in that his real interests go beyond the clarification of language. In his follow-up article (1979a) he utilizes Freire's sociopolitical theory of education to provide an alternative approach to the assessment of educational needs. This moves Monette's theoretical approach beyond language analysis into the area of a political theory of education.

The field of adult religious education needs more attention to language clarification. An attempt will be made in later chapters to clarify a number of concepts commonly used in the field. Language analysis brings to the field a clarity and a quality of reasoning that challenge loose language and slogans, unpack metaphors, and show the vague and ambiguous use of words. At times, however, language analysis may lead to unwarranted consequences, as is the case of Moran's rejection of the term "adult education" in favor of "education toward adulthood." Though I agree with his point that "adult education" has connoted a lack of continuity with education of children and a static view of adulthood, I contend that there are good reasons not to abandon this phrase but rather to retrieve it along lines that he has proposed. The language is well-established in common usage. It focuses upon a large span of life that is neglected by educators. A field and a profession has developed around this particular term.

A second danger of analysis, one which both Moran and Monette avoid, has been its stance of providing a methodology that is value free or netural. Both Lawson and Paterson argue for an adult education tha has no direct social purpose. Paterson contends that "the commitment of education is to knowledge, understanding, insight (1979, p. 256)." From this he concludes that "it is not the purpose of education either to vindicate the status quo or to advocate social change, whether gentle and piecemeal or radical and sweeping (1979, p. 256)." Both Moran and Monette and other adult religious educators appear to reject this position.

ADULT LIBERAL EDUCATION IN RELIGION

While language philosophy is a rather recent approach to educational theory, liberal education has a long and venerable tradition in education. This approach also focuses on language, not, however, on ordinary language but rather on the language of the great classics in literature, history, science, philosophy, and religion. The focus in liberal education is upon the ideas and values contained in classic works of Western civilization. The emphasis in this theory is upon liberal learning, the organization of bodies or disciplines of knowledge, and the development of the rational powers of the mind.

The fortunes of adult liberal education in North America have known both rise and decline. It was prominent in colonial colleges and in such experiments as Franklin's Junto. Jefferson espoused it in his plans for a nationalized form of education. The lyceum movement was strongly influenced by this perspective as was the Chautauqua movement. The popularity of this theory declined with the rise of the practical thrust of progressivism and pragmatism in the later part of the nineteenth century. After World War I there was renewed interest in this theory when people searched for values upon which to build a new society. Eminent scholars advocated adult liberal education: Robert Hutchins, Mortimer Adler, Gilbert Highet, Mark Van Doren, and Jacques Maritain. Great Books Clubs, discussion groups, lectures, and cultually oriented programs developed at this time. This tradition is still strong in some sectors of the adult education movement (Elias and Merriam, 1980, ch. 2).

Adult liberal education has enjoyed great favor in religious education. Religions place great emphasis on the truths and values contained in the writing of their traditions. Study of the Bible, commentaries on the Bible, classical writings of theologians, and contemporary efforts to relate religious traditions to present culture and experience form the basis of liberal religious education and are found in adult religious education. John Vincent, the founder of the Chatauqua movement, expressed this philosophy when he urged that participants should "read the same books. . . . Let the course of prescribed reading be broad and comprehensive (Vincent in Grattan, 1959, p. 67)."

The theory of liberal education utilizes classics to promote three types of growth: rational and intellectual; development of the esthetic sense; and spiritual and religious growth. This last dimension was strongly advocated in the classic work of Jacques Maritain, *Education at the Crossroads* (1943), in which he argued against the purely pragmatic view of education. In his theory of education the prime goal was the conquest of internal and spiritual freedom. Such goals as problem-solving, social adjustment, and social change were to be subordinated to the primary goal of intellectual development.

Adult liberal education in religion places primary focus on education in religious classics, ancient and contemporary. Greater importance is given to the content of education than to processes of education, though the latter are not ignored. Though many religious educators have developed theories in this tradition (Burgess, 1975, chs. 2, 4), the most comprehensive effort in adult religious education is Schaefer's *Program Planning for Adult Christian Education* (1972). In this work Schaefer clearly places classical theological writings of the Christian tradition at the center of his theory. Liberal learning, organized learning, and intellectual development are primary though not exclusive focuses in Schaefer's theory.

Schaefer's work is a theoretical one in a professional sense. It is directed to academics and utilizes the language of the curriculum theorist. After establishing the principles of curriculum theory in general terms (objective, personnel, scope, process, context, timing), Schaefer develops principles for adult Christian education in each of these areas. The main organizing principle for program planning, however, is the scope or content. The objective of Christian adult education is that mature Christians learn "the meaning of the Church's experience of the mystery of Christ (p. 109)." The scope of Christian education includes a knowledge of the mystery of Christ as event (Biblical dimension), as horizon (theological dimension), as celebration (liturgical dimension), and a moral imperative (ethical dimension).

Closely related to scope in importance is the process of adult Christian education. Schaefer describes this process as interpersonal appropriation by faith. Methods of disclosure are appropriate for producing a historical knowledge of Christ as presented in the Scriptures. Methods of inquiry are suitable for promoting cognitive understanding of theological approaches to the mystery of Christ. Methods of initiation are suggested for bringing persons to an appreciation of the liturgical celebration of the mystery of Christ. Finally, problem-solving approaches are recommended for creating a sense of responsibility to moral imperatives contained in the mystery of Christ (Schaefer, 1972, p. 167).

Though this brief summary does not do justice to the precision and complexity of Schefer's theoretical approach to adult religious education, it does present its essential features. The major dimensions of liberal religious education are represented: the wisdom presented in theological classics is the primary focus of education; intellectual understanding of ideas and values found in these classics is promoted; moral education takes place through exposure to and dependence on values in religious classics; and religious and spiritual growth is through initiation into a way of living and a way of thinking celebrated in a religious community. Though Schaefer places major emphasis on religious or theological classics, he recognizes that learning begins with the needs and interests of learners and the competencies of teachers. Yet he makes it clear that a distinctive Christian education does not take place until adults are involved with meanings that pertain to the

Church's understanding of the mystery of Christ in one or more of its fourfold dimensions (1972, p. 198).

Since an alternative analysis of the process of program planning will be presented in a later chapter, no extended critique of this position is presented here. Suffice it to say, Schaefer's analysis does not do full justice to the dimension of the religious or theological. A broadened view of human learning and modes of learning is needed. The starting point of the educational process must be more clearly within persons in human communities. The objectives of adult religious education must be broadened to include the personal, interpersonal, social, and political. (These criticisms come from one who considers Schaefer's work a classic in the field, uses this work in his graduate classes, and has profited greatly from contact with it.)

Schaefer's work clearly raises the issue of the role of theology in adult religious education. I identify adult liberal education in religion with theological approaches that Tracey describes as orthodox or neo-orthodox (1976). Burgess (1975) does something similar when he describes the traditional and the contemporary theological approaches to religious education. Schaefer's work is neo-orthodox or kerygmatic in its theological understanding. Biblical theology and the theological method of Lonergan are most influential in key sections of his work. The modes of education most appropriate to these theological approaches are preaching, teaching through instruction, a study of classical religious sources, initiation into sacred rituals, and a theologically founded moral education.

I bring up the issue of theology in order to emphasize the pluralism in theology that Tracey has so brilliantly analyzed. A pluralism in theology has led to a pluralism in theories of religious education. It must also be recognized that some theories of religious education take a non-theological or anti-theological stance. Pluralism in theology and religious thought, dependent as it is on more critical understandings and correlations of religious traditions and contemporary secular experience, is partly resposible for the diversity of theoretical approaches found in adult religious education. For example, it was Protestant liberal theology that in part provided the basis for progressive adult education and for what Burgess terms the social-culture approach to religious education (1975, ch. 3).

PROGRESSIVE ADULT EDUCATION IN RELIGION

Progressive education had its intellectual origins in the various movements of the Enlightenment: naturalism, romanticism, and empiricism. The authority of classics in philosophy and religion was questioned. Natural feelings, reason, and scientific observation became the acceptable ways of arriving at knowledge. Traditional education with its dependence on classics was criticized by such Enlightenment figures as Comenius, Rousseau, Pestalozzi, Hegel, Loche, and Bacon. The effort of many religious thinkers was to develop an approach to religious truth that would depend upon feelings, reason, and scientific knowledge.

Progressive education in the United States was part of a complex social and political movement. The educational movement had a least three phases. Early progressivism was student-centered in its focus upon the natural development of the person, especially the child, and its attack on the subject-centeredness of traditional liberal education. Secondly, in connecting its educational theory to progressive social and political movements, progressivism became keenly interested in the power of education to bring about social change. A third aspect of progressive education, represented best in the work of John Dewey (1916; 1938), focused on the role of experience in the educational process. Dewey was interested both in the formative power of our interactive experience with the environment in socializing us into the values of society and in the power of human intelligence acting through the experience of problem solving to bring about changes in our environment.

The theological counterpart to progressive or pragmatic thought were Liberal Protestantism, Modernism, and Reform Judaism. In these theologies human experience, reason, and feeling become the major source of theology. The religious tradition was no longer viewed as a divine and supernatural message. Religious symbols were reinterpreted to correspond to contemporary human experience. These liberal theologies took seriously the challenge of Enlightenment thought but the judgment of history is that they may have jettisoned valuable elements of their religious traditions.

The foremost work of a religious educator within the progressive tradition was George Coe's *A Social Theory of Religious Education* (1917). Religious education in his view had to take account of the natural development of the person in faith, account for human experience in a meaningful manner, and point the way to the solution of social problems. Religious education is not the means of transmitting revealed doctrines of a tradition but a process by which doctrines and values are created or revised. Coe's focus, like that of most progressive educators was on children. For him the aim of religious education was "growth of the young toward and into mature and efficient devotion to the democracy of God, and happy self-realization therein (1917, p. 55)."

At the same time that men like Dewey and Coe were developing the progressive theory of education, the adult education movement was beginning in this country in efforts to socialize immigrants, address social problems that came with urbanization, and prepare workers for a more industrialized nation. Dewey's ideas formed the basis of a classic work in adult education, Eduard Lindeman's *The Meaning of Adult Education* (1926). Life's meaning for Lindeman was to be found "in the things for which men strive, the goals which they set for themselves, their wants, needs, desires, and wishes (1926, pp. 13-14)." The teacher in the educational process was not to be an authority but a guide who also participates in learning. As a professor of social philosophy Lindeman was especially interested in adult education as an instrument for social action. It was his contention that all successful adult education would sooner or later become social action.

Though Cremin (1957) appeared to have written an epitaph for progressive education, a neo-progressivism appeared in the 1960s and 1970s in the writings of John Holt, Paul Goodman, Jonathan Kozol, and others. In religious education it was Gabriel Moran who articulated the position of neo-progressivism most forcefully. Moran first critiqued the neo-orthodox theology found in the kerygmatic catechetical movement imported from Europe (1967). He then presented a theory of ecumenical religious education that is clearly within the progressive tradition (1970). Where Moran differs from most progressives is that he places the education of adults (1974; 1979) at the center of attention. Dewey's classic statement of a theory of education, *Democracy and Education* (1916), is in reality a theory of schooling.

As a religious educator Moran has generally preferred to avoid the language of Christian theology in order to move religious education into dialogue with education in general and with world religions. This has led one interpreter to classify him as a liberal theologian or a theologian of culture (Tracy, 1976). My view is that Moran's type of theological revisionism as found in *The Present Revelation* (1972) is more radical than is currently acceptable to some parts of the theological community which does not generally encompass the broad ecumenical scope of his religious concerns.

The concerns of the progressive or neo-progressive adult educator in religion are with personal growth, the totality of human experience, and social change. Religious traditions are respected but their particular elements are to be subjected to ongoing critique and revision not only from revised understandings from within these traditions but also in the light of new knowledge from secular understandings of human life and culture. How one remains faithful to traditional interpretations and at the same time allows for revisions and transformations is a problem that theology and religious studies face together with all other thought systems. The progressive mentality is to be more open to these possibilities than traditional or orthodox theologies since it places human growth, human experience, and social change at the center of both thought and action.

Progressive education in religion has greater protential for adults than for children. Religious education for children is primarily a process of religious socialization and enculturation into the religious views of family, church, and community. This situation gradually changes as children mature into adolescence and young adulthood. The context of educating children is not usually a fruitful one for revising or transforming theological understandings. Though religious enculturation also takes place in adulthood, this time of life offers the opportunity for a more critical investigation and interpretation of received doctrines. The religious faith of adults confronts greater problems of growth, changing and expanding experiences in and of the world, and demands and opportunities for involvement in social change.

Though the late 1970s and early 1980s have thus far witnessed in some circles a retreat from the enthusiasm for educational reform in the progressive mode, progressive thought is still present in the theories which are in reaction to it—new orthodoxies—and in theoretical approaches which put particular emphasis on one or more dimensions of the progressive thrust: attention to environmental and social factors that shape individual growth (behaviorism, socialization, and enculturation); a focus on human growth through openness to the full range of human experiences (humanistic theories); and attention to the possibilities of achieving social and political change through educational processes (socio-political theories of education). The key to understanding all theories of education, including theories of religious education, is to understand progressivism—what it reacts to and in what forms it persists. Likewise the key to understanding theological or religious thought is understanding theological liberalism—why it rejects orthodox or neo-orthodox thought and in what forms it remains in theological and religious systems of thought. With this perspective we can examine three remaining theoretical approaches to adult religious education.

SOCIALIZATION-BEHAVIORISTIC THEORIES

One of the major components of progressive thought was its reliance on the newly developing psychological, sociological, and anthropological theories for understanding the development of individuals and institutions. This is most apparent in Dewey's statement on moral education, *Human Values and Conduct* (1922). In this work Dewey explains how the learning of values is similar to other forms of learning. Social and environmental factors are powerful determinants of moral values. A major thrust in Dewey's theory of education is to explain how these factors are powerful but not determining influences on human behavior. Dewey resolves this issue by ascribing to the human person a basic freedom and flexibility to make choices among possible interpretations of experience.

The progressive concern with socialization and enculturation has found its way into both education and religious education theories. A radical socialization theory is found in Skinner's behaviorism (1971), which considers the force of environmental factors so powerful that one can set up environmental conditions in such a way that peoples' behavior will be modified in a predetermined manner. Parsons (1970) in his functionalist theory of social systems placed great emphasis on the influences of family and school in socializing persons into the values of a society. Mead (1963) examined the broader cultural factors in the education of persons. Finally, Berger and Luckman (1967) presented a theoretical understanding of how the knowledge and values of individuals are both shaped by and help to shape the social reality of the world in which we live.

An awareness of the influence of such environmental, social, and cultural factors in religious education is found in Bushnell's classic work *Christian Nurture* (1861). Bushnell focused on the child and considered it an educational ideal for children to grow up Christian and never know themselves as being otherwise. For him, home and experience were central in religious learning.

In more recent years a number of religious educators have utilized findings of psychology and the social sciences in developing theories of religious education that place major focus on environmental and cultural factors. Lee (1971) has been the major proponent of a social science approach to religious instruction that utilizes behaviorist principles of learning. A major theme in behaviorism is the power of a reinforcing social environment. Lee's major focus is on the school and even more narrowly on the acts of teaching and learning that take place in the classroom. His theory has been valuable in its questioning of the dominant role that theology has had in religious education and in the attention it gives to the dynamics of the instructional environment. Lee has not explicitly related his theory to the field of adult religious education though much of what he suggests is relevant to this field.

Adult education has received explicit attention in Nelson's classic work in educational theory, *Where Faith Begins* (1967). Drawing on mainly sociological and anthropological sources, Nelson interpreted the power of culture in forming religious traditions, developing faith and identity, producing a religious perception and world view, and forming religious values. Though Nelson's work was primarily concerned with how children are enculturated into the faith of a family and congregation, he also made a strong case for the importance of adult education because of adults' prominent role in congregations and their ability to evaluate religious traditions critically.

Nelson clearly recognized that the strategy of progressive religious education in focusing on the education of children in Sunday Schools had to be reversed. But he was unwilling to advocate changing the strategy to adult education because of difficulties in motivating adults to learn religion, lack of knowledge of how adults learn in informal, voluntary associations such as churches, and a lack of dependable knowledge about how adults change their values and world views (p. 194).

While Nelson advocated an enculturation theory for religious education but stopped short of advocating a new strategy, John Westerhoff in a number of works has reworked the enculturation theory and presented new strategies for implementing the theory. In the clearest statement of his position, *Will Our Children Have Faith?* (1976), Westerhoff has challenged the schooling paradigm that has so long been associated with religious education. Drawing on many of the criticisms that such romantic and revisionist critics as Goodman, Illich, Holt, and Kozol made of the public schools, Westerhoff concluded that schooling is an inappropriate mode of communicating faith. The new paradigm for religious education described in his writings is a community of faith enculturation paradigm. Education in this paradigm focuses around the rituals, experiences, and actions of persons within communities.

Westerhoff's enculturation paradigm deals seriously with adult religious education. Enculturation "emphasizes the process of interaction between and among persons of all ages (1976, p. 80)." This interactive process is one of growth in faith from the experienced faith of childhood to the affiliative faith of adolescence, to the searching faith of late adolescence and young adulthood, and finally to the owned faith of mature adulthood (1976, ch. 4). This faith journey is presented as an ideal, though Westerhoff recognizes that many adults do not reach owned faith. Westerhoff's main educational strategy is active participation in the rites, symbols, beliefs, morality, and life-style of a faith community. His focus is on faith enculturation in the Christian faith.

Socialization theory has been given a strong theoretical foundation in the writings of Marthaler (1978; 1980). Utilizing both empirical research and theoretical inquiry into understanding the socialization process, Mathaler proposes a model of religious socialization that identifies it with the "catechesis" language of documents of the Roman Catholic Church. Both terms emphasize education into the faith of a particular community by participation in the symbols, rites, values, and life-styles of members. Marthaler stresses the importance of adult education in the faith when he states that success in socialization is to be judged not by numbers of children initiated into the community but rather "by answering how well adults are assimilated into the faith community and how closely they identify with it (1978, p. 82)."

Despite their strengths, behaviorist, socialization, and enculturation theories have a number of limitations. Though these theories focus on how faith is transmitted and communicated, they do not appear to contain a critical principle whereby religious faith and religious traditions are evaluated, renewed, and revised. These educational theories appear more appropriate to orthodox theologies and traditional religious systems of thought than they do to liberal and revisionist theologies and religious systems that are open to criticism from both within and without religious communities. Westerhoff seems to reinforce this in his characterization of faith communities as countercultural. Though this is true, religious faith, as all of life, must live in a broader and pluralistic community than this theory envisages (Nicholson, 1980).

Many adults need the types of educational and socialization experiences that these theories recommend. The clearly defined elements of religious knowledge, attitudes, and behaviors described in the social science approach and the more broadly defined Christian life-styles, values, and community ethos emphasized in socialization—enculturation theories are important objectives for adult religious education. More attention, however, must be given to psychological dimensions of personal and interpersonal growth and to the implications of religious faith in particular socio-political contexts. Though these theoretical approaches address these issues, I do not feel that they have done this adequately. The two theories that remain to be treated give particular attention to these aspects.

HUMANISTIC ADULT EDUCATION IN RELIGION

While theories of behaviorism, socialization, and enculturation continue the progressive tradition's focus on environmental factors in education, humanistic educators have stressed the progressives' deep concern for the total experience of human persons. In the past three decades person-centered and experience-centered humanistic theories of education have been powerful influences in all of education, especially adult education. Two major theorists in adult education are clearly in the humanistic tradition, Malcolm Knowles and J. R. Kidd.

Humanistic adult education draws on a number of sources. It is indebted to the liberal tradition for its emphasis on personal freedom and dignity, though it differs from this tradition in not placing classical writings of the past at the center of the educational process. Though it takes its person-centeredness and experience-centeredness from the progressive tradition, humanistic educators tend to place more emphasis than progressives on emotional and affective dimensions of education. Also, some humanistic educators utilize the methods and themes of existentialism and phenomenology. Thus within humanistic education is found a considerable amount of variety.

The chief theorists within this approach are humanistic psychologists Carl Rogers and Abraham Maslow. In Chaper Four I presented the major contributions of these men to the understanding of adult learning. Here I draw attention to their educational theories which have as their major thrusts the facilitation and promotion of personal and interpersonal growth and fulfillment. Humanistic educators are optimistic about human potential for freedom and creativity. They reject the environmental determinism of behaviorism and the biological determinism of Freudian psychoanalysis. They are deeply concerned with insight into problems, intuition, understanding, and subjective experience.

Though much of the practice in adult education is behavioristically motivated, a great deal of the theory is humanistic. Knowles's (1980) andragogical assumptions (discussed in Chapter Four) are drawn from humanistic psychology. The underlying theoretical assumption in Kidd's work (1973) are clearly within this tradition. Tough's research (1979) on self-directed learners also establishes the humanistic premise of intrinsic motivation.

In the field of adult religious education McKenzie has developed a strong theoretical approach which utilizes both existential and personalistic principles. He presents as the major objective of adult education the enabling of "adults to actualize their potentialities to the end that they become more fully liberated as individuals and more fully prepared to participate in bettering the life of the communities to which they belong (1975, p. 13)." Such education becomes religious either by reason of the religious content of the education, e.g., scripture, liturgy, or by reason of the religious intent of the educator, e.g., religious convictions in teaching any content. (The notion of religious in adult religious education is examined in Chapter Nine.)

Humanistic principles are among the key concepts for adult educators that McKenzie draws from the work of Paul Bergevin. These principls include: affirmation of the adult as learner; respect and consideration for persons; promoting of adult freedom in the learning situation; meeting the needs of individuals and institutions; promoting continuing and lifelong growth; and involving adults in a civilizing process (1975, ch. 3). In his defense of andragogy McKenzie also utilizes humanistic and existential theory (1975; 1977). He argues that existential differences between children and adults call for an existentially different theory of learning and teaching. This position has been discussed in Chapter Four.

McKenzie's espousal of humanistic education is made clearer in his more philosophical position in *Adult Education and The Burden of the Future* (1978). In his proposals for adult education McKenzie recommends facilitating in adults a rejection of a deterministic world view. He argues for an adult education that will facilitate the development of proactive and self-directed adults who are responsible for evolving a more enlightened human existence. Adult educators should promote concern for human welfare, a spirit of interdependence and cooperation, and courage in learners. These should be done through self-directed learning and facilitation of groups.

As of yet McKenzie has not treated the specifically religious content of adult religious education. This has been done in general terms from a humanistic perspective by Girzaitis in her *The Church as Reflecting Community: Models of Adult Religious Learning* (1977). This book is written from the standpoint of a perceptive practitioner who combines practical skills with theoretical understanding. Girzaitis presents as the major task of adult education the promotion of adult reflective growth. Adult religious education is to "free self from a narrow and closed vision of life in order to see everyday experiences as a call to growth (p. 20)." Religious growth is described as the increasing capacity to care for oneself as God's image and the striving to know and to accept oneself and others in both strengths and weaknesses. This growth also entails a commitment to meet the needs of others.

The specific goals Girzaitis suggests for adult religious education are aiding persons: (1) to discover and develop their potential as persons created according to the image of God; (2) to recognize the meaning of life and to respect it in all its dimensions; (3) to incorporate the message of Jesus into one's personal life; (4) to articulate and to share the teachings of Jesus with others; (5) to understand and reflect upon the signs of the times so as to give direction to change in order to shape the future; (6) to provide opportunities for ongoing learning at all periods of adult life; (7) to participate in and celebrate life in the church, the community of believers; (8) to aid committed Christians to serve the needy, the poor, the lonely, the outcast, the discriminated against, and the segregated (177, p. 20). These rather lofty ideals for adult Christian education are clearly representative of the humanistic approach. Girzaitis's work directs attention to processes and resources that can be utilized in the local congregations for working toward these ideals.

A major focus of humanistic adult education is education through participation in group activities. Adult education has been greatly influenced by the work on groups by such theorists as Lewin (1951), Rogers (1969), and Miles (1981). Much of adult education in religious bodies takes place in small groups: prayer and meditation groups, discussion groups, support groups, sensitivity or encounter groups, inquiry groups, and action-reflection groups. Both McKenzie and Girzaitis give detailed suggestions for the development of such groups. In Chapter Nine a fuller treatment of groups in adult education is given.

Humanistic theory of adult religious education has also had an impact through a number of popular published programs that incorporate its principles. Genesis II, Romans VII, and the Serendipity Bible Series are three examples of such humanistically oriented programs. The goal of these programs is to promote religious and spiritual growth. Greater emphasis is placed on processes that will lead to growth than on the content of religious teachings, though content is not ignored. The humanistic psychologies of Rogers and Maslow explicitly inform these programs. Such programs also make extensive use of small group processes.

The influence of humanistic theories in adult religious education has been extensive, as might be expected, given the compatibility between its goals and the goals of religious bodies. As one who has both participated in and directed programs of humanistic orientation, I can attest to the practical value of this theory. Yet experience has also taught me some of the pitfalls and limitations of this approach to adult religious education. Since its goals are so idealistically stated, it is difficult to evaluate programs and groups that utilize this form of education. Sparse attention to the content of religious traditions and contemporary thought often promotes an anti-study or anti-intellectual attitude toward adult religious education. Rather extended attention upon the self-growth and group life is often accompanied by a lack of attention to broader social and political concerns.

Notwithstanding these problems it must be conceded that humanistic principles must be part of the adult religious education enterprise. Sensitivity to personal spiritual growth within small communities that share their visions of faith in the world are essential components of sound adult religious education. When these components are combined with a clearer and more realistic setting of goals, a recognition of the importance of serious inquiry, and a commitment to the social and political imperatives of religious faiths, then we have the essential ingredients for an adequate theory of adult religious education.

SOCIO-POLITICAL ADULT RELIGIOUS EDUCATION

It has always been recognized that education is related to the social and political life of a society. Theories of education arise within particular historical circumstances and are related to the social and political goals of society in which they develop. Derr (1973) has classified the socio-political purposes of education in categories of stabilization, reproduction, modification, and replacement. Each theory presented thus far has social and political purposes, though these have not been explicitly drawn. The only theory that clearly presented a replacement or reconstructionist purpose was progressivism's articulated belief in the power of the schools to reconstruct society.

Among progressive educators George Counts (1932) was the strongest advocate of a reconstructionist point of view. In the midst of the Depression he issued a clarion call to teachers to become the revolutionary class that would usher in a socialist revolution. For a brief time his call was debated in educational circles. Most educators, however, considered the indoctrination into socialism that Counts advocated a contradiction to the quality of freedom demanded in the educational process.

The reconstructionist theory of education took on a radical aspect among some educators in the 1960s and early 1970s. A number of educators accepted some Marxist tools for social analysis: class struggle, alienation, and revolutionary praxis (Bowles and Gintis, 1975; Kozol, 1975). Both Goodman (1970) and Illich (1970) argued for an anarchist society, though Illich's utopia included some elements of small capitalism and an implicit socialism. Other educators called for reforms and modifications in both education and society (Silberman, 1970).

For the most part adult education was not the focus of educational reformism or educational radicalism in this period. The publication of Freire's work (1970; 1973) in English did, however, encourage a number of adult educators who contributed to Grabowski's *Paulo Freire: A Revolutionary Dilemma for the Adult Educator* (1972) to consider social and political problems in this country in light of Freire's work in conscientizing impoverished adults in Brazil to the oppressive social reality which made up their world.

Social and political purposes have also had an important place in some religious education theories. The social change orientation that was found in Coe's progressive theory of religious education reappeared in the neo-progressivism of Moran's *Design for Religion* (1970). In this work Moran emphasizes the importance of focusing on "changing the social structure for the increase of freedom (p. 52)." For Moran the presuppositions of all social systems have to be challenged, social organizations should be promoted that increase individual choices, and human resources should be allocated in a way that is proportionate to need (pp. 54-56).

Social purposes of education are also of concern to Moran in *The Religious Body* (1974). Moran analyzes some problems that must be faced in order to reform both religion and society. Bureaucratic societies resist changes in distribution of power, status, and possessions. These societies can be reformed through development of communities dedicated to education and religion. Moran devotes most of his attention to the reform of religious bodies, a concern for which he has many helpful suggestions and criteria. When he takes on the broader problems of society, however, his treatment is not adequate to the task. His analyses of social problems are often general and sketchy. When he treats the role of education in such societies, he makes many fine linguistic distinctions but fails to show what role education can make in addressing some of these problems.

The political purposes of education have been addressed in Groome's *Christian Religious Education* (1980). That education is political activity is demonstrated by Groome through an examination of curriculum. Curricular decisions are political decisions: how is history to be taught? what is to be read? Education is also political because it is an exercise of power of teachers and institutions over people's lives (pp. 15-17). In this excellently conceived work, Groome gives a strong theoretical rationale from Christian and philosophical sources for a shared praxis approach to religious education. He utilizes the Christian symbols of the Kingdom of God, salvation, liberation, and a critical theory of praxis as major elements in his theoretical approach to Christian religious education. For the purposes of this chapter, however, Groome's work is limited in not treating the political purposes of religious education in concrete detail and in not giving particular attention to *adult* Christian religious education. His theory, however, has potential for extension in both of these areas.

A reconstructionist theory of adult religious education is clearly presented in Wren's *Education for Justice* (1977). This work is deeply indebted to Freire's insights on knowing, education, dialogue, and conscientization. This work takes on the difficulties any political theory of education faces: uses and abuses of power, definitions and issues involved in the concept of justice, dealing with conflict, vested interests, overt and subtle forms of oppression, and educational and political strategies.

Wren's work raises the important question that any education for justice must raise, the ideological issue. Most educators avoid this issue and thus remain at the level of either platitudes or overly general principles when it comes to moving from theory to practice in education for justice. Wren examines the conservative view (individual freedom and capitalist economics), the liberal view (freedom, justice, and reason), and the socialist view (equality, redistribution, and conflict). Working and writing in the British socio-political context, Wren agrues for a radical socialism which is willing to dialogue with opposing viewpoints (Ch. 9).

The issues that Wren raises are crucial in education for justice. His small work does not do justice to the complexity of the socio-political analysis from a religious perspective. Though a work of social ethics and not one of educational theory, Wogaman's *A Christian Moral Judgment* (1976) deals more fully with the ideological question in its analysis of the compatibility of the Christian tradition with different economic and political systems. His conclusion is that the greatest possibility of compatibility exists with democratic socialism, though he admits possible compatibility with other ideologies.

I raise this issue not to bring it to any conclusion in this work but to indicate an important dimension of religious education for justice that is most often neglected. If adult religious education is to deal seriously with social and political issues, more attention must be given to sociological and political analysis and to strategies for action in these areas. These are precisely the areas where there is greatest complexity and greatest divergence of ideologies and opinions. Yet an adult religious education that does not deal with these issues may easily remain tied to privatistic and institutional concerns.

Education for justice is most appropriate for adult religious education. Adults are more deeply involved in institutions and organizations of society than children and youth. The dangers of indoctrination, manipulation, and ideological propagandizing are less possible in dealing with mature adults than with pre-adults. It is easier for adults to make the move from discussion and consensus to involvement and action since they are situated more deeply in socio-political contexts.

The risks of this form of religious education are well-known if one recalls the price that Christians in South and Central America and Jews in the Soviet Union have paid in their attempts to educate and act for justice. The exile of Freire and many others from their native countries, the killings of hundreds of activists motivated by liberation theologies, the struggles between church leadership and governments and among members of churches, and the personal affronts to political dissenters attest to the realities of the risks of education and action for justice. Religious bodies in this country that have attempted to bring their religious visions to bear on social, political, and economic issues have also known and experienced the risks involved in political education and politics.

CONCLUSION

Looking back over these six theoretical approaches to adult religious education, one is struck by the depth and range of writings in this field. The field of religious education and the field of adult education are both in ferment. Foundational issues are being actively discussed in the journals of both fields. Adult education has in the past been overly concerned with practical programming. Religious education has been biased toward methods of teaching. It is clear, however, that no matter where one begins in practice, the importance for the development of theory to undergird, explain, and reflect upon practice soon becomes apparent.

In reviewing these theories it is clear that a certain arbitrariness is involved in this classification system. In some sense all theories deal with language clarification, transmission of content, problem-solving processes, behavior and socialization, personal and community growth, and social and political consciousness raising. The classification system is based on perceptions of emphases that exist among different theorists. The perceptions may of course be biased in some ways. Yet attempts at classification, arbitrary as they may appear to some, have a number of advantages. Classifications are useful in introducing persons to a field. They make sense of what is happening in a field of study and practice. They indicate similarities between theorists of different times and places. Such classifications also point out where major differences lie among theorists. The debate over andragogy and the debate over the very names used to describe the field (religious education, Christian education, Jewish education, and catechesis) may appear to some as exercises in semantics; but in reality profound theoretical differences are involved in these debates.

The saying goes that there is nothing so practical as a good theory. This chapter assumes but does not confirm the truth of this statement. The remaining chapters in this book are an attempt to confirm this statement. Theories act as bridges between research foundations and the field of practice. An approach to the field of practice of adult religious education will be developed that is based on major theoretical positions developed in this chapter.

Theoretical approaches are influential in shaping the administrative structure and educational climate for adult religious education. There should be a compatibility between the organization which sponsors adult education and the forms of adult education that are offered. Theory also suggests the types of climates in which it is conducive for adult religious learning to take place.

Educational theory is vital in determining the true needs of individuals and the objectives of adult religious education. The balancing of individual, institutional, and political needs demands an attention to philosophical and theoretical consideration of values. At times planners in adult education think that needs assessment and setting objectives are merely matters of finding out the interests of people and making these the objective in programming. This is a rather simplistic approach to this crucial issue.

Educational theory is involved in decisions about design: scope and process in adult religious education. Theories differ on what is the essential content of religious education, what are the appropriate processes for realizing objectives, and what are the relationships that should exist between scope and process.

Finally, there are implications in educational theory for management and evaluation of programs and learning in adult religious education. Especially in the area of evaluation there are differences among the different educational theories.

CHAPTER VII
ORGANIZING FOR ADULT RELIGIOUS EDUCATION

The major purpose of this chapter is to show that religious bodies should and can become adult learning communities. From a sociological point of view religious bodies are organizations with goals and purposes. In general terms these goals and purposes are personal growth, interpersonal support and fellowship, and societal improvement and change. The values that religious bodies promote at the personal, interpersonal and societal levels are love, peace, justice, equality, and freedom. The major means of achieving these goals and promoting these values is through adult learning and education broadly conceived. Adult education is a dimension of all functions of religious bodies. Worship is in part a learning experience. Service to one another and to the needs of society include a learning component. Pastoral care and counseling depend in part on educative and learning processes. Besides education's inclusion in all functions of religious bodies, it also exists as a separate function of its own.

Religious bodies become adult learning communities if they have an awareness of the importance of adult religious education and learning in its threefold dimension. Adult religious learning can be broadly conceived as part of each person's daily life and experience. In this sense it is not restricted to learning that is directly connected to membership in religious bodies. Times of reflection and meditation, encounters with others, work and leisure time pursuits, and other activities in life provide opportunities for growth in religious learning, growth in awareness of divine presence, and growth in love for others. Secondly, adult religious education is, as explained above, a dimension of all functions of religious bodies: worship, service, care, and counseling. Thirdly, and what will receive greatest treatment in the remaining chapters of this book, adult education should be a specialized function in all religious bodies. There are connections among these three forms of adult learning. For example, a specialized adult religious education may promote and foster religious learning in daily life and in the various functions of religious bodies. The first two forms may call forth the development of a specialized adult religious education.

This chapter is based on the theory that there are desirable forms of organization of religious bodies that will make these bodies adult learning communities. In the first section of the chapter desirable forms of religious bodies are described in terms of community, structures, leadership, and purposes. In the second section the desirable organization of adult religious education is described in terms of these same four components. This chapter establishes the organizational context for adult religious education. The remaining chapters will describe the planning, design, management, and evaluative processes for adult religious education within organizational contexts.

ORGANIZATION OF RELIGIOUS BODIES

Religious movements usually begin with the religious experiences of founders and their disciples. At the onset little attention is paid to matters of organization. With the death of the founder a crisis of continuity arises. The charisma of the founder is not sufficient to keep unity in a religious movement. With the founder's death a crisis of succession arises: who will succeed the founder? in what form will the organization be continued? Other crises develop concerning the teachings of the founder and the nature of group activities. In order to survive, the new group must embody the charisma of the founder in some association or organization (O'Dea, 1966, ch. 3).

Religious organizations arise because of a need to address certain important issues. Most religious associations in their origins were at odds with existing and established societies. Religious associations usually offer a new community and a new way or pattern of life. The association attempts to mark out its differences in rituals, beliefs, norms, and forms of organization. While some religious organizations maintain a distance from the society in which they develop, gradually most make some accommodations to existing societies and their norms and values. These developments are seen in the origins of the Christian church and in such modern religions as the Mormons, the Jehovah Witnesses, and the Unification Church.

A major crisis in the development of a religious movement is the crisis of leadership that comes with the death of the founder. The charismatic leadership of the founder must give way to a more institutionalized form of leadership. Thus there is usually a great emphasis on the office of leadership in the early years of an organization. This is seen in the development in Christian church of a multiplicity of offices, the emergence of bishops, and eventually the Pope. As is well-known, the problems of succession, office, and leadership are occasions for great disagreements and divisions in many religious bodies.

Organizational and leadership issues are most often the target of protest movements within religious organizations. The Protestant Reformation is the best known example of such a protest movement. Rejection of the authority of the Pope was as much an issue as the doctrine of justification. Other protest movements include monasticism, which often decries the moral laxity of leaders, mysticism which appeals to higher authorities in the search for authentic religious life, and communal forms of church organization. One of the major issues of Vatican II was the issue of collegiality or shared responsibility between Pope and bishops. The declaration of this principle has had broad effects in all of Catholic life, even down to the level of the local church.

This explanation of the origins of religious organization is indebted to Weber's classic *The Sociology of Religion* (1922). This work broadly encompasses the great world religions in establishing general patterns of organizational development. A strong case is made for the necessity of organization. But organization brings about certain dilemmas for religious bodies which must be faced. O'Dea (1966, ch. 5) has insightfully outlined these: (1) *the dilemma of mixed motivation* (While a singlemindedness prevailed in the beginning, in time this gives way to a multiplicity of motives for belonging.); (2) *the symbolic dilemma: objectification versus alienation* (In time the symbolic activities become routinized through repetition and lose their power.); (3) *the dilemma of administrative order: elaboration and alienation* (Since structures become over-elaborated or bureaucratic, members become alienated from structures and leaders.); (4) *the dilemma of delimitation: concrete delimitation versus substitution of the letter of the law* (Concrete decisions that are made to keep the religion relevant often result in an undesirable legalism.); (5) *the dilemma of power: conversion versus coercion* (Alliances are formed with political powers to buttress and supplement voluntary adherence.).

Though it is not only religious organizations which face these dilemmas but all organizations in society, these dilemmas do highlight some of the issues that emerge with increased organization of religious bodies. Many who belong to religious bodies do not want to accept the fact that they belong to large organizations which experience all of the problems of such organizations. Recognition of this fact is a step in the direction of facing up to organizational problems that often produce alienated members, burned-out leaders, and non-achievement of goals.

Now that the general origins and potential dilemmas of religious organizations have been sketched, some of the main components of religious organizations can be considered. Those components will be emphasized that are most relevant to making religious bodies adult learning communities.

The Community

The first component of a religious organization is the community of people who are members. Religious bodies exist in different types of communities and reflect the character of these communities. Religious bodies grow and develop as their communities grow and develop. Leadership and members have to spend a great deal of time understanding the community in which the religious organization is situated: individuals, families, classes, races, political parties, and other organizations.

Religious bodies should clearly define the communities for which they are responsible. Anderson and Jones (1978, pp. 31-34) describe six types of religious bodies based on the type of community which they serve. The *neighborhood* church or synagogue is located in a fairly well-defined and contained geographical area. A *metropolitan* or regional religious body serves a larger area but rarely the entire inhabited area. Churches and synagogues are located in *downtown* business areas of cities in order to reach both residents of the city and suburbs. Communities of *special purpose* are not defined by geography but rather by a unique theology, distinctive style of ministry (e.g., for homosexuals, workers, or professionals), or other exceptional quality. The *small town* organization serves people in outlying and sparsely populated areas. Finally the *open* country church or *rural* parish is located at a crossroads or on a secondary highway in rural areas. These different types of communities call for different structures, leadership, purposes, and programming in adult religious education.

Understanding a community means understanding the social processes that make up the community: systems and networks (schools, political parties, labor unions, street gangs, social groups, etc.); power blocks and lobbies (unions, coalitions, organizations, etc.); issues and problems (taxes, drugs, Sunday sales, crime, etc.); status and class differences (rich and poor, blacks and whites, national and ethnic groups); accepted norms, values, and morality codes; institutions, agencies, and organizations; community ethos (increasing conservatism, middle-class values, etc.). These processes, pointed out by Anderson and Jones (1978, pp. 35-37), need to be considered in shaping a religious organization. They are of great importance in developing a stance and program for adult religious education.

Religious communities, like individuals, are not static. They have a life cycle of their own with particular problems and needs at each stage of development (Anderson and Jones, 1978, pp. 38-42). The *newly developing community* needs the development of basic services and delineation of clear goals. *Stable communities* require efforts to avoid complacency and accept modifications. *Pre-transitional communities* prepare for the entrance of new and different groups of residents and require awareness and sensitivity to problems that will soon be faced. *Communities in transition* (mixed racial and ethnic communities) require efforts in inter-group communications and cooperation. Finally, *post-transitional communities* have needs for stability and the development of new leadership patterns and processes.

Religious organizations can be understood according to the basic distinction between client-centered and member-centered organizations (Hargrove, 1979, pp. 261-263). The former are less affected by mobility and change since persons are oriented towards services provided by religious bodies. A member-centered organization is more deeply affected by mobility because relationships with other members are severed through mobility. In client-centered organizations persons can more easily shift to another organization to meet their needs. While sociologists have in the past viewed Protestant and Jewish bodies as member-centered and Catholic parishes as client-centered, this distinction is generally less important as a result of changes in Roman Catholic parishes.

Winter (1961) pointed to an interesting phenomenon in how religious bodies reacted to rapid turnovers in membership. Religious bodies often fabricate a community through such activities as fund raising and cooperative work. Church work thus becomes for many an outlet for energies and a chance to achieve status. Activities serve the purpose of promoting organizational unity. As religious bodies move from client-centeredness to member-centeredness a greater percentage of the community is involved in the activities of these bodies. Changes such as this begin to effect shifts in basic purposes of religious bodies.

Purposes

The purposes of religious organization are many and complex, Dulles (1974) has presented a historical perspective on the multiple purpose of Christian churches in his description of five models of the church. This analysis can be extended to other religious bodies. *Church as Institution* places greatest importance on regular worship, acceptance of teachings, and obedience to authority. The major focus of the membership is on achieving eternal life with God. *Church as Communion* places great emphasis on the spiritual fellowship among members and has as its chief purpose leading a united people into communion with God. *Church as Sacrament* focuses on the worshipping community and attempts to strengthen members' responses to God. *Church as Herald* is most concerned with proclaiming and teaching basic teachings in order to promote the faith response of members. Lastly, *Church as Servant* stresses mutual brotherhood and service to those who are in greatest need.

The theological approaches of such theologians as Dulles are valuable for providing historical perspective and grand purposes for religious organizations. This approach must be complemented by attempts to analyze purposes from a social science vantage point. Though it is difficult for social sciences to describe the distinctive religious ethos or organizations, the analyses they provide do enable us to go beyond the general purposes presented in the broad models of theologians.

Social scientists of a functionalist orientation prefer to speak of goals, tasks, and functions instead of purposes. Tasks are those things an organization must do to survive in an environment at a given time. Some tasks are primary while others are secondary. The primary tasks of religious organizations are to meet the religious needs of its members. Religious organizations promote the life of faith in individuals and in communities. They give members a sense of purpose, identity, meaning, and stability. Religious organizations also make contributions to the well-being of society by supporting laws, governments, and values of the existing society.

Functionalist sociologists (Parsons, 1951; Yinger, 1970) tend to see religious organizations as stabilizing, integrating, and conserving forces in society. Critical sociologists prefer to explore that aspect of religion which is a force for change in individual and societal life (Mills, 1959; Gouldner, 1970; Baum, 1975). Both aspects are important tasks for religious organizations if they want to be sensitive to needs of individuals and needs of changing environments.

A sociological distinction that is important in analyzing functions of religious organizations is manifest and latent function. Manifest function is what the organization states it intends to do. Latent functions are hidden functions such as maintaining class, racial, sexual, and generational discriminations. Because he perceived certain latent functions of religion as producing complacency in its members, Marx labeled religion the opium of the people.

Wallace's (1966) anthropoligical analysis of religion clarifies a number of important functions of all religious organizations. Religious faiths function as technologies in that they provide people with power to accomplish things in their lives. Religions are therapies for many persons. They provide ideologies and belief systems. The promise of salvation here and hereafter is an important function. Finally, religions revitalize individuals and societies.

A useful summary of the functions of religions has been provided by O'Dea (1966). Religions offer an opportunity for *identity* by giving individuals a coherent system of beliefs. Religious faith provides impetus to individual *growth and maturation*. Religions provide *support, consolation, and reconciliation* by uniting persons with a world that is beyond. Religions furnish the ground for *security and firm identity* by offering transcendent help through cultic actions. Religions often *sacralize the norms and values* of a given society by emphasizing group goals over individual goals. At times religions exercise a *prophetic role* in society by providing the standards by which existing arrangements are criticized and the motivation by which protest and reform efforts are mobilized.

Theological ideals for religious organizations are important for keeping primary purposes in the minds of leaders and members. Social analyses are valuable for keeping the reality of what is happening in the forefront. What groups desire or intend is not necessarily what they accomplish. Religious leaders must be sensitive to the latent and negative functions of religions. Adult education, broadly conceived, can make religious organizations sensitive to negative functions and consequences of the life of religious organizations. A real danger arises when such functions are embedded in the structures of an organization.

Structures

Structures, the third component of religious organizations, should ideally be developed in relationship to the purposes of the organization and the communities which it serves. Various attempts have been made to analyze the structures of religious organizations. A good starting point is Etzioni's (1964) work which traces the development of modern organizations. The value of this work is that it treats not only industrial organizations but also hospitals, armies, and churches.

The first type of organization is the *formal organization* characterized by scientific management. In this form of organization great stress is placed upon accountability, expertness, efficiency, economy, level of conflict settlement, policy development and program planning (p. 25). In decision making the advice of experts is extremely important. In programming the emphasis is on service to clients and on the development of profit making products. A key characteristic of formal organizations is centralized authority.

The *informal organization* is a product of the human relations school of social psychology. Emphasis is placed upon the social capacity of members, non-economic rewards, and less specialization. In this type of organization members share in decision making and the organization is sensitive to the needs of its members. Freedom of expression and availability of information characterize this form of organization. Mutual responsibility exists in defining goals, planning activities, implementing decisions, and evaluating outcomes. Leadership is more democratic than in formal organizations. One of the major goals of leadership is to enable participation by as many members as possible.

In his critique of these organizational forms Etzioni faulted the formal organization with presuming that the goals of the organization and those of the members are the same. The formal organization presumes that efficiency of organization leads to happy members. The weakness of informal organizations is the presumption that happy members mean an efficient organization. Good social relations do not of themselves lead to a good and efficient organization. The informal organization also fails to realize that alienation and conflict are both inevitable and occasionally desirable. Conflicts are often opportunities for organizations to make decisions that may lead to productive growth.

Etzioni's *structuralist* approach to organizational theory attempts a synthesis between formal and informal organizations and also draws on the work of Weber and Marx. Structuralists face up to a major organizational dilemma: there are inevitable strains between organizational and personal needs; between rational organization and sensitivity to nonrational elements; between the need for discipline and the need for autonomy; between the need for formal relationships at some times and informal relationships at other times; between managers and leaders and members and workers (p. 41).

The structuralist viewpoint is important for an analysis of structures of religious organizations. Though some religious organizations are small enough to be considered associations, many are closer to true organizations in their structures. Religious bodies are often large social units in which many subgroups interact. Among these groups there are shared interests and values, but there are also opposing viewpoints and interests. Conflicts between leaders and members and among different groups of members are inevitable. Forms of alienation also exist in religious bodies: from religious norms, laws, beliefs, structures, and leadership. Human relations theory is helpful in indicating how some of this alienation can be handled, but there are limits to what can be done through their methods of conflict resolution. The demands that religious bodies make on their members and leaders can often be alienating. It is important to find the important social functions of the alienation and conflicts which often arise in religious bodies. In the human relations approach people are often made to feel better without there being any real change in their objective situation.

The structuralist approach to religious organizations views them as multipurpose organizations that have added social and community purposes and structures to the more properly religious goals of worship, education, counseling, and service. The structuralist approach recognizes that it is most difficult to evaluate religious organizations because their goals are nonmaterial. Too much insistence on testing and evaluation might lead to an emphasis on elements that can be easily measured (numbers, money, buildings, etc.). The adding of nonreligious goals to religious organizations presents the problems of building structures in areas that overshadow the more specifically religious goals of the organization. Adding goals entails more attention to setting priorities in goals and structures for an organization.

This approach to religious bodies will not be satisfying to many. The models of religious bodies often preferred are those which emphasize smallness, intimacy, communion, and fellowship. In the thinking of many, religious bodies are like families and natural communities. There is, however, another reality. Religious bodies are very often large social units with a few thousand members, numerous staff persons, many committees and councils, large budgets, and specialized functions. The task of these bodies is to have some of the good characteristics of families, communities, and organizations without the negative aspects. It is not an easy task to so structure religious organizations to achieve these differing values. The Latin American experiment of establishing within large parishes small basic communities for prayer, worship, dialogue, and social action, attempts to achieve these ends. Many members of large religious organizations find that some of their religious needs are met in smaller subgroups. If, however, religious organizations are to have the happy combination of communal and organizational values that appears to be ideal, they will require leaders who have this vision of religious organizations.

Leaders

The problem of leadership in religious organizations, as in all organizations, is critical. Organizations do not continue in existence unless effective leadership is exercised. Leadership in religious organizations takes a number of forms. Synagogues are led by rabbis and councils. Christian churches are led by bishops, priests, pastors, ministers, elders, and councils. The history of religious bodies indicates that changes in forms of leadership occur with the passage of time. Most often these are brought about through changed communities that are served through and interactions with different environments.

Leadership is usually treated in theological writings under the concept of ministry. Niebuhr (1956) described five models of ministry that have emerged in Christian history. In each model the task and the source of authority for ministry are different. The *pastoral ruler* was concerned with the governance of souls and possessed institutional authority through ordination. The *preacher* proclaims the good news of forgiveness and receives authority from having personally appropriated the Sacred Scriptures. The *evangelist* intends to bring about personal conversion and draws authority from personal religious experience and conversion. The *priest* celebrates the liturgy and rites of the church and receives power for this through ordination by the religious body. Niebuhr saw the emergence of a new model in churches of North America, the *pastoral director*. In this model the major task is the building up of the church, with authority coming from the community through more democratic procedures.

Sociological analysis of what religious leaders do has led to a rather broad conception of leadership. Fichter (1954) listed nine functional roles of the Roman Catholic parish priest: communal (relating to parishioners and community); administrator of activities and groups; business man; civic leader; recreational role in leading youth athletic groups; ameliorative (supervising and performing works of mercy); educational; socio-spiritual; and liturgical. How the multiplicity of functions produces role conflicts was reported by Blizzard (1956). Although leaders are expected to be persons of faith, they are also expected to manifest personal faith only on certain occasions. They are expected to be both persons of action in leading large organizations and also persons of scholarship in reading and teaching. They have both private roles (pastors, directors, and counselors) and public roles (preachers, teachers, administrators). Though they are generalists in treating all aspects of life, they are expected to be specialists in religion. Religious leaders have professional status, but very often they are unable to organize their lives like other professionals.

The role conflicts within leaders, together with other factors, have led to a crisis among leaders and ministers in Christian churches. Holmes (1971; 1976) has addressed this crisis as a theologian in touch with social science research and perspectives. His analysis is that ministers have attempted to resolve the conflict by making their primary identification with a secular profession or function: counselors, social activists, group leaders or builders, or administrators. His contention is that this approach is doomed to failure because it does not make central the sacramental or spiritual role of the minister. Holmes does not describe this in any narrow cultic manner but more in terms of the holy person through whom and in whom individuals come into contact with The Holy.

A recent comprehensive study of ministry in religious bodies in the United States (Schuller, Strommen, and Brekke, 1980) shows the broad range of expectations that members have of the religious leaders. The rank-order of expectations rated highest were: open affirming, style; caring for persons under stress; congregational leadership; theologian for life and thought; ministry from personal commitment of faith; development of fellowship and worship; denominational awareness and collegiality. Two items were rated as somewhat important: ministry to community; and world and priestly-sacramental ministry. The study shows a number of significant differences among religious bodies. From the data the authors develop four models of ministry found among religious bodies: *spiritual awareness* (e.g., evangelistic churches); *sacramental-liturgical emphasis* (e.g., Roman Catholic and Orthodox Catholic); *social action emphasis* (e.g., Jewish bodies, United Church of Christ, and Unitarians); and *combined emphases* of the first three (United Methodist, Lutheran).

The social science literature on leadership is voluminous. Burns has extensively reviewed this literature in his valuable work *Leadership* (1978). Burns's model of transforming moral leadership is most suited for leaders of religious bodies. Persons exercise moral leadership when there is a relationship not only of power but also of mutual needs, aspirations, and values. Members have an alternative choice of leaders and programs. Leaders take responsibilities for their commitments. This type of leadership is transforming leadership since it brings about social change by raising the level of ethical conduct and aspiration.

Moral transforming leadership can be exercised in religious bodies in two chief ways. The spiritual direction of individuals through preaching, teaching, and counseling is concerned with challenging members to form ethical commitments and to live by these commitments. The efficient management of an organization can promote ethical values and social changes through attention to values in planning and goal setting, organizing and recruiting, staffing and training, directing and supervising, and controlling and evaluating.

Most religious bodies are moving away from focusing attention on the single leader by attempting to involve many members in leadership roles. Leadership styles are changing from autocratic to more consultative and participative modes. Ministry teams and shared ministry have become important concepts in renewing leadership. The inclusion of more women in leadership positions has also been a strong force in changing the form and style of leadership in religious bodies.

In this section four important components of religious organizations have been considered: the communities served by religious organizations; the purposes, tasks, and functions of these organizations; the appropriate structures of a religious organization; and the role of leaders in such bodies. From the theory and research on these items, those elements were chosen which are of particular importance to making religious organizations adult learning communities. Attention is now given to these same components in the organization of adult religious education.

ORGANIZATION OF ADULT RELIGIOUS EDUCATION

This section of the organization of adult religious education considers this function both in a broad sense of an activity included as part of activities of religious bodies and in a narrower sense of a specialized function. This section treats the organization of adult religious education in relationship to the same four components of religious organizations: community, purposes, structures, and processes.

The Community

To be successful, adult religious education must be sensitive both to the immediate community that the religious body serves and to broader regional, national, and international communities. The local community provides the context, needs, issues, and interests for which adult religious education is primarily developed. The broader communities provide both broader contexts and broader issues that ought to be focuses for adult religious education.

Adult religious education should first of all be directed to the members of the religious body. The needs of these members need to be assessed according to principles outlined in the next chapter. One of the assumptions behind adult education is that though there are similarities from community to community, each community is unique in its needs. The more adult religious educators know about the interests, problems, and issues within the local community, the more they are able to address these in an effective manner.

Religious bodies are also interested in persons in communities who are not members of their group. Attempts to reach these members differ from religious body to religious body. Some groups make aggressive efforts to attract new members, while others strongly oppose any efforts that border on proselytizing. In a pluralistic society it would appear preferable to relate to broader communities through meeting the needs of members and through strong and manifest commitments to the betterment of all persons and communities. Many religious bodies rightly desire to share their life and teachings with nonmembers. But before embarking on efforts at doing this, they should seriously question both motives and strategies in their approaches.

An interesting development in recent years is the use that religious bodies, especially those in the evangelistic tradition, make of television and radio for preaching and recruiting. The effectiveness of these efforts is a matter of some controversy. The same issues of motivation and strategy must be raised with regard to these efforts. There is no doubt that these media are valuable sources of religious learning for many persons who do not participate actively in a religious organization. However, the strong dose of commercialism that is often connected with these newer forms of religious programming and a number of alleged financial scandals reported make one hesitate to consider present efforts in this area as boding well for the future.

A major thrust of adult religious education should be to sensitize its members to concerns and problems beyond those of the local community. Regional, state, and international issues should be the focus of adult education efforts. Religious bodies have opportunities to provide this broader perspective since many of them are part of worldwide organizations. A major task of education is to foster an awareness of the problems that people experience in the world community. Efforts at global education such as those provided by Global Education Associates and Bread for the World are valuable tools for promoting this broad perspective on adult religious education.

A number of concrete suggestions have been offered by Anderson and Jones (1978, pp. 139-142) for making the ministry of religious bodies more responsive to community needs and interests. I take the liberty of adapting these for the specific function of adult religious education. Adult religious education should be made *visible and available to the community*. After working as a volunteer director for adult religious education in my local church for three years I am surprised how few people know that programs exist for adult religious learning. Concrete suggestions for making programs visible and available are included in Chapter Ten of this book.

Adult religious education will be responsive to the community if it *encourages people to talk* about their needs, problems, concerns, and yearnings. Many people attend services who are never listened to or who choose not to speak. Programs have to be so structured that people will feel the freedom and the confidence to speak about those things that deeply affect them.

Adult religious education must *target specific groups* within the community. Categories of concerns and common interests have to be differentiated. In programming for adult religous education in my local church we attempt to reach at least one new group each year. Our experience has been that the most difficult age groups to reach are young adults and older adults. Most programming is targeted for adults in middle age groups.

To be truly effective adult religious education must *recruit and train indigenous leaders*. This is extremely important in communities which are in various stages of transition. Many religious bodies have the problem of leaders not living in the community where they work. This is not an ideal situation since it fosters an unhealthy distinction between leaders and members of a religious body. In these less desirable situations it is especially important to recruit and train indigenous leaders.

Religious bodies should *cooperate among themselves* in adult religious education programs. In many situations like cities and small towns cooperative ventures can be valuable for participating communities and for the entire area. Cooperation is especially desirable around social and political issues that affect the entire community.

Adult religious education must be organized differently according to the type of community the religious body serves. The task of the neighborhood church is to meet individual needs and to expand the vision and concerns of members. The metropolitan or regional church is strategically located to take on cooperative ventures with other religious bodies and civic groups. The downtown church or synagogue can develop programs appropriate to business persons, shoppers, and inhabitants of downtown areas.

Special purpose churches usually have clearly defined concerns: integration of homosexuals into the religious community; ministry to college students. The small town and rural religious body must take advantage of times when people are gathered for worship and include elements of adult religious education in conjunction with these services.

Adult religious education also takes on different forms according to the place where a community is in its development. The newly developing community has great needs for establishing a clear religious mission identity. The enthusiasm surrounding the development of a community usually provides a strong motivation for educational efforts. Stable communities need educational efforts to avoid dangers of complacency and stagnation. Education can be directed towards modification and growth. For communities in transition, adult religious education must take on the complex task of preparing attitudes for change, developing new leadership, and handling conflicts and tensions. While many religious bodies were powerful forces in providing smooth transitions in communities, others acted too late or not at all in preparing members for the problems that accompany community transitions.

Perhaps the most important community function that adult religious education can provide for religious bodies is its power to build a sense of community among small groups. Religious bodies have many small groups besides educational groups that accomplish this. Adult education, however, is especially valuable for this purpose since it can include a strong component of faith and values sharing. We develop a sense of community with those with whom we share faith, values, history, traditions, and common concerns. It is the sense of community experienced in small family, neighborhood, and particular concerns groups, out of which concern and action for the broader human community develop.

In summary, adult religious education has the potential to relate to the various communities in which it takes place. It can also build a sense of community among many members of religious bodies. But in order to do this effectively it must attend to other components of organization. It must have some clearly defined purposes. It must be adequately organized. It must have competently trained leadership.

Purposes

The purposes of adult religious education in religious bodies need to be clearly stated. This section considers general statements of purposes as these are related to the organization. In the following chapter a more thorough treatment of assessment of needs and determination of objectives will be presented.

Most religious bodies are in need of a strong policy statement of purpose in adult religious education. Religious bodies generally are more concerned with the education of children and youths than they are with adult education. It would appear preferable to work for gradual modifications in policy and structures that would enable adult religious education to become an important and integral function of a religious body.

The movement toward improving adult religious education in a religious body can begin with the development of a policy base as suggested by Knowles (1980). The highest governing board should have the task of formulating this statement. An adult religious education council or committee can participate in the formulation process, but the policy should be endorsed by the chief governing body and the membership.

Knowles has given a number of criteria for such a policy statement or convenantal agreement. Adapting his criteria to religious education, the following components should be included in a policy statement for adult religious education:

1. The unique role of adult religious education should be stated. Use can be made of authoritative sources, including major documents of the religious body, and the writings of theologians and educators. A commitment to lifelong religious learning needs to be clearly expressed.

2. The specific purposes and objectives of adult religious education should be spelled out in terms of individual, social, and community needs. Special attention should be paid to the faith needs of individuals and the religious needs of specific communities.

3. A strong commitment of resources to be allotted to adult religious education should be expressed. This should be expressed in terms of personnel and financial arrangements. Budget statements are theological statements of priorities.

4. The relationship between adult religious education and other functions of the religious body should be spelled out. This includes relationships to leadership; the chief governing board; committees for worship, finances, service, and fellowship; and other related committees. The importance of collaborative efforts should be highlighted.
5. The preferred types of teachers and leaders to be involved in the program should be specified. This includes the types of educational experiences desired. Diversity in both of these areas is desirable.
6. The statement should list the target groups for adult religious education: young, middle-aged, and older adults; married and single; divorced, separated, and widowed; parents of children and youth; workers and retired persons; persons with special needs; minority groups.
7. The relationships of adult religious education to other functions and organizations outside the religious body should be stated. These include ecumenical efforts with other religious bodies, relationships with civic organizations, and other adult education programs. Linkages with other associations and organizations are important because religious bodies cannot provide for all the needs of their members.

The importance of a policy statement on adult religious education cannot be underestimated. The process of developing such a document is as important as the product. The process includes study, consultation, sharing of views, and resolution of conflicting opinions. As many people as possible should be involved in the deliberations in order to insure that the views of the entire organization are considered. Those who are not involved in the process should be informed about the deliberations. This process can be used effectively both by religious bodies which already have established adult education programs and those which want to establish them. Once a policy has been formulated, it should be promulgated for the entire religious body.

A policy, once formulated, should not be considered unrevisable. Periodically it should be reviewed, especially with the purpose of evaluating what progress has been made toward achieving the goals that were established. Too often little effort is made in evaluating programs that have been established in religious bodies. The matter of program evaluation will be treated in Chapter Ten.

The establishment of policies is an important step in making religious bodies adult learning communities. The implementation of these policies, however, demands both structures and leadership. The remaining parts of this section are devoted to these components.

Structures

If a religious organization is structured according to Etzioni's model of the structuralist organizational theory, then it will need structures that provide both for efficiency and good human relations. This can be provided for in the establishment of an adult religious education council, committee, or team. This group should be established as a work or task group. The elements of a task group identified by Anderson and Jones (1978, p. 144) form the basis of this treatment: the composition of the group, the nature of the task, and the working procedures.

It takes time *to form a task group*. This is best done at a long session where there is time not only for work but also for prayer, enjoyment, and community building. Qualities to look for in potential members are interest in adult religious learning, representativeness of the attitudes of the religious bodies, and some competence in adult religious education. Teams should have enough diversity to represent the entire religious body and enough similarity to have common ground for working together. Between five and ten members is ideal for a task group. Members should be invited to remain on the committee for a specified period of time, preferably two to three years. The group should have a leader with a similar specified term. From experience I have learned to encourage members to make a definite commitment to adult religious education and not to become involved in other time-consuming volunteer work in the religious organization during their term.

The *nature of the task* for the adult religious education committee should be clearly defined and achievable. People remain in volunteer groups only if they consider their time well-spent.

The first task of the group is to study and discuss many of the issues in adult religious education treated in this book: what is adulthood? what are the social contexts of adult learning and development? what are the implications of psychological research on adult development and learning? what are good models for adult religious learning? how does planning, design, management, and evaluation of adult education take place? The group may want to use an outside consultant for part of this training. Groups have also started effectively with group learning procedures utilizing one of the practical handbooks developed by Bergevin and McKinley (1958), McKenzie (1975), Girzaitis (1977), or Deboy (1979).

Members of a task committee consider their participation worthwhile according to a number of criteria. They desire to contribute their valued skills to the group and its task, especially if they feel that their skills are underutilized in other spheres of life. The nature of the task should be clearly identifiable. Expectations and goals need to be set. Members must feel that their work has an impact on the lives of individuals, the religious organization, and the broader community. As time progresses committee members expect some degree of responsiblity for the outcomes of the work and thus they expect knowledge of what has been accomplished (Anderson and Jones, 1978, p. 147).

A task group needs *efficient working procedures*. Efficient procedures include the use of an action list that comprises the following: what task will be done, by whom it will be done, and by what time will it be done? Though a great deal of discussion takes place in task groups, it is important that decisions are made and tasks are assigned. Task groups must avoid the extremes of endless group discussions and overdependence on parliamentary procedures. It is the responsibility of leadership to prevent the group from falling into bad working procedures. The main task of leadership in a task group is to move toward group consensus around issues where there is greatest agreement and to see that someone is responsible for carrying out the decisions of the group. The other roles and functions of task group leadership will be treated in the concluding section of this chapter.

Task groups need *accurate records and reports*. Agendas need to be set. A four-part agenda format is recommended: item, background, action needed, and action taken. The agenda is important in focusing attention on tasks, decisions, and actions. Priorities need to be set among agenda items. Members should feel free to modify and add to the agenda during the progress of the meeting.

Though task groups are businesslike in their goal orientations, this does not mean there is no room for small talk, camaraderie and humor. Certainly no volunteer group can function well without these elements. People work well together if they share a bit of themselves, enjoy one another's company, and have a chance to relax, while at the same time accomplishing something valuable. Task groups, however, differ from discussion groups, sensitivity and encounter groups, and other growth-centered groups in that they engage more of our social and working selves than our personal selves. Leadership and members in the group must be sensitive to this distinction (Miles, 1981).

One thing that work groups require is a prudent honesty. Many groups have what Steele and Jenks (1977) call supernorms or unspoken rules that bind members. In religious organizations these often control the relationship between leaders and members. Norms include not speaking about embarrassing issues, avoiding telling particular members about their monopolizing discussions, and not offering criticism when it is called for. We have all been in groups where there is a sigh of relief when someone honestly says what needs to be said to move the group forward. On occasion a group must look at itself and the way in which it functions to determine what might make the group more effective.

One reality that adult education committees must face is that they are not the only structures within religious bodies concerned with adult religious learning. Almost all groups, committees, and councils in religious bodies promote in some way adult religious learning. My experience has taught me not to duplicate efforts of other groups but to look for tasks which are not being done and issues which are not being addressed. Most religious bodies are so diverse in their membership that it is beyond the competence of any one committee to provide all the educational experiences that are necessary.

Structures are all important. But structures are developed, maintained, revised, and evaluated by competent leadership.

We have saved to last a consideration of the important role of leadership in adult religious education because of the logic of our treatment and importance of this function.

Leaders

Leadership in adult religious education must be provided at various levels in religious organizations. The most essential leadership is given by pastors, rabbis, and ministers. These persons set priorities in a religious organization. Their commitment to making religious organizations adult learning communities must be manifest in their administrative styles, preaching and teaching, conduct of worship, and personal relationships. Leadership is also given by the main governing bodies in their development of policy statements and setting of budgetary priorities. The styles and stances of these leaders create the climate within which adult religious education can flourish.

Adult religious education should also be the responsibility of a particular person in the community. Preferably this position should be filled by a paid professional adult educator. Realistically this is often impossible because of the size of the congregation and the urgency of other priorities. The situation in many religious organizations is that adult religious education is one of the functions of the director of religious education. Since the director usually has broad responsibilities in the areas of child and youth education, the work of adult religious education receives secondary attention.

One of the major goals of this book is to argue for a shifting of attention from the education of children and youth to the religious education of adults. One of the best ways to accomplish this is to change the primary focus of the director of religious education to lifelong education. A concept of lifelong religious learning demands attention to the entire life span and not just to earlier periods of development. The work of initiating the young into the community is important but equally important in changing societies is the lifelong learning of adult members.

If the work of adult religious education is not the primary function of a professional religious educator, then a search should be made for a committed and competent volunteer. Within many religious organizations there are trained teachers or administrators who can competently perform this function. Once a person has been selected, opportunities for training should be provided. Many colleges and state universities have developed specializations in adult education. Within these programs there are often courses in various aspects of adult education: administration and organization; adult learning and development; and program planning in adult education. If courses are not available, then training can be sought through workshops, institutes, conferences, and study. Religious organizations that expect persons to do competent jobs should provide the necessary training opportunities.

The training of leaders in adult religious education must focus in a particular manner on knowledge and understanding of religion and theology. Opportunities for education in this area are available in the same forms mentioned above. The formation of a good leader takes time and effort. But once a leader has been properly formed and trained, the organization will reap benefits from this specialized training.

The director of adult religious education needs support from various elements in the religious organization: from the leadership and governing body of the organization; from other groups, committees, and councils. The greatest need, however, is for a group of persons who make up a council or committee for adult religious education as described in this chapter. It is the director's role to get the most competent and representative persons for this committee. This group is critical for planning, designing, managing, and evaluating programs. It is with this small group that the director spends the greatest amount of time. The effectiveness of the group is related to the leadership that the director gives to the group.

In treating leadership in religious bodies Burns's (1978) concept of moral transforming leadership was used. After developing this concept of leadership utilizing political figures, Burns gives a number of practical implications that can be adapted for leaders in religious bodies and for leaders in adult religious education (1978, pp. 452-455).

Leadership is collective. One-person leadership does not exist; it is a contradiction in terms. Leaders are defined in terms of the groups that they lead. Leaders must be sensitive to the motives, values, needs, and problems in groups of which they are leaders. People respond to leadership if it addresses what concerns them deeply. Leaders in adult religious education must see themselves working with members of a committee and with the entire membership of the organization.

Leadership is dissensual. The task of leaders is to produce or allow to arise meaningful conflicts and differences of opinion. This characteristic of leadership is especially needed in religious organizations that take the model of "one big happy family" or "one loving community." The religious movement toward unity and harmony often leads to covering up serious needs and differences. Meaningful conflict can organize the motives of people, sharpen their demands, strengthen their values, and mobilize them for action. There are advantages in the two-party system in politics. I see my role as teacher and director of adult education in terms of bringing out the other side, the neglected position, and the unheard voice. Not just the truth but often the good program evolves through a dialectical process.

Leadership is causative. It is not merely symbolic or ceremonial. Leadership brings about changes in people's motives, goals, and aspirations. True leaders are changed in the process of leading others. Often leaders enjoy most the symbolic and ceremonial aspects of their role: appearing at nonthreatening functions, being acclaimed, receiving recognition, and having the place of honor. Causative leadership is at times exercised in public and dramatic events but more often it is exercised in private, boring, and tedious committee meetings. Committee meetings may be the contemporary form of asceticism for leaders and members of religious organizations.

Leadership is morally purposeful. Burns contends that there are plenty of leaders but not enough moral leaders. Moral leaders have key values which they attempt to achieve through social structures and programs. Leaders in adult religious education need values and goals to motivate and shape their efforts. The setting of priorities is a matter of making choices among competing values. The moral leader taps the needs of individuals, raises their expectations, helps shape their values, and thus mobilizes the efforts of members of religious organizations.

Leadership is elevating. Leaders raise the moral expectations of membership. Burns makes the point that they do this through asking sacrifices from members and not merely promising them goods. He gives as an example of elevating leadership the activities of a leader like Martin Luther King in the civil rights movement. King appealed through religious teaching and civic understanding to deep moral convictions within people. He was able to tap a reservoir of moral force in individuals. Leadership in adult religious education does not often have this dramatic potential, but the principle of elevating leadership applies. People have a deep need to develop their potential, use their talents and abilities, learn more about themselves and their religious traditions, and utilize this knowledge, talent, and potential for the betterment of society.

These characteristics of leadership may seem far from the small details of exercising leadership for transforming religious organizations into adult learning communities. The details will come in the next three chapters. What is important to establish in this chapter is a vision of moral leadership that can be seen above all the details of programming. This is a vision of a person who has deep principles of faith and morality, and a person with skills to inspire and lead others to rise above a narrow self-interest and become deeply concerned with transforming their organizations into communities of understanding, love, and action.

CONCLUSION

This chapter has presented principles for enabling religious bodies to so organize themselves that they might become adult learning communities. This is not an easy task, especially in religious bodies where for decades almost exclusive attention has been given to the formation of children and youth in the faith. From my experience I judge that many adult members of religious organizations experience within themselves needs and aspirations for more intense religious learning. These needs can be met only if religious bodies organize educational ministries for adults. This chapter has included general principles and suggestions for organizing an adult religious education program that is sensitive to the needs of various types of religious communities. The chapter has also described appropriate structures, purposes, and leaders for religious organizations that desire to become adult learning communities. The following three chapters deal more in detail with the processes of planning, designing, managing, and evaluating efforts in adult religious education.

CHAPTER VIII
PLANNING FOR ADULT
RELIGIOUS EDUCATION

The treatment of program planning in adult religious education began in Chapter Seven with suggestions for the development of policy statements, the establishment of committees, and the training of leadership to respond to various communities in which religious bodies are situated. The next step is to develop a process of program planning, design, management, and evaluation. This is a crucial decision for a group because the choice of a program planning process may well determine the direction that adult religious education takes in that religious body.

Though treated in separate chapters, the processes described in Chapters Eight, Nine, and Ten are closely related. This chapter presents a process for planning adult religious education. The emphasis in planning is on the investigation of values and the establishing of objectives. Chapter Nine describes the design of educational activities appropriate for adult religious education. Formats and processes for individual, group, and mass education are presented. Chapter Ten treats the management and evaluation of adult religious education programs. Important issues considered in Chapter Ten are the selection of teachers, the establishment of climate and environment, budgeting, and promotion. Planning is thus presented as a complex of interacting functions.

SYSTEMATIC APPROACHES TO PLANNING,
DESIGNING MANAGING, AND EVALUATING
ADULT EDUCATION

In the past sixty years a number of distinctive systematic approaches have been developed for planning, designing, and managing adult education. Houle (1972) described five of the most common approaches. These are briefly sketched to present a context for developing a theory of adult religious education.

The first systems were based on *Dewey's thought*. Lindeman (1926) and Kotinsky (1933) developed pragmatic approaches to adult education by extending Dewey's problem solving method to adult education. This method is actually the very act of thinking: a felt difficulty, the definition of a problem, the formulation and testing of possible solutions, and the choice of the best solution. Lindeman explained the approach succinctly: "In conventional education the student is required to adjust himself to an established curriculum; in adult education the curriculum is built around the student's needs and interests (1926, p. 9)." This primary focus on adult needs and interests has become a major component of almost all program planning in adult education.

For three decades *Tyler's theory of curriculum development* (1950) has been a dominant system for designing adult education programs. The system includes four components: (1) the programmer defines the purposes by considering studies of learners, of contemporary life, and of subject matter specialists; (2) this data is screened through the educational and social philosophy of the programmer and through the findings of psychology of learning studies to produce specific objectives; (3) educational experiences are chosen and organized in such a way as to achieve desired results; (4) evaluation processes are designed to identify whether or not the objectives have been achieved.

Tyler attempted to remedy the lack of attention to academic disciplines that was found in the Deweyan models. However, though Tyler's approach is extensively used, it has also come under criticism on a number of points. Among others Eisner (1967) has attacked the behavioristic approaches to stating and evaluating objectives. Lawson (1975) and Monette (1977; 1979b) have criticized the utilization of needs language without sufficient attention to values and norms for determining what objectives and educational experiences should be utilized. The importance of these criticisms is that they highlight the fact that this system, as all systems, is limited in the types of adult education for which it is appropriate. It is appropriate for basic knowledge and basic skills, but less suited for interpersonal growth, social reconstruction, philosophy, literature, and the arts.

Systems based on the *social psychology of Kurt Lewin* constitute another approach to adult program design (1951). These systems include group dynamics and change theory. *Group dynamics* is concerned with the education of adults for group work. It includes such concepts and techniques as feedback, role playing, buzz groups, hidden agenda, and nondirective leadership. When group dynamics became more concerned with learning about relationships, it became known as sensitivity training, human relations training, and encounter group training.

Lewin's ideas also gave rise to *change theory* which assumes that in every situation there are forces to support change and forces to prevent it. The task of the change agent is to determine what these forces are and to enable the client or client system to deal with these forces. The process includes these elements: (1) clients are made aware of a problem; (2) the motivation and capacity of clients to change are assessed; (3) change agents assess their own motivations and resources; (4) appropriate change objectives and targets are worked out; (5) suitable strategies are identified and applied; (6) attention is given to determining structures to stabilize and maintain changes; (7) the helping relationship is ended.

The major questions about this theory are questions of values. Who makes the judgments on what changes will be promoted and for what reasons? Some attempt to utilize the method in a value free manner. Others have explicit progressive, liberal, or radical ideologies. The method is also open to conservative or reactionary ideologies. The method appears to be radical in Alinsky's usage (1971) and liberal in Myles Horton's educational approach at the Highlander School (Adams, 1973).

The fourth systematic approach to adult education program planning is *community development*. The primary purpose in this approach is to help members of a community act collectively on some common problem. As a result of this process, it is hoped that members of the community develop skills that can be transferred to handling other problems. Dewey's problem solving technique is utilized here. The approach is similar to change theory in its purposes but differs from it in not attempting to bring about change in a specific direction. Community development is at times an extension of a University, or, in some countries, a separate function of government. Problems with this approach lie in the habit patterns of communities that resist change and the difficulty of transferring learning from one situation to another.

Systems analysis approach is the fifth approach to planning in adult education. The systems analyst approaches programs in a theoretical and abstract manner—as sets of interrelated ideas, principles, or practices which have a coherent unity. Analysts are interested in building models or diagrams of how a process can be conceived. This highly sophisticated approach is valuable for analyzing a program on a wide scale, but its complexity has prevented it from having a great impact in adult education programming.

After reviewing these systems, Houle presents his system (1972, p. 47) which is largely an expansion of Tyler's approach. Houle's system has seven components: (1) a possible educational activity is identified; (2) a decision is made to proceed; (3) objectives are identified and refined; (4) a suitable format is designed attending to resources, leaders, methods, schedule, sequence, social improvement, individualization, roles and relationships, criteria of evaluation, and clarity of design; (5) the format is fitted into larger patterns of life through counseling and attention to lifestyles, finance, and interpretation; (6) the plan is put into effect; (7) the results are measured and appraised.

The best known and most widely utilized approach to programming for adult education is presented by Knowles (1980). Knowles's eclectic approach combines elements of Tyler with elements of human relations theory. His process entails: (1) assessment of needs and interests of individuals, organizations, and communities; (2) the translating of needs into program objectives (operational and educational) by screening them through the criteria of institutional purposes, feasibility, and the interests of the clientele; (3) the design of formats for individual and group learning and for community development; (4) the operation of a program (selection of teachers, management of facilities and procedures, promotion and public relations, budgeting and financing); (5) the evaluation of program objectives through standard methods.

The approaches of Knowles and Houle are complementary. While Houle has provided a detailed logical analysis of the program planning process, Knowles has included many excellent examples and practical suggestions. Both approaches are comprehensive in their attempts to include all possible forms of adult education. Given the dominant pragmatic character of adult education in this country, these pragmatic approaches, especially Knowles's, have great appeal to adult educators.

Criticisms of these approaches have come from a number of sources. Humanistic educators are opposed to behavioral definitions of objectives. My study of Houle and Knowles on this issue is that they do not favor *narrowly* defined behavioral objectives. Analytic philosophy advocates have criticized their lack of attention to values, the vagueness of the "needs meeting" language, and the "service" or "market" approach found in these theories. These criticisms have some basis in that though both speak of using philosophies in determining objectives, insufficient attention is given to the issue of values in these pragmatic approaches. Finally, criticism comes from educators who feel that social and political values should have a more prominent role in the development of adult education programs.

In the 1970s adult educators were challenged to think more deeply about the question of values in programming and specifically social and political values because of the work of *Paulo Freire* (1970; 1973). Freire's work in literacy education and political education in the Third World presented an alternative approach to adult education programming. This approach is closest in intent and method to the community development system. It differs from this approach in the revolutionary political principles that inspire it.

Freire's method begins with a study of the context: a study of generative words for literacy education and generative themes for political education. The words and language of the people are carefully recorded. A selection of words and themes is made. Motivation sessions are used to raise consciousness about the ability of people to control their lives. Teaching materials are developed, using words and pictures (process of codification). Words and themes are broken down and analyzed (process of decodification). A coordinator is responsible for the group learning, which emphasizes the process of dialogue.

The power of this educational process is in the issues that become the focus of dialogue. While involved in literacy education, persons also discuss poverty, property rights, distribution of wealth, the meaning and value of work, just wages, the power of government over individuals' lives, and the evils of prostitution. Two major criticisms this theory has received are charges of subtle indoctrination or manipulation and failure to move beyond conscientization to politicalization (Elias, 1976).

Monette (1979b) has attempted to reconceptualize the process of program planning in light of an analysis of needs language and an analysis of Freire's method of conscientization. Though he admits his effort is incomplete, he is hopeful that alternative models will develop from his analysis. Programmers, he suggests, should be concerned with three sets of questions: (1) what are the values we want to promote or maximize in a given sociocultural context? (2) what are our views of human persons, human learning, and human learning experiences? (3) given answers to one and two, what are appropriate learning activities? With regard to the first question, Monette is careful to describe values not as predetermined outcomes but as directions that need reevaluation. As possible general values in contemporary contexts, he offers liberation, pluralism, or personalism. As an example of a response to the third question, he gives the steps in Freire's process of conscientization.

Monette's effort to reconceptualize the process of program planning in adult education is a valuable one. Though I believe he may have slightly caricatured Tyler, Knowles, and Houle by not attending to some nuances in their thought, he has raised issues about language, values, politics, educational theory, and learning theory that demand serious inquiry. My approach to program planning in adult religious education depends in part on Monette's insightful reconceptualization.

PROGRAM PLANNING AND DESIGN IN ADULT RELIGIOUS EDUCATION

The systems treated in the preceding section are applicable to adult religious education. *McKenzie* (1975) has utilized the Knowles approach in his work on planning programs. Also, given the specific nature and scope of religious education, various educators have developed approaches to curriculum planning that take into account the specific nature of religious education. A number of these approaches will be reviewed in this section.

In a number of influential writings, *Wyckoff* (1961; 1967) presented a theory and design for Christian education curriculum. Wyckoff's major thrust has been the establishment of Christian education as a particular discipline. His theory is dependent on the work of Tyler and John Goodlad, who refined Tyler's work. The basic categories for a discipline are the objectives and purposes, scope or essential content and experience, context or setting in which education can take place, process (procedures or methods), personnel or partners in the enterprise and their roles, and timing or sequence to be anticipated and planned. These six categories make up the conceptual framework for planning, conducting, and evaluating the practical enterprise of Christian education (1967, p. 390).

Wyckoff's work had a great influence on Schaefer's *Program Planning for Adult Christian Education* (1972), the most thorough treatment of this topic. Schaefer has changed the sequence of categories but not the substance. His sequence is objective, personnel, scope, process, context, and timing. Three general curriculum concerns that touch on all six categories are organizing principle, administration, and evaluation. Schaefer provided in his work both formal and substantive principles in that he not only raised the curricular questions for the programmer but also argued persuasively for particular answers. He presented a thorough discussion of Christian education as interpersonal appropriation of the mystery of Christ in all its dimensions (historical, theological, liturgical, and ethical). Schaefer adopted a situational approach to programming whereby programs are developed at the local church level and not at a centralized level.

Some dimensions of Schaefer's work were discussed in Chapter Seven. At that time the strengths and weaknesses of his educational theory were indicated. More attention is given to his substantive principles as a design for adult religious education later in this chapter and in following chapters.

The most recent work by a religious educator to attempt to present a curriculum design is Groome's *Christian Religious Education* (1980). Groome's work, like Wyckoff's and Schaefer's, is clearly a theory of *Christian* religious education. The objectives of Christian religious education are to educate for the Kingdom of God, Christian faith, and human freedom. Each of these objectives is clearly and fully explained. An approach of shared praxis is proposed as most suitable for attaining these objectives. As Groome presents this approach, he describes it in terms of a teaching-learning method. His approach, however, can also be viewed as a system of curriculum design or program planning.

The shared praxis approach has five movements. (1) *Present Action*: participants are invited to name or explain their own activity with regard to the topic under discussion; (2) *Critical Reflection*: participants reflect critically on why they so act and what are the consequences of their activity; (3) *Story and Its Vision*: the educator presents the Christian story concerning the topic and invites the faith response to it; (4) *Dialectic Between Story and Participants' Stories*: the participants are invited to appropriate the story to their lives in a dialectic with their own stories; (5) *Dialectic Between Vision and Visions*: participants have the opportunity to choose a personal faith response for the future.

Groome is not wedded to this particular sequence. He also recognizes that the method must be adapted for different age groups. His interpretation of Christian story and vision is a carefully nuanced one since he tries to maintain a balanced position between faithfulness to tradition and openness to criticisms of that tradition by participants' stories and visions.

The shared praxis approach moves beyond the work of Wyckoff and Schaeffer in its theological sophistication. Groome utilizes critical or revisionist theology and theology of liberation in defining the purposes of Christian religious education. His theory of knowing is informed by critical social theory and Freire's theory of conscientization. His treatment of socialization theories is well balanced in pointing out what he accepts and what he rejects in these theories.

Since Groome's work is a successful attempt at a comprehensive theory of religious education, it is helpful to define one's own theory by describing differences with his system. My major difference, developed in Chapter Six, is in advocating an even more political form of religious education. When describing objectives and epistemology, Groome draws on liberation theology and a socio-cultural-political concept of praxis. But in describing his educational approach, praxis appears to be reduced to individual and private activity. It is not clear how critical reflection that is primarily on the self "is ultimately on the social context by which the self comes to its self-identity (1980, p. 185)." The starting point must be both on self and on themes, issues, and problems in the political context. If the starting point is merely on self, the theory may remain idealist and removed from broader political concerns.

The weakness in dealing with the political in this educational approach may be brought about by a too great dependence on theological and philosophical sources. To Groome's skepticism about the data collected by the research of social scientists (p. 235), one can add a skepticism about theological and philosophical theory that avoids empirical data. The profession of education (a practical field relying on theory and data) needs grand theory (from theology, philosophy, and social sciences—and education), middle range theories from the social and human sciences and education, and empirical data from these same disciplines. One's present action is to be critiqued not only by theology but also by data and theories in other fields.

An additional criticism of Groome's approach is the lack of fit between his theology, theory of knowing, and educational theory. The first two are rather broadly and grandly presented. The focus of the educational approach, however, is narrow and limited, as presented. Groome states that "shared practice takes place in a situation of shared dialogue (1980, p. 185)." A theory of education must focus upon organizations, groups, individuals, and masses. A theory of education, if it is to be more than an instructional theory or an educational method, must consider the interrelationships among the various educating institutions of society: family, work, religious bodies, and media. The concept of shared dialogue can only with great difficulty be broadened to encompass the many activities that are involved in education.

Groome's theory of education is a general one but does have applicability to the education of adults. The theory embraces Moran's ideal of education toward adulthood. A number of examples of shared praxis come from the author's experiences with adult groups. Groome considers Fowler's stages of faith development as providing important guidelines for religious education. The shared praxis approach, with the examples that Groome gives from his practice, are valuable tools for thinking through the planning and conducting of adult religious education.

PLANNING ADULT RELIGIOUS EDUCATION

The process of planning adult religious education demands attention to four areas: values, interests, needs, and objectives. Planners should be aware of their own values and the values they wish to promote through education. Secondly, they must be aware of felt interests and needs in those for whom they plan educational activites. Thirdly, they must establish goals or objectives for educational processes. In Chapter Nine the particular formats and processes for adult religious education are presented and evaluated.

Investigation of Values

Planning should start with the questions suggested by Monette: "What are the sociocultural forces operative in society which we as educational planners choose to maximize or perpetuate? What are, in other words, our value commitments within this context? (1979b, p. 91)." For religious educators the focus is upon *religious values*. It is preferable to begin with values—those things or activities considered worthwhile—instead of needs and interests because these latter have no educational significance unless value judgments are made about the appropriateness of meeting needs and interests according to a particular value system. Also, the use of the term values makes it clear that education always takes place in a context of commitment to a course of action in different realms of life.

The concept of values used here is of "end states or collective goals or explicit purposes ... and standards in terms of which specific criteria may be established and choices made among alternatives (Burns, 1978, p. 74)." Besides being standards, values are also modes of conduct, such as faith, love, and fairness. Values have cognitive, affective, and behavioral components; they are also strong motivating forces.

Religious values exist in all areas of life. Religious education finds values not only in theological sources but also in the humanities, science, social sciences, and ordinary experience. What makes something valuable religiously is its connection with *some transcending purpose or end*. Transcendent ends can be found at personal, interpersonal, and socio-political levels of human existence. An examination of religious values at these levels is important at the start of the planning process.

Adult religious education is concerned with promoting *personal values*. Psychoanalytic and humanistic psychology indicate how human life is a movement toward self- and ego-transcendence. The chief symbols in modern psychology around which personal values are grouped include self-fulfillment, self-realization, individualization, the heroic individual, and the person of integrity. Connected with these symbols are a number of secondary values: authenticity, identity, awareness of weaknesses and limitations, creativity, honesty, acceptance of darkness in self, patience in suffering and in face of death, trust, love, wholeness, and freedom. Many of these same values are those emphasized in religious traditions.

An important personal value that religious education should promote is a sense of meaningfulness of life. Psychology and sociology of religion have emphasized this function of religion. Religious creeds (belief systems), religious cults (ritual systems), and religious codes (ethical systems) provide individuals with resources for developing a coherent philosophy of life. Personal religious experience and membership in a religious organization are also aids in this quest for meaning. These five phenomenologically derived dimensions of religion both point to transcending ends and meanings and offer the possibilities of attaining these for religious believers (Smart, 1969, pp. 6-12).

Religious meaning and religious values are *mediated through symbols* in the form of phenomena, events, and persons in daily life that keep before us transcendent ends and the means of advancing toward these ends. The value of religious symbols is that they are open-ended and thus allow us to bring some of our own meaning to them. There is room in symbols for improvisation and development of personal perspectives. Such powerful religious symbols as Christ, Moses, the Torah, and the Buddha have a richness of meaning for individuals in their search for personal religious faith and value in their lives.

People reveal their personal religious values most clearly through the *stories* they tell about themselves. Story is overworked in religious circles today, yet it still seems an excellent medium for people to use in determining religious values and meanings. Stories capture the narrative and dramatic character of experience. In telling stories, we recall the past that has shaped our present experience and convictions about what is truly important now and for the future. In urging people to tell their personal stories we should ask them to use either, or both, religious symbols and images and contemporary forms. The two types of symbols interpret, correct, and complement each other.

In examining classic religious stories there is one recurrent theme that touches a deeply personal value. This religious story has a plot in which the central person is brought to *"salvation"or healing or wholeness*. In Slater's interpretation of religious stories he finds that these stories "communicate some affirmation of identity with integrity, some hope of personal fulfillment or self-realization, which enables its characters to transcend the negativities of existence (1978, p. 58)." Religious stories are about individuals transcending themselves and forming new characters or values systems. Different ways of transcendence are found in religious traditions: redemption, resurrection, renunciation, reconciliation, and revolution. Some of these are more properly interpersonal or socio-political values, though no clear-cut distinctions can be made among these values.

A most common religious story entailing personal values is the *conversion story*. This type of story has been more common in Protestantism than in Catholicism. Protestantism in this country has focused more on the dramatic story of religious conversion from sinfulness to holiness, from hope to despair. Catholicism has stressed more the gradual movement to holiness through growth in virtue. In more recent years, however, personal revivalistic movements have appeared in Roman Catholicism. At the root of the conversion experience is an awareness that we have many more potential selves than we can ever hope to actualize (James, 1902; 1974 reprint). Some symbolic event, phenomena, or person dramatizes this potential for us and empowers us toward a new end state or value.

Contemporary religious conversion stories take forms not found in the classical works of James and Starbuck. People today feel free to draw symbols from a number of different religious traditions, both East and West. While rootedness in a particular tradition may be desirable for some, others prefer a "polysymbolic religiosity and a conscious eclecticism (Shepherd, 1974)." Persons in life transitions most often are groping for new symbols and stories that can become the center of personal values. For some modern Jews the Holocaust or State of Israel has replaced the Exodus and Torah as the central symbol of their lives. The political struggle for liberation is a central symbol for others. The deepest meaning of the death of God movement in theology since Nietszche's time is that many people need to replace in their personal lives the symbol of the Absolute God with something like Bonhoeffer's symbol of Jesus as the Man for Others. For others the individual self and authentic self-realization are central symbols that motivate conversion.

One thing appears to be clear. People need symbols and visions around which to center their lives and values. Religious faith is present only when symbols are unified and visions hold out the hope of changing our daily lives. What a religious vision of transcendence entails is made clear by looking at Camus's vision of *The Plague* in which there is a rejection of the vision of transcendence. The only absolute reality is the plague. Relationships with others are possible but transcending encounters are impossible. Symbols, like philosophies of life, do not have to be refuted. They simply die in the life of a person or group.

Interpersonal Values. The second realm of life where transcendent religious values are to be promoted is in the area of interpersonal relationships. No precise distinction can be drawn between personal values and interpersonal values since a mutual relationship exists between the two. Promoting personal growth must include promoting values that enhance human relationships and life in communities. Thus for the purposes of planning adult religious education, it is beneficial to be aware of promoting religious values that more clearly define our relationships with others and our life in groups.

The religious philosopher Martin Buber and the humanistic psychologist Carl Rogers have both explored the deeper dimensions of our relationships with others. Buber (1958) contrast the objectivity of the I-It relationship with the subjectivity of the I-Thou relationship. The religious significance of interpersonal relationships is highlighted in Buber's view that in every I-Thou encounter there is an encounter with an Eternal Thou.

Interpersonal values that are given great prominence in the psychology of Rogers are empathy or placing oneself in the frame of reference of another; congruence or participating in the life of another; acceptance of the failings and weaknesses of others; permitting others to be fully themselves; and unconditional positive regard and caring for others (Rogers, 1961). Other values also promote interpersonal growth: self-understanding, self-identity, self-acceptance, self-direction, and love of others.

Interpersonal values, like personal values, can be transcendent values and thus have religious significance. Oden (1966) made a careful comparison of Roger's theory of interpersonal relationships and therapy with traditional religious symbols of sin, redemption, and grace. It is Oden's contention that an analysis of other psychological theories on human relationships would bring similar results. Though I am not sure of this contention with regard to some forms of behaviorism and psychoanalysis, this reservation does not weaken Oden's thesis about the values promoted through the practice of humanistic psychology. These values certainly enable persons to transcend themselves and open themselves to transcendent reality.

Interpersonal values are also important in our life in communities: families, churches and synagogues, schools, work, etc. We need interaction in communities of relatives, friends, co-workers, and co-members of religious groups to enable us to know the truth about ourselves and the world in order to correct our own versions of this truth.

Religious bodies have always been places where emphasis is placed on interpersonal values. Friendship, fellowship, common brotherhood and sisterhood, and the loving community are powerful religious symbols. Religious bodies promote these values through experiences where faith is shared in ritual, myth, and other symbolic activities. One task of adult religious education is to ensure that these symbols do not become stereotypes.

Though it is easy to talk about interpersonal and community-building values in general, it is difficult to attend to specific situations. Interpersonal values include acceptance of all human beings, regardless of race, sex, or social status. To promote religious interpersonal values entails that a community extend friendship to all peoples, especially those who have suffered discrimination. It involves helping those in need even though they do not belong to our community.

Promoting interpersonal values entails the difficult task of dealing with emotions. Both positive and negative feelings should be released and understood in order to promote healing of differences, reconciliation of separated persons, and personal renewal of individuals. Religious symbols of confession, forgiveness, and reconciliation are powerful forces in promoting these values unless these symbols have become routinized and devoid of real meaning.

An organizing principle around which interpersonal religious values can be grouped is love. Love is a central symbol in many religious traditions and it is found in various forms; paternal, maternal, love of friendship, and erotic love. Love that is self-seeking, self-giving, and self-denying is found in religious symbols and stories. The highest form of love is found in symbolic persons who realized that there were situations in which it was necessary to risk their own lives: Socrates, Moses, Jesus, Mohammed, Ghandhi, Martin Luther King, and countless other martyrs for noble causes.

Political Values. Personal and interpersonal values are closely related to the values of the political community. Political values include the values that should characterize social systems and structures, economic systems, and political systems. It is not an easy task to spell out these values.

The major value to be promoted in all social institutions is justice. Rawls (1971) enunciates the two basic principles of justice. According to his first principle each person has a right to the most extensive liberty compatible with a like liberty for others. Basic civic liberties include the right to vote and stand for public office; freedom of speech and assembly; liberty of conscience and freedom of thought; and freedom to hold personal poverty. Rawls's second principle applies to the distribution of wealth and to arrangements of power and authority. Rawls contends that inequities in wealth, power, and authority can be just in a society only if they can reasonably be expected to work out to the advantage of those who are most deprived. They are not justified as rewards. Examples are the education given to doctors at public expense, and the rewards for being an entrepreneur. All religious traditions recognize that religious faiths include ways of devotion, contemplation, and action. Religions include those who are contemplative but pregnant in silence, those who win us over with their poetry and songs of devotion, and those who spend time "instigating a flurry of political movements, writing pamphlets, leading marches, training cadres of activists, finding truth in praxis (Slater, 1978, p. 62)." The future that religious stories present is a vision that demands collective political action for its realization. Such images of the future as the Kingdom of God, Paradise, Nirvana, and Enlightenment tell more about the quality of life to be achieved now than they do about what the future state will be. Religious stories raise the question of how to move between the present situation and the future hope.

The religious symbols that reveal the future lack specifics since they invite our participation in shaping the transcending political goals of religious bodies. The stories present the future as unfinished and undetermined. The good life, the achievement of justice, and the state of peace envisioned demand struggles, at times even violent struggles. Central stories of death and resurrection, renunciation, and revolution indicate that transcendent peace and justice come only through struggle.

When we move from the level of stories and symbols in an attempt to draw concrete principles for religious action in the political order, we encounter a number of different approaches. Neibuhr (1951) classified five approaches within Christian history, which also appear to be applicable to other religious traditions. Some religious groups have advocated strict separation from and opposition to the entire culture in which they exist. Other groups become totally conformed to the culture. A third position is the development of a synthesis of best elements in religion and culture. A fourth view is living in tension or paradox with a culture that is viewed as basically opposed to religious ideals. A final position takes the stance that it is the function of religion to bring about a transformation of the culture.

All five positions are political stances intended to bring the power of religion to bear upon social institutions. At the heart of these positions are a number of values that religions try to foster in society. Wogaman (1976) has described common religious values that need to be promoted in the social and political order. He presents these not as absolutes but as presumptions which allow for exceptions in some cases. *Positive* values include the goodness of created existence, the value of individual life, the unity of the human family, and the equality of persons. *Negative* presumptions are human finitude and human sinfulness. A number of values—*polar* presumptions—need to be carefully balanced: the individual and social nature of human persons; freedom and responsibility; subsidiarity and universality; conservatism and innovation; and optimism and pessimism. Wogaman's treatment is carefully nuanced and filled with practical examples of how these values can help shape the social, political, and economic institutions in which we live.

In summary, the first task of planners of adult religious education is to make decisions on values to be promoted at personal, interpersonal, and political levels of life. This entails both a self-analysis and a socio-political analysis. Sources for this analysis are contemporary experience, contemporary cultural analyses, and the wisdom of religious traditions. A second step, closely connected with this, is the assessment of interests and needs of potential participants. Educational objectives are determined by evaluating needs and interests by particular standards.

Assessment of Religious Needs and Interests

One of the great contributions of progressive educators was their insistence that educational planning begin with the needs, interests, and wants of learners rather than with academic subject matter. The progressive teacher was to direct and guide the natural impulses and drives or instincts of learners into areas of traditional subject matter. Adult educators have followed this practice. The starting point is the Knowles system of program planning in assessment of needs and interests (1980).

While the criticisms leveled by Lawson (1975) and Monette (1978) against an exaggerated dependence on needs assessment in determining educational objectives are helpful correctives, assessment of needs is still a valuable step in program planning if done in conjunction with investigation of religious values. Wants and needs are powerful motivating factors that cannot be ignored is establishing educational objectives.

In his study of political leadership Burns (1978) concludes that effective leaders are able to take the felt or expressed wants and needs of individuals and turn them into powerful motives for seeking values that both leaders and people really want. Burns accepts as valid the hierarchy of needs described by Maslow (1954): biological, safety, esteem, belonging, and self actualization. In this theory lower needs must be met before others can be sought. Burns contends that a "congruence between the need and value hierarchies would produce a powerful potential for the exercise of purposeful leadership (1978, p. 44)."

There are a number of *reasons for assessing needs and interests* in adult religious education. This process helps to ensure that programs will be of interest to members of religious bodies. Planners should know where people are with regard to values at personal, interpersonal, and political levels. A needs assessment may indicate particular deficiencies in one or more of these areas. Such an assessment gives members an opportunity to express what they think should be offered in adult religious education. Given the voluntary nature of most adult education, needs assessment is valuable, since planners need to be constantly informed of members' sentiments and desires.

While the criticisms against the exaggerated emphasis on needs assessment in adult education are valid, my experience is that they have less validity in adult religious education. Most often programs in adult religious education are determined merely by planners working out of their own sense of what is valuable and needed. A needs assessment of a particular local church or synagogue will surface many varied interests and needs, all of which are important and valuable indicators for programming. The task is then to decide which needs to attempt to meet through educational processes.

The focus in needs assessment in adult religious education is upon the *religious needs of adults*. Adult religious needs can be analyzed in a number of ways. Schaeffer (1972) is most concerned with needs that come from an analysis of the basic elements of Christian faith: knowledge of the sacred literature, understanding of contemporary theological interpretations, intelligent participation in worship and ritual, and a commitment to the ethical teachings of Christian faith. In a general sense members of religious bodies are aware of a need to achieve these intellectual and moral values. However, needs assessments also require additional starting points of a more personal nature.

The approach to values presented in the last section can serve to broaden the scope of needs assessment in that it takes in three dimensions of life: personal, interpersonal, and political. In *humanistic personality* theory personal needs are considered primary motivating factors. Needs are the outcomes of internal and external occurrences. Needs come and go in our lives; needs are subject to many changes. A basic need for all persons is to find meaning in life and to live a meaningful existence. Many persons at one time or another express needs for higher and more spiritual values than those to which they are presently committed.

Religious needs of individuals are often related to *developmental changes* in their lives. In Chapter Three I indicated the religious significance of the search for identity and intimacy in young adulthood, the generativity crisis in midlife, and the struggle for integrity in late adulthood. Values sought in attempting to resolve these crises are personal, interpersonal, and socio-political. My experience in programming indicates that individuals will most often express interpersonal needs before personal and socio-political needs: family relationships, friendship, sexuality, guidance of children, dealing with aging parents, and coping with work relationships. Needs that are deeply personal tend to be felt but not readily expressed. Needs of society that demand personal commitment and action are least often found in replies to needs assessments.

What this experience indicates is that great attention should be paid in programming to needs individuals have for help in fulfilling their particular social roles and life-styles in family, work, community, and religious bodies. The religious dimensions of these roles can be integrated with psychological and sociological understandings. In the process of meeting these interpersonal needs there often surfaces needs of a more personal nature, for example, identity crises, particular sufferings and trials, and awareness of limitations. At times these can be addressed in an educational setting; at other times personal or group counseling is indicated.

The most difficult needs to address in adult education are the *social and political needs* of the broader community. As a planner I find that this is the sphere of needs that I have to continually bring before a planning committee. The obvious reason for this is the immediacy of the personal and interpersonal needs that we face. We do not often realize how these needs are related to social, political, and economic issues in our communities. The planning process in adult religious education must focus attention on the full range of human needs, interests, and values. Often it is by grappling with broader social issues that we gain the perspective and insight into how to meet needs at more personal levels.

Once needs are assessed a determination must be made of what needs can be met through *educational processes*. Some individual and societal needs can be met through education. Others clearly cannot. Some distinctions must be maintained among religious education, counseling, social action, worship, and pastoral care. Education broadly conceived is a dimension in all of these activities. Yet is also distinguished from these activites in important ways. Religious education as such does not involve counseling persons in emotional problems, direct political strategizing and action, ritual celebration, or tending to the spiritual crises. Though religious education deals with personal problems, social action, ritual, and concern for others, it does so in contexts that stress explicit and direct intentions of teaching and learning, wide range of understandings, freedom of inquiry, suitable processes, and appropriate methods of evaluation. It is important for adult education committees to come to an understanding of what their scope is in order that energies are not extended into areas beyond the competence of the group.

I have kept to last a discussion of methods of assessing needs and interests. A number of good resources exist that can be useful for planning adult religious education. *Assessing Needs, Evaluating Programs* (Catholic Education Office, no date) has many sample surveys. *GIFT: Growth in Faith Together* developed by James Schaefer (1973) has been found useful by many religious bodies. This program has three parts: *research* of religious attitudes and beliefs; *reflection* on the findings from this research; and a *response* in the form of development of educational and liturgical programs.

While religious educators may find the above-mentioned programs helpful, it is also necessary for planners to have a broader view of methods of needs assessment. A helpful analysis of approaches is found in McKinley's (1973) threefold classification system.

1. *Individual Self-Fulfillment Models.* Two examples of this model are given: (a) the *random approach model* attempts to sample all adults in the organization. Its purpose is to determine what are the topics of interest to the largest number of people. Data is gathered through telephone surveys, questionnaire surveys, advisory committee recommendations, suggestion boxes, interviews, and combinations of these procedures; (b) the *selective appeal model* focuses on the needs of a particular segment of the population, e.g., young married adults. The same techniques are utilized, but with only a specified population.

2. *Individual Appraisal Models.* In this approach individuals are consciously and directly involved in determining their own learning needs rather than in selecting from a proposed list. Individual appraisal is done in collaboration with guidance counselors and independent study consultants. Scales for self-analysis or diagnosis might be utilized. Individuals can analyze their performances in simulated situations.

3. *System Discrepancy Models.* These models attempt to determine the gap or discrepancy between what is and what ought to be in a system, organization, or group. One approach is to infer the existence of needs from problems that exist in the system. Problems must be clearly defined and a determination made on what education can contribute toward their solution. Needs assessment begins with the goals and stated purposes of an organization.

I believe that all three approaches can be utilized in adult religious education. Periodic surveys of the entire membership and frequent opinion samplings from particular groups are valuable planning tools. If these are done with the thoroughness of the GIFT program, the process itself is educational and ideas are produced for years to come. Adult religious education needs more models for individual appraisal. I consider it an ideal that each person who enters an adult religious education program has an opportunity to do a self-diagnosis on religious knowledge, attitudes, and practices. Planners should also be sensitive to problems that exist in their religious organizations and in the community. Often these are valuable indicators of educational needs.

The investigation of values and assessment of needs are the first two elements in planning for adult religious education. Planning must proceed from these activities to a consideration of objectives and ends to be sought through educational processes.

Determination of Objectives

The movement in educational planning is from values to needs and interests to objectives or purposes. All theories of program planning include a treatment of objectives, though the term is used in different ways. McKenzie (1975, pp. 67-69) gives five usages for the term educational objective. It refers to the activity of a teacher, the topic to be treated, a task of the learner, a general outcome for the learner, and a specific outcome for learners. This specific outcome is often expressed in behavioral terms.

Knowles in his treatment of objectives for adult education makes a number of important distinctions (1980, ch. 7). He distinguishes *general purposes*—the broad social and institutional goals of adult education—from *program objectives*—the educational and operational outcomes toward which a program is directed. Program objectives are *operational* if they are concerned with such matters as finances, scheduling, and public relations. They are *educational or learning objectives* if they define the kinds of behavioral outcomes that participants are invited to seek. Knowles's espousal of behavioral objectives in this chapter seems somewhat inconsistent with his humanistic learning theory where he emphasizes the self-directiveness of adult learning.

A careful analysis of objectives is found in Houle's system of planning (1972). Houle makes distinctions among *motives*—inciting causes which help determine an individual choice of an objective; *aspirations*—desired perfections or excellences based on an ideal or theoretical statement; and *objectives*—intended results of an educational activity. An objective in Houle's view exists only when a decision has been made to perform a definite action and when effects are intended through these actions. Thus an objective is a practical end to which actions are directed.

Educational objectives according to Houle have a number of attributes (1972, pp. 139-142). They are *rational* in imposing a logical pattern on educational activities. Objectives are *practical*, i.e., directed at some concretely defined changes in specific persons within a specific time frame. A *plurality* of objectives should be developed to meet different needs. Some *hierarchy* or priority should be established among objectives. Objectives should have a *discriminative* quality, i.e., rule out other goals and objectives. Finally, objectives need to be *open to change* if it is realized during the educational process that other objectives are more appropriate.

It is clear from Houle's analysis that the refinement of educational objectives is a creative and judgmental process. Planners must think creatively about context, the aspirations and motivation of learners, content, and design. Any one of these elements may be the starting point but all should be considered in the planning process.

The highly debatable issue about educational objectives is whether or not planners should decide beforehand what specific behavioral outcomes ought to be realized. This issue is at the heart of philosophic differences between behaviorists and humanists in education. My view is that while specific objectives are beneficial in areas of basic knowledge and skills, they are not appropriate in most areas of religious education. Though educators might desire behavioral responses in religion (and other areas of study), the freedom of individuals to respond or not respond must be respected, as well as the mode of response.

The fact that objectives are not defined behaviorally does not make planning aimless or directionless. Planners should have some general expectations of what they want to accomplish. It is preferable to state these in general terms of what people might learn or do, or how they might respond. However, objectives in religious education should neither be stated or pursued to *ensure* that people do precisely what we desire.

The development of objectives in adult religious education

should be *a cooperative effort*. As much as possible planners, administrators, teachers, and learners should be involved in the process. While there are certain areas where the contribution of learners may not be great because of lack of knowledge, these learners still need to be involved in order to ensure that the program has comprehensibility and relevance to their situation. This principle of shared responsibility in program planning is especially important in adult religious education because of differing perceptions of religion and differing expectations of religious education.

Thus far our treatment of objectives in adult religious education has dealt with formal principles. *Substantive principles* have to do with a determination of what adult religious education should attempt to accomplish. The clearest presentation of substantive principles is found in Schaefer's work on adult Christian education (1972). A summary of his position is found in Chapter Six of this book. In brief, Schaefer argues that the objective of Christian adult education is that mature persons appropriate in faith the mystery of Christ as presented in the Scriptures, explained by contemporary theology, celebrated in worship, and made relevant in ethical teachings.

Substantive objectives for Christian religious education are also found in Groome's work (1980, Part II). Religious education is to lead people to a faith lived in response to the Kingdom of God in Jesus Christ and to human freedom. As in Schaefer's treatment, each of these words is thoroughly defined in its Biblical and theological language. Groome's advance over Schaefer's work is his inclusion of human freedom within the objectives of Christian religious education.

My view of the objectives of adult religious education is implicit in my treatment of values earlier in this chapter. I believe that the general objectives of religious education should be stated in terms that are common to all religious faiths and that transcend particular expressions of religious faith. The language of personal, interpersonal, and political values appears suitable to accomplish this.

There are certain dangers in using such central symbols as "mystery of Christ," "Kingdom of God" as meta-purposes or meta-objectives in Christian education. These heavily Biblical symbols continue the theological domination of religious education in religious bodies by tending to reduce the religious to the theological. I also feel that the symbols, though deeply rooted in the tradition, are not central in the pattern of current life and thought and thus are not primary symbols. Central symbols in religious bodies should not identify end-states (Kingdom of God, Nirvana, Salvation) nor central truths (Mystery of Christ) nor means of achieving these states or truths (Faith). The central symbols of a religion should describe "a religious way of life." They should call a person to the "discovery of oneself as well as of the Christ, the Buddha, or the law (Slater, 1978, p. 36)."

In this view of central religious symbols in religious education, the emphasis is on imitation of a particular person, actions according to standards found in the religious tradition and in the culture, and on religious self-realization. It is clear that central religious symbols include Christ, Torah, Buddha, Enlightenment, and the Way of Confucius. Yet these central symbols take on different meanings in different cultural epochs according to which values need to be promoted. At times for a large number of people there develops a new symbol around which a group coalesces and is motivated to religious thinking and living. The Holocaust, the Great March, Liberation, and Arab Nationalism have become central symbols. For some people the old symbol is replaced by the new. For others two symbols exist side by side mutually illuminating and correcting each other.

These remarks should not be interpreted as a rejection of the use of historic symbols in religious education of particular groups. I question rather the prominence given to these symbols in religious education and the nature of the central symbols chosen. I believe those symbols should be chosen which clearly invite people to a way of life. Religious symbols by nature are not totally clear on what they propose and thus invite different responses at different times. If, however, they require elaborate historical and theological explanation, one wonders about their power as objectives for adult religious education.

In religious education it is important that objectives include initiation into central stories and grappling with classic arguments and classic authors. This is so not that we might make these our own but in order to better think and decide for ourselves. Good religious education entails in part going through familiar stories and earlier expressions of religious faith and coming to new conclusions which may have some continuity with earlier versions. The goals and objectives of these educational processes, however, are not more beautiful thoughts on love and justice but just and loving lives (Slater, 1978, p. 166).

While I have argued for the necessity of objectives in adult religious education, I also recognize that all education has to be open to the surprise that often comes when free persons encounter transcendent elements in themselves, in others, and in the world. In my theistic vision, God is integral to all these forms of transcendence. Religion sets forth a way, but not the single way. People are invited to judge, participate, adapt, and live. The stories and teachings of all religions are incomplete. They are not just about past events. They are also about a present opening out to the possibility of a better future. Even in the face of a terrible present and seemingly demonic reality such as the Holocaust, people were able to share a vision of future hope. People are ever able to find new ways to affirm transcendent personal, interpersonal, and political values.

CONCLUSION

This chapter has attempted to describe a planning process for adult religious education. The excellent work that has been done in this area in the past fifty years was briefly reviewed. A basic similarity was found among the various systems: needs assessment, setting of objectives, designing of programs, managing programs, and evaluating programs.

This chapter focused on three critical elements in the planning process: investigation of values, assessment of needs and interests, and setting of educational objectives. The view was taken that the investigation of religious values at personal, interpersonal, and political levels is the most critical element in the planning process. It is according to these values that felt needs and interests are evaluated and placed in a priority listing. It is also these values that constitute the objectives for adult religious education.

Once planners have set educational objectives for adult religious education, they can move to decisions about how this education should be carried out or designed. The design of adult religious education involves formats and processes that are appropriate for achieving objectives. The next chapter suggests suitable formats and processes. Chapter Ten treats practical issues involved in the management and evaluation of adult religious education programs.

CHAPTER IX
DESIGNING ADULT
RELIGIOUS EDUCATION

The planning for adult religious education should include careful attention to the design of educational activities and experiences. The development of objectives through processes of values investigation and needs and interests assessment is the first step in designing programs. Once planners have established objectives, they should then turn to questions about formats, processes, and methods. Objectives can be achieved through various processes. The task of planners is to determine the most suitable program design. This chapter examines the most commonly used formats, processes, and methods in adult religious education.

BASIC PRINCIPLES FOR DESIGNING PROGRAMS

Before describing particular formats and processes I first want to present a number of principles or assumptions that planners should consider before deciding upon particular formats and processes. Though some of these ideas have been presented in previous chapters, some repetition may be helpful here in order to make clear how the concepts developed in earlier chapters are related to the practical task of designing programs.

A Comprehensive View of the Religious

Planners should have a broad view of the religious. The concept of the religious is commensurate with the concept of the human. All personal, interpersonal, and political human experiences are open to a transcendent dimension that make them religious. The religious includes personal religious experiences, rituals, stories and doctrines, codes of morality, organization of religious bodies. These are the fundamental elements of the religious. Yet the religious includes other aspects of human life that are not clearly contained within these categories.

The religious is found in elements of personal development such as the struggle for identity and intimacy, the quest for love and friendship, and engagement in the world of work and leisure. Passage events of life have potential for religious transcendence: birth, puberty, marriage, child-rearing, divorce, sickness, retirement, and death. Religion is also a dimension of our interpersonal, community, and political lives. Religious faith is closely related to mental health and the search for meaning.

The religious is closely related to aesthetic appreciation and artistic creation. The religious finds expression in works of literature and the various art forms—drama, dance, music, architecture. In recent years religious educators have begun to explore more deeply the relationship beween the arts and religious education (Durka and Smith, 1979).

Adult religious education should attempt to ground people in their own religious traditions and invite them to a study of the great world religions. Only one who is grounded in a particular tradition through life and understanding can begin to appreciate fully other religious traditions. In the pluralistic societies in which most people live a mutual understanding and appreciation for commonalities and differences among religious bodies can promote civic harmony and cooperation.

In planning programs for adult religious education this comprehensive view of the religious is a necessity. Programs should be developed with a sensitivity to the religious aspects of the personal, interpersonal, and political values and needs that pertain to religious life. Programs planned solely around the traditional religious elements of creed, code, and cult do not do justice to the full meaning of the religious.

A Comprehensive View of Learning

Planners for adult religious education need a comprehensive view of forms of human learnings. I believe that planners can find a beneficial analysis of forms of learning in well-known taxonomies for the cognitive domain (Bloom and Associates, 1956) and the affective domain (Krawthwohl and Associates, 1956). These objectives do not have to be interpreted in any narrowly behavioral sense.

For the cognitive domain five types of learnings are described. These are described in hierarchical order from basic learnings to more complex learnings.

1. *Knowledge*: a recall of specific terms, facts, trends, and categories. It includes a knowledge of universal patterns, abstractions, principles, theories, and structures.
2. *Comprehension*: an understanding of terms, facts, trends, and categories. This is manifested by an ability to *translate* or paraphrase, to *interpret* (explain, summarize, reorder, rearrange, or present a new view of the matter), and *extrapolate* (determine consequences, corrolaries, and effects).
3. *Application*: the use in concrete and particular situations of general ideas, rules of procedures, generalized methods, and technical principles, ideas, and theories.
4. *Analysis*: the ability to break ideas and theories down into constitutive parts or elements such that the relative hierarchy of ideas is made clear and the relations between ideas expressed are made explicit.
5. *Synthesis*: the ability to put elements together to constitute a pattern or structure not already there. Forms of synthesis include the detailed expression of ideas and feelings, and experiences; the production of a plan or proposed set of operations; the classification of data or phenomena.
6. *Evaluation*: judgments about the value of material and methods for given purposes. It includes both quantitative and qualitative judgments about the extent to which criteria are satisfied. Judgments are made in terms of internal criteria—logical accuracy, consistency, etc.—and external criteria—confirmation by facts and theories.

All educational activities have a knowledge or understanding dimension that planners need to be concerned about. At times in religious education there is a tendency to minimize understanding in a desire to affect attitudes and behaviors. All analyses of religious faith include a knowledge or understanding dimension. In many forms of adult education—study groups, discussion groups, individual learning, courses, lectures, independent study— this form of learning is specifically desired.

While faith as cognitive understanding may include such learnings as knowledge, comprehension, application, analysis, synthesis, and evaluation, faith as attitude and action entails other learnings that comprise learnings in the affective domain. The learnings in this domain have been classified into five general types.

1. *Receiving*: awareness of the existence of a situation, phenomenon, object, or state of affairs. It includes the ability to receive the impact of a phenomenon through the process of selective attention.
2. *Responding*: show of feeling or emotion with regard to the perceived phenomenon, situation, object, etc.
3. *Valuing*: includes three steps: *accepting* values (persons, positions, ideas, groups, and causes) as worthwhile; manifesting a *preference* for these values by desiring and pursuing them; making a *commitment* to such values. At times persons attempt to convert others to their values.
4. *Organization of Values*: values are conceptualized in some manner, often in some symbolic form. Values are so organized that the dynamic relationships among them are seen.
5. *Characterization by a Value or Value System*: the development of a personal moral character that enables one to act consistently and effectively in this world. A person internalizes a value or value system in such a way that there is identity between the person and the value or value system.

This analysis of valuing found here is similar to that given by Raths and Associates (1966) in the rationale for their approach to values clarification. Seven criteria are given to establish whether or not there is a true valuing process. Persons must *choose* (1) freely, (2) from alternatives, (3) after thoughtful consideration of alternatives. Persons must *prize* objects (4) by cherishing them and being happy with their choices, and (5) by being willing to affirm their choices publicly. Finally, persons must *act* on their values (6) by doing something about their choices, (7) repeatedly in some pattern of life. Though there is some legitimate concern about the exaggerated relativism of values in this system, the process described is generally a good description of the valuing process.

Since I take the view that the promotion of values is of paramount importance in planning adult religious education, I find this analysis helpful in expanding a view of learning at the personal and interpersonal levels. When it comes to the promotion of political values, Derr's taxonomy (1973) referred to in Chapter Six can supplement these individualistically oriented taxonomies by drawing attention to social and political purposes of religious education. Though this taxonomy was developed to classify social purposes of public schools it can be adapted for purposes of adult religious education.

1. *Maintenance*: the desire to perpetuate the use of desirable values norms, and beliefs, in the community or society;
   a. *Stabilization*: seeking to induce adults who are using desirable values, norms, and beliefs in the community or society to continue to do so;
   b. *Reproduction*: recreating the use of desirable values, norms, and beliefs in the community or society by developing prospective users to use them;
2. *Improvement*: seeking to increase the use of desirable values, norms, and beliefs, and decreasing the use of undesirable ones;
   a. *Modification*: seeking to induce adults who are using undesirable values, norms, and beliefs in the community and society to commence using desirable ones;
   b. *Replacement*: seeking to reduce the use of undesirable values, norms, and beliefs in the community or society by developing prospective users of desirable values, norms, and beliefs.

Derr's taxonomy gives formal principles for planners and needs to be supplemented by substantive principles about social, political, and economic values. A discussion of appropriate political values for adult religious education was presented in Chapter Eight.

A Comprehensive View of Modes of Teaching-Learning

A third major principle for designing adult religious education programs is a comprehensive view of possible modes of learning. The most helpful work in this area has been done by Weil and

Joyce (1978a; 1979b) and Weil, Joyce, and Kluwin (1978). Though these models were developed from theorists concerned primarily with education of pre-adults, they deal with fundamental modes of learning that can be readily used with adults. A parallel can be drawn between these models and educational theories (Chapter Six) and systems of program planning (Chapter Eight). Four families of teaching-learning models have been developed in the cited works.

1. *Information Processing Models.* The major emphasis in these models is upon gathering and organizing data, sensing problems, generating concepts and solutions to problems, and employing verbal and nonverbal symbols. These approaches to teaching-learning are often concerned with productive thinking or general intellectual ability. Thus these models are most appropriate for learning in the cognitive domain, though they can be adapted for personal and social goals. Major examples of these models include approaches to inductive thinking, inquiry training, concept attainment, developmental models, and the advance organizer model. The emphasis in all of these models is upon learning to reason and to meaningfully absorb and relate bodies of knowledge.

2. *Behavioral Modificaton Models.* Skinnerian operant conditioning and reinforcement theory is the prime example of this model. The emphasis is upon changing or shaping the external behavior of learners and a description of learning in terms of visible behavior. Human learning is the learning of behaviors. The role of teachers is to decide what behaviors are to be learned and to so arrange the environment that the desired behaviors will be achieved. The model has been applied to a wide variety of goals in education, therapy, and industrial organization.

3. *Personal Models.* These models include processes for personal construction of reality and for integration of personality. The major focus is upon the emotional life of individuals and the relationships of individuals with other persons and with their entire environment. The model is designed

primarily for objectives in the affective domain. Primary examples of this model are the Rogerian Non-Directive Model and Fritz Perls's Awareness Training. The emphasis in this model is upon self-understanding, self-discovery, and self-concept. The attempt is also made to increase interpersonal awareness and understanding.

4. *Social Interaction Models.* These models emphasize the relationships of individuals to society and culture. They draw on social sources and are designed to improve life in community and society. Examples include group investigation of social problems, social inquiry through academic and logical reasoning, role playing around social values, and social simulation models. At times the social action model includes direct social action and involvement.

All of these models of teaching-learning have relevance for adult religious education with the possible exception of the behavioral modification model, if this is given a radical behaviorist orientation. Each model is best suited for its primary purpose. But this does not mean each one cannot be expanded to include the purposes contained in the other models. What these models emphasize is that the complexity of human learning is such that organized designs and formats are needed for both teaching and learning. In discussing the formats and processes for adult religious education I will draw on some of the concrete examples of models described by Weil, Joyce, and Kluwin.

FORMATS FOR ADULT RELIGIOUS EDUCATION

The most comprehensive analysis of formats for adult religious education is found in Houle's *Design for Education* (1972). In this work Houle classifies adult educational formats into eleven major categories. The categories are grouped around contexts of individual learning, group learning, mass education, and formation of educational institutions. In this section I will make use of these categories to present appropriate designs for adult religious education.

1. Individual Design: Independent Study

In this format individuals design education activities or experiences for themselves. Tough (1979) has done extensive research on the wide range of self-directed learning that takes place. For some learners such self-directed learning is an inherent pattern of life; for others it is necessitated by work or profession; for still others it takes the form of hobbies and leisure time activities.

Self-directed learning is not usually organized in a systematic manner. Many people seek the help of others in planning and carrying out their learning projects. People make use of both human and material resources in their independent learning projects. Programmed instruction, reading, and correspondence courses are the most common forms of this type of learning.

Wickett's study (1980) cited in Chapter Four is the only report on adult learning projects in the area of religious and spiritual growth. Among the examples he gives of independent study were persons who made a study of psychiatry, Bible, Hinduism, the dance, and racism. He found little evidence that people utilized the materials that were developed by religious bodies. Wickett's study is only a glimpse of the independent learning that takes place in the area of religion.

It has always been my conviction that religious educators need to develop ways to promote this form of learning. Educators can function as helpers, planners, and motivators for independent adult learning. Many adults are interested in learning about religion who cannot or who prefer not to work in groups. The role of the adult religious educator in this area can be likened to an educational consultant who would put persons in touch with resources (books, tapes, films, etc.) and aid them in planning their learning projects. Many educators perform this role with teachers of religion. But this particular adult education role needs greater emphasis and visibility.

A helpful manual for independent learning in Ronald Gross's *The Lifelong Learner* (1977). Gross recommends the keeping of a learning log or recorder of learning experiences. He calls attention to the invisible university that we have about us in the form of libraries, museums, selective television viewing, learning networks and exchanges, cassettes, and tapes. Gross offers a simple plan for an independent learning project which could be adapted to religious learning:

What, exactly, do I want to learn, understand, know about, become, be able to do?
1. How and where can this best be learned? What resources would be useful?
2. When is the best time to learn it, and what would be a desirable schedule?
3. Who could help?
4. How much is it worth to me? How much will it cost—in time, energy, and money—through various means?
5. How will I know I've achieved the goal, and what documentation or product would it be useful to have?

2. Individual Design: Tutorial Teaching

Many adults are tutored by private teachers each year and pay for this tutoring. Supervisors, readers' advisors, and counselors also perform tutorial functions. The range of learning in this form goes from Platonic dialogues to programmed tutorial instruction. Tutorial teaching can also be group planned, e.g., specialized training in Clinical Pastoral Care at a hospital. Apprenticeships and internships are commonly used forms of tutorial teaching.

There are various steps in the tutorial process. An agreement is made on learning objectives and an indication is given of the various routes that can be taken to achieve these objectives. Tutor and learner determine what the best mode is, though in some situations there is not a clearly defined direction. Learners should have some idea of how to gain the desired knowledge or skills. The tutor should take cognizance of improvements and problems and give necessary criticisms and suggestions. Finally, the tutor has the responsibility of evaluating the progress of the learners toward their goals.

In my experience I have not encountered many examples of designs for tutorial teaching in adult religious education. This form is at times used in introducing new members into a religious body when a one-to-one instructional relationship is used. This design for teaching needs more exploration by leadership in religious bodies. Tutorials could be a valuable design for teacher education, parent education, and the training of people for specific roles in religious bodies: administration, stewardship, counseling, pastoral care, and worship. Peer ministries and like-to-like ministries that have been developed in some religious bodies have some of the characteristics of tutorial relationships. Use of tutorials would enable more people to pass on the knowledge and skills they have acquired through years of membership.

3. Group Design: Learning Group

A group (with or without a continuing leader) designs an activity for itself. Such groups are autonomous, independent, self-governing groups with no outside allegiance or relationship. Learning groups are of various types. Groups come together to study particular subjects. Groups also take the form of literary clubs and scientific societies. Still other groups focus on increasing interaction among individuals. The scholarly professions often have advanced study groups for professional development.

The research of Allen Tough (1979) indicates a great appreciation for learning groups among the general population. They are veiwed as efficient and economical. Motivation and emotional benefits are provided through the group. Learning about the problems, needs, frustrations of others is found helpful. People develop a sense of responsibility to a group and at times feel free to express their deepest convictions in a group context. Some persons have reported negatively on their experience in groups: fearfulness of criticism, not meeting their wants and needs, and lack of sensitivity among members.

Gross (1977) has a number of practical suggestions about such groups. Groups should have a name, meet in member's homes, allow great flexibility and variety, take notes on significant developments and insights, and use resources. Groups should not be afraid to dissolve when there appears to be a waning of interest. Gross reports on a fourfold process that one group developed: opening up at the emotional level; sharing information and experiences; analyzing the meaning of these experiences; and abstracting information into an integrated perspective on life.

Learning groups have become increasingly common in adult

religious education. Many people prefer to share their religious faith in small intimate groupings of equals. Many of the newer programs in adult religious education include such learning and sharing groups. Bible study and prayer groups, faith sharing groups, and other types of groups fit into the category of learning group. For the past two years my major learning group has been a small group that comes together to share insights on a book or article on a religious topic. I have found the experience both supportive and challenging. Members suggest readings and the group has no formal leadership. The only rule is that the person who suggests the reading must be present at its discussion!

The basic Christian communities that have developed in Latin American countries are in part learning groups. These groups appear to fulfill the hopes of Erich Fromm who saw small groups as advancing the "revolution of hope" in satisfying "the need of the individual to work actively together with others, to talk, plan, and act together. . . . To relate in a less alienated fashion than is customary in most relations to others, to make sacrifices . . . to be open and vulnerable, to be imaginative, to rely on one's own judgment and decision (Fromm in Gross, 1977, p. 112)."

4. Group Design: Teacher-Directed Group Instruction

A teacher or group of teachers designs an activity for, and often with, a group of students. In this design there is a clearly defined role for the teacher, and instruction is provided for a group. Although this design is a schooling model, it is also widely used in adult education. The design makes efficient use of expert knowledge by bringing a large group of people into contact with experts. Many persons prefer this mode of learning because of the relative anonymity it provides and because of the expertness of the instruction given.

Though the tendency among some writers in adult education is to be critical of this design because of lack of teacher-student interaction and learner self-directedness, my experience is that in adult religious education it is a valuable design if used creatively. I would not make this design the dominant mode of instruction, but would always include in a comprehensive program lectures, courses, and institutes that utilize this mode.

When this design is used, it is preferable to group the courses, lectures, etc., into an integrated program rather than have isolated individual courses. It is also good practice to make some distinction between courses that are introductory and those that demand some previous knowledge. Variety in courses is most desirable. Courses should also be kept topical. In scheduling courses attention must be paid to patterns of life. Short or mini-courses held in mornings and evenings appear to be preferred in many areas (Knowles, 1980).

The most crucial decision that planners have to make concerning this design is the choice of teacher. Successful courses or lecture series most often involve the teacher or lecturer in the planning process itself. This mutual planning clarifies the goals and processes of the educational experience. In introducing an unknown person to speak to a community it is my practice to schedule only one session with the hope that at the end of the session people will make a commitment to continue the learning experience for a specified period of time. This practice spares the teacher and the planning group unnecessary embarrassment.

The most important thing that planners can do for teachers of courses (besides involving them in the planning process) is to give them immediate feedback about the course. This should be in the form of suggestions, questions, criticisms, and encouragement. As one who gives such courses from time to time, I can attest to the value of such feedback in helping me to tailor topics and processes to needs and interests of particular groups.

5. Group Design: Committee Guided Group Learning

A committee designs an educational activity for a larger group. Very often committees are formed to guide learning for larger groups that cannot or do not want to plan such learning activities. Many organizations have program committees that plan educational experiences. Though committees may plan courses, most often they plan for the membership of their organization conferences, workshops, institutes, field trips, seminars and other forms of education.

Bergevin and associates (1963, pp. 55-63) have presented a good description of the procedures of a committee. Committees are responsible to parent organizations. Members are appointed by the parent organization and specific charges are given to the committee by this organization. A committee should have a chairperson to give direction and guidance and committee members to accept responsibility and carry out tasks to their completion. At times committees make use of consultants or resource persons.

The advantages of a committee include the spreading of responsibility among different persons, the possible emergence of new leaders, an efficiency in use of time and effort, the opportunity for exploration and study, and the utilization of talents of diverse people. Disadvantages and limitations of committees include the difficulty of finding a group of persons who can work together, the tendency to delegate to committees responsibilities that a person or the group as a whole could perform, and the danger of manipulation by a skillful chairperson or member.

Some procedures that make for good functioning committees are: a clear view of goals and objectives, suitable physical arrangements for meetings, a prepared (tentative) agenda, minutes of meetings, respect for people's time in starting and ending promptly, a limit to discussions, some concrete action steps, regular reports to parent organization, and procedures to evaluate the work of the committee. From years of experience I have concluded that committee work is often boring, at times frustrating, and occasionally interesting and productive. A description of the types of educational activities that a committee might plan is given in the next section of this chapter.

6. Group Design: Collaborative Group Education

Two or more groups design an activity that will enhance their combined programs of service. To accomplish this groups must be able to transcend their own particular interests and join in a common effort. Usually a special planning committee is formed from members of the participating groups. Members of this committee participate as representatives of their own groups and should not promise more than their groups are prepared to do. Close communications should be maintained among members and their parent groups.

This educational design needs to be utilized more often, both within religious bodies and among different religious bodies. Adult education committees should regularly schedule educational activities in conjunction with committees that are concerned with worship, social action, ecumenical relationships, family enrichment, and other religious concerns. Cooperative efforts should also be developed with other religious bodies and civic organizations. Fortunately, in many areas exclusive group loyalties have lessened to the extent that such efforts are both feasible and desirable.

One of my most valuable educational experiences came from planning and participating in a three day educational conference for Jewish and Christian teachers of religion. Working closely with rabbis and Jewish lay teachers gave me an appreciation of Judaism as a living tradition which my previous education through reading did not provide. After initial amenities and acceptance, people felt free to speak about deeply sensitive and potentially divisive issues. The Christian teachers came to respect the practice of serious study of Jewish history and traditions that was manifested in the discussions during the conference.

The six designs developed by Houle presented thus far have dealt with individual and group learning. The next four designs are concerned with educational institutions. Houle uses the word *institution* to embrace both associations and organizations. Associations are distinguished from groups by reason of size and complexity. In *associations* (e.g., of professors, workers, and artists) there is an equality among members while in *organizations* (e.g., corporations, schools, government, and most religious bodies) there is hierarchical flow of authority and responsibility from the top downward. Neither exists in a pure form since an association often becomes bureaucratized and an organization often has within itself various associations (e.g., faculty and student associations within a university).

7. Institutional Design: Creating an Educational Institution

A new institution is designed for an educational purpose. In adult education new institutions are constantly being formed. A study of the creation of five dissimilar adult educational institutions revealed a common pattern of six stages (Griffiths, 1965, pp. 139-142): (1) a potential founder or founders sense a need that is not being met by existing systems; (2) the founder gathers a group to refine objectives, structures, methods, and functions for the new organization; (3) the institution comes into existence and acquires its identity or personality; (4) the institution expands in accordance with the original plan and procedures; (5) a strain develops, adjustments are made, and the institution becomes mature; (6) the institution achieves a steady state in which a constant level of inputs and outputs are maintained. Once a steady state is achieved institutions remain in place until there is a need for major institutional reconstruction.

At times wholly new institutions are created. At other times institutions are imitations or adaptations of other institutions. Of the many institutions that are formed, only a few become permanent fixtures in society. Few persons have the opportunity and freedom to establish totally new institutions. A necessary quality in establishing a new institution is flexibility. Plans often need to be changed before they have been put into action.

Descriptions of the creation of new institutions in adult religious education are not common. The most interesting account I have read is Bernier's description (1980) of the establishment of a regional adult religious education program in the diocese of Portland, Maine. Bernier presents a detailed description of how he and a group of people formed a school for adult religious education in which many local churches participated. His struggles with church leadership and structures, the quest for economic stability, the discovering of communal religious needs, and the process of implementation and evaluation are clearly presented. The work ends with projected visions and dreams which one can only hope will be achieved.

8. Institutional Design: Designing a New Institutional Format

At times an institution designs an educational activity in a new format. In recent years colleges have developed new formats for attracting the nontraditional college student: Weekend College, intensive summer programs, off-campus centers, and TV courses. It is my view that religious bodies have not shown the same initiative in developing educational programs and programs of service for their membership.

Houle gives a number of reasons for the addition of new institutional formats: response to expressed need or demand, meeting a need perceived by the leadership, providing a broader base of service than previously done, or taking advantage of resources which are made available (1972, p. 119). The process of adding a new format is at times a painful one especially in institutions which have achieved their identity through a particular format or program. The history and tradition of the institution has an important influence on the design of a new format. Some members may not accept the new direction. It is wise to proceed first with pilot studies before introducing new formats for which possible negative consequences are foreseen.

An example of this process in adult religious education is the development in Roman Catholic dioceses of new institutions for the training of lay persons for ministry and leadership in the church. Tensions have developed between these new institutions and the traditional institutions of seminaries and religious education offices. This new educational format attempts to respond to needs which cannot easily be grouped under the accepted scope of religious education. It is also a threat to seminaries which have traditionally trained all the leaders that were needed by the local church.

9. Institutional Design: Designing New Activities in Set Formats

Institutions need to constantly design new activities in established formats. New courses must be provided, along with staple courses. An appeal should be made to new groups. Planners need to be open to ideas from all sources: members and leaders of the institution, the availability of a new resource, the example of other comparable institutions, and systematic study of community values and needs.

In my work as a director of adult religious education in a local church it is one of my goals each year to develop one different type of program and to plan a program for a particular group that has not been the focus of attention in previous years. I have found that this practice both strengthens the program and brings more persons into contact with the educational resources of the church. As I mentioned in an earlier chapter the two age groups that appear to be least attracted to adult religious education are young single adults and older retired adults. I also make it a habit to collect advertisements from local religious bodies on the adult programs that they sponsor.

10. Institutional Design: Collaborative Institutional Planning

Two or more institutions often design an activity that will enhance their combined programs of service. Since many institutions are involved in adult education, there are great possibilities of cooperative efforts among institutions. Very often different institutions in a community serve the same broad clientele. Collaborate effort is necessary to avoid unnecessary duplication and to strengthen community efforts in adult education.

Collaborative efforts often face difficult problems of coordination. Various types of coordination are possible. *Multilateral* coordination is usually accomplished through a separate governing body which practices a form of representative democracy. *Bilateral* cooperation involves two organizations which are attempting to reinforce or strengthen each other's efforts. In *unilateral* coordination one institution, such as a library, sets itself the task of assisting other institutions in their educational efforts (Houle, 1972, p. 124).

A form of collaboration that is open to adult religious education groups is promoting the work of other institutions. This can be done by publicizing their efforts, referring to them potential students or members, and making suggestions to them about possible programs. Adult religious education institutions should also look to co-sponsor programs with other institutions in the community.

It is an interesting task to attempt to analyze the reasons for the lack of many collaborative efforts in adult religious education. At times there are longstanding hard feelings or apathy that prevent such efforts. What it often takes in such situations is a local or national crisis to force institutions to develop modes of collaboration. Some transcendent goal is often necessary to enable institutions to forego narrow loyalties and look for ways to mobil-ize the efforts of all institutions in a community. It is often diffi-cult for institutions to forego their own programs for the common good.

It seems that cooperative efforts among religious institutions have diminished after a period of heightened activity in the 1960s and 1970s. Ecumenism had a popularity then which it does not have in this decade. Perhaps these efforts go in cycles. Historical and theological differences, together with such divisive issues as abortion, contraception, and capital punishment, seem to have cut off collaborative efforts. Given these differences, it would seem even more imperative in pluralistic societies for religious bodies to attempt to present opportunities for discussion and debate on such issues. This would certainly be an important contribution for religious bodies to make to the common welfare.

11. Mass Audience Design

The final general educational design entails the development of an educational activity for a mass audience by an individual, group, or institution. A mass audience exists where the individual learners are unknown as individuals to those who conduct the program. Forms include large lectures, conventions, radio and television courses and presentations, expositions, fairs, and congresses.

The advantage of mass education lies in the large number of people who can be reached. The major disadvantage is the lack of contact with the educator. Mass education appears to be mostly individual activities rather than episodes with continuity. Some success has been reported in the use of television in mass educa-tion in the British Open University system. Efforts are under way in this country to develop a similar system of education for those who are not attracted to traditional college programs.

Mass education is valuable in introducing learners to new and renowned educators and speakers. It is also valuable in introducing people to current issues. But because of the lack of personal con-tact with an educator, other purposes are often added such as entertainment, amusement, or fund-raising. Also, it is difficult to evaluate the impact of such experiences on individuals and to determine just what is achieved through such educational activities. These activities are good, I believe, as enticements for more sustained programs.

The revolution in telecommunications—television, cable TV, two way cable systems, and other forms of technological communications—demands a rethinking of forms of mass education. The two way systems appear to have the greatest potential for they provide for interaction between educators and learners. The history of technology in education, however, makes one more than cautious about predicting the long range effects of rather expensive technology.

In adult religious education mass education has the same advantages and disadvantages that have been mentioned. The lack of personal contact and interaction is an even greater disadvantage in forms of religious education which are deeply concerned with promoting personal and interpersonal values. Mass education does not appear to be conducive to achieving this purpose. If forms of mass education are connected, however, with some activities and learning experiences that provide for interaction and evaluation, then they would appear to have greater potential in adult religious education.

In this section I have adapted for adult religious education the eleven categories of designs that Houle has used to analyze adult education. These categories give planners and educators a way to grasp the full range of the designs that are possible. Once a design is chosen attention can be given to different processes that help to fulfill the objectives of the designs more effectively. In the following section I will present some useful processes for adult religious education. For this material I will be drawing to a large degree on Bergevin and associates (1963), Kidd (1973), and McKenzie (1975).

TECHNIQUES FOR ADULT RELIGIOUS EDUCATION

These processes for adult religious education are appropriate for group, institutional, and mass education designs. The processes can also be called techniques and methods of adult education. Though a confusion of terminology exists in this area, the terms methods, techniques, and processes will be used interchangeably.

All three terms refer generally to the practical dynamics of teaching-learning. Processes are related to design as tactics to strategy.

Lecture-Type Processes

A review of processes in adult education reveals the continuing popularity of lecture type processes. A number of these are briefly described in order of increasing participation by an audience. Since active and intelligent participation in these activities is most desirable, a number of subtechniques that have been devised to increase participation are also described.

Lecture (Speech). This is a carefully planned oral presentation of a topic by a qualified person. Its purpose can be to present information in an organized manner, identify or clarify problems, present an analysis of controversial issues, or to stimulate and inspire an audience. Critical to the success of a lecture is the recognized competence of the speaker and the relevance of the topic to the potential audience. The advantages (large numbers, organized learning) and disadvantages (views of one person, little participation and interaction) of this technique are well-known. This method is common in adult religious education and is now used with a number of subtechniques to promote audience participation and interaction.

Symposium. In a symposium two or more speakers give prepared presentations on the same or related topics. Each speaker has an allotted amount of time. A symposium is useful for presenting an organized view of a topic, showing differences of opinion and approach among experts, clarifying closely related issues, and helping people to see a topic in both breadth and depth. This method has an advantage over the lecture in that it presents a variety of views. However, it has limitations in the area of participation and interaction. Symposia are most commonly used in adult professional education.

Panel. A panel is a discussion of a topic by a number of people (six to eight) before an audience. A moderator guides the discussion with prepared questions. The advantage of the panel over the speech and symposium is the opportunity it affords for the audience to hear discussion among experts. A possible limitation as a learning method is the lack of orderly presentation of ideas.

Critical for the success of the panel is a skilled and informed moderator who is sensitive to interests of the audience and is able to maintain necessary control over the process. With such a moderator a panel can be a lively and informative educational experience.

Forum. The term forum has different meanings. In an *open* forum a moderator leads the discussion of a large group (more than twenty-five persons) with one or more resource persons. A *public* forum is a meeting with one or more speakers, interaction between forum participants, and interaction with members of the audience in the form of questions, comments, and observations from the floor. A successful forum must have a skilled moderator, informed resource persons, and an interested and informed audience. Forums are often frustrating for the loose ends they leave and the lack of time for participation by all members of an audience.

Colloquy. A colloquy involves six to eight persons (half of whom are resource persons and half of whom are representatives of the audience) in a broad discussion of views on a topic. Audience representatives ask questions of the resource persons. At the end of the process the entire audience is invited to participate in the discussion. The colloquy goes beyond the previous methods in formalizing the participation of the audience. In my experience colloquies are not commonly used methods in adult education. The element of audience participation provided for should recommend this method for adult religious education.

Subtechniques for Lecture-Type Processes

Because of the lack of opportunity for participation and interaction in lecture-type methods a number of subtechniques or devices have been developed for use in conjunction with lectures, panels, forums, etc. A brief description of these techniques is given in this section.

Audience Reaction Team. A small number of representatives from the audience are designated to interrupt a speaker at appropriate times to ask for clarifications and assist speakers in meeting the needs of the audience.

Buzz Groups. The audience is divided into small groups for a short period of time to discuss a topic or perform a specified task.

Such groups may meet before the presentation to provide questions, during the session to give feedback, or after the presentation to give reactions.

Idea Inventory. The audience is invited at the beginning of a presentation to give ideas about their expectations and desires. It takes a skillful speaker or moderator to integrate these concerns into the program.

Listening and Observing Groups. The audience is divided into groups which are assigned clearly defined listening and observing tasks. Audiences are often divided according to seating in an auditorium: left, right, center. Each part of the audience can be given a different listening and observing task.

Question Period. At the end of a talk the audience is invited to ask questions. These can be written during a break. My practice is to gather a number of questions at the beginning of the question period and arrange them in an appropriate order. It is very important that a question-and-answer sessions gets off to a good start with questions that are relevant to the topic.

Screening Panel. Members of an audience discuss in small groups their concerns relevant to a proposed presentation. The presenters listen in on their discussions in order to better adapt material to group needs. This technique can be used either before or during a presentation.

It is important that some of these methods be used in programs of adult religious education that involve large audiences. Too often such programs become drawn out and boring for the audience. Efforts should be made to engage as many persons as possible in learning activities.

Methods for Group Discussion

A common design for adult religious education is the learning or discussion group. The very nature of religious faith as an experience that one share with others leads to the value placed upon small groups for faith sharing and probing. The broad design of group discussion was drawn in the last section. In this section some practical methods for group discussion are presented.

The subject matters for group discussion in adult religious education are greatly varied. Subject matter may focus on the teachings of the religious bodies, the relevance of these teachings to contemporary life, or a probing of personal, interpersonal, or political values and issues. Good topics for discussion lend themselves to differing perspectives, views, opinions, and experiences. Questions for discussion should be focused but open ended. It is better for groups to choose their own topics for discussion rather than have them imposed from the outside or from some prepackaged material. These materials can be used beneficially if they are handled with flexibility. McKenzie suggests a method of focused topic, clearly defined goals, and outline of the steps for discussion (1975).

Successful discussion groups have a number of *different roles* that members assume. *Participants* prepare for the discussion by study, help to clarify topics and goals, contribute their ideas and experiences, actively listen to other members, help to resolve differences of opinion, and evaluate the group. The group *moderator* initiates discussion, keeps all involved in the process, summarizes, prevents individuals from dominating the discussion, and offers support to all members of the group. If appropriate, a group may have a *recorder* to write down main ideas or viewpoints that the group has reached. From time to time a group may bring in *a resource person* to provide expert advice on a particular topic. A group may also ask an *outside evaluator* to observe a session to analyze the group processes and to make suggestions to the group.

A number of helpful *group norms* are suggested by McKenzie for promoting effective participation and learning. Members should *accept* one another's ideas, viewpoints, and experiences. While this does not preclude disagreements, it does counsel respect and tact. Groups need members who are truly *willing to listen* to one another. This norm flows from mutual acceptance. From experience I know it is my most difficult norm to respect. Participants have to be *willing to share* with members their ideas, perspectives, and experiences. Of course some persons are more comfortable with this than others. The task of the moderator is to bring out the ideas of as many persons as possible. Members should participate *freely and voluntarily.* Moderators should not ordinarily put people on the spot by directing questions to them. A little gentle nudging of some people is, however, a way to get more people involved in the discussion. Finally, participants must have *a commitment to the task* of the group and to the group itself. This commitment means that members participate even when they do not have great enthusiasm for the topic at hand when others have such an interest.

Groups can be inhibited in their progress by certain types of behavior described by McKenzie (1975). Some person may dominate a group by talking too much. A *dominator* is a poor listener. It is easy for a person in authority in religious bodies to tend to dominate a group. Groups at times have *dropouts* who continually refuse to share their experiences and points of view to the embarrassment of others. Group progress is impeded by the *blocker* who inserts irrelevant ideas and suggestions at crucial points, carries the discussion beyond decision-making points, or asks meaningless questions. Finally, groups are impeded by *distractors* who carry on side conversations or do things which in one way or another disturb the group or moderator.

McKenzie (1975, pp. 104-106) describes five behaviors that enhance the growth of groups. Groups need *the builder* to make connections between what different members say. *The gatekeeper* in a group is sensitive to inviting persons to participate who ordinarily do not make contributions. *The harmonizer* in a group attends to differences and conflicts that arise in a group. Harmonizers try to see truth in all sides of an argument or disagreement. Groups often have *an encourager* who makes members feel content about the contribution that they are making to the group's activity and growth. In groups where ideas may be complex or where some members may have difficulty following what is said, *the clarifier* repeats statements in ways that enables all to understand. Good moderators perform some of these roles. They are also aware of those in the group who carry out these useful functions.

A specialized form of discussion group is one whose task is the solving of a particular problem. Very often a discussion group grows into a discussion-action group. Kidd (1973, p. 254) presents a pattern such groups may follow in their activities: (1) ensure that the problem is recognized; (2) define the problem in terms that all members have the same understanding; (3) discover the nature and cause of the problem and agree on a standard by which potential solutions can be evaluated; (4) examine the possible solutions; (5) choose the solution that best fits the situation;

(6) evaluate the solution in terms of the original definition of the problem. Though such a pattern is not to be rigidly followed, some method of proceeding is important.

Simulation Methods of Learning

It is an obvious truth that persons learn from real life experiences. Because of this, it has always been the goal of education to develop learning processes that closely approximate real life situations. A few examples of such simulation methods are presented as illustrations of methods that attempt to simulate the real world.

Role Playing. Role playing is a spontaneous portrayal or acting out of a situation by a group. The acting out process is usually followed by a discussion to determine the relationships among people. This method has a strong emotional dimension and is thus useful for exploring situations in which hostility may be present. There are a number of uses for this method: leadership training, human relationship training, sensitivity training, stimulation of discussion, values clarification and analysis, and training in problem solving. Persons involved in the method include the leader who plans the situation, the players, and the audience.

Some advantages of this method are the stimulation of audience participation; an insight into how persons think, feel, and act in certain situations; and a clear view of differences among people in various roles. Limitations of the method include the danger of using the method as a gimmick, its unsuitability for highly complex problems, the need for other methods such as discussion to supplement it, and the possible fear and anxiety it may produce in players and audience.

There are designs in adult religious education where this technique is useful. Role playing attempts to get people to probe values and attitudes. Miles lists some possible task situations: ranking and consensus, choice, value surfacing, creativity-generating, belief-clarification, and bargaining (1981, p. 225). Religious education programs such as Genesis II and the Serendipity Bible Series make effective use of some of these procedures.

Case Method. The method of case analysis has long been used in legal and business education. This method is also appropriate in religion, philosophy, and ethics since it has a major component "analysis, identifying fact and opinion, weighing and testing alternatives, and considering values (Kidd, 1973, p. 1973)." The explicit purpose of the method is to apply what is learned into an actual situation in human life. Though this methods is a particular form of role playing, it places greater emphasis on analysis of a particular problem. Moral dilemmas that individuals face in their lives lend themselves to case analysis.

Demonstration. This method involves showing and telling how something is done. The participants have opportunities for practice after a particular procedure has been demonstrated. This method not only shows how something is done but also promotes confidence and interest in performing a specific function. The limitations of the method are difficulties in finding good demonstrators and in finding time for many participants to practice their skills. Demonstrations are useful in teacher education and for training for specific roles.

Methods for Extended Educational Experiences

Institutional and mass audience designs often call for educational experiences that last over extended periods of time. The following formats for learning can be from one day to a number of weeks. The methods that have been described above can be used within these different formats which have become part of the ecology of education in this country.

Clinic. The purpose of a clinic (a medical term) is diagnosis, analysis, and prescription of solutions to problems that have arisen in fields of practice. The most common methods for a clinic are demonstrations, case studies, field trips, and role playing. Lecture-type activities can be beneficial, provided the speakers make presentations from practical or research experience. Clinics in adult religious education have been concerned with teacher and parent education. They have also focused on such problems as drugs, alcoholism, and care of the elderly. This method can easily be adapted to probe both individual, institutional, and social problems.

Institute. An institute is concerned with instruction from authoritative experts. Various lecture-like methods are used to present organized bodies of knowledge and training in skills. Large group education is most common in institutes though efforts are often made to promote small group interaction and individual study. Though some institutes exist for a specified period of time, e.g., teachers' institutes, others take on a somewhat permanent existence, e.g., Jungian Institute.

Workshop. Although the term workshop has a great deal of flexibility, it usually emphasizes the development of individual competencies and understanding. Both theory and practice are part of workshops. General sessions usually consist of lecture-like activities while subgroup meetings utilize discussion and simulation learning activities. Four types of subgroups have been identified by Bergevin and associates (1963, pp. 224-225): *special interest groups* in which a small group of persons with similar concerns learn under the guidance of a resource person; *work groups* in which tasks, assignments, and projects are the focus; *discussion groups* in which some topic is examined under the guidance of a leader; and *practice groups* in which participants have the opportunity to demonstrate a skill under expert guidance.

McKenzie (1975, ch. 9) gives a number of similar suggestions to prevent a workshop from becoming a "spongeshop." He recommends supplementing lectures with group discussion, buzz groups, panels, and multiplying dyads. In the multiplying dyad method two persons discuss a matter for a few minutes and then join another dyad to form a group of four. After a period of discussion, groups of eight are formed. This process offers many persons the opportunity to enter the discussion.

Workshops are very often used in adult religious education at both local and regional levels. Nearly every phase of adult religious education lends itself to this form of educational activity. Such short term educational experiences often suit the schedule of teachers and planners of adult religious education.

Convocations, Conferences, and Conventions. The largest forms of informal adult education are found in convocations, conferences, and conventions. Though these terms may refer to small meetings, they are increasingly used for large gatherings of people. Such large meetings serve a number of purposes: education, fellowship, contact-making, promotion of motivation and group spirit, and exposition of new materials by publishers and producers. The planning of these events is usually in the hands of a committee. A variety of educational methods are used at these large meetings.

These large gatherings have become valuable to the field of adult religious education in achieving for religious educators the purposes outlined above. On the national level, a section on Adult Religious Education meets annually with the Adult Education Association. The Religious Education Association sponsored a conference on adult learning in 1976 and one on adult faith development in 1981. Many large meetings of this kind also are held at regional and local levels. As the field of adult religious education expands, one can expect more developments of this kind.

CONCLUSION

In concluding this chapter I have the feeling that though much has been written, much more needs to be said about the design of programs in adult religious education. My attempt has been to stress general principles, broad program designs, and commonly used methods. More detailed treatment of methods can be found in the works that I drew on in developing this chapter.

CHAPTER X

MANAGEMENT AND EVALUATION
OF ADULT RELIGIOUS EDUCATION

The planning and design of adult religious education programs must be complemented by effective management and evaluation. Many good programs have failed even though they have been carefully planned and designed. Where failure often takes place is at the level of management and evaluation. Adult religious educators need to put into practice sound management and evaluation principles to complement planning and designing activities.

The last three chapters have treated principles of management in a general sense. The activities involved in organizing, planning, and designing programs pertain to management. However, this chapter has as its principal focus those management activities that pertain to the actual operation of programs: selection of teacher and leaders, creation of educational environments, promotion and public relations, and budgeting and finance. A second section is devoted to evaluative processes.

Some repetition is found in this chapter. This repetition is inevitable because of the interconnection between foundations and practice and the unity of the planning process. A certain amount of repetition is also desirable since this final chapter is in some way a practical summary of major topics treated in this book.

PART I: THE MANAGEMENT OF
ADULT RELIGIOUS EDUCATION

Selection of Teachers, Leaders, and Facilitators

The selection of teachers should be in accordance with the type of educational program designed. In Chapter Nine four basic types of teaching-learning modes were developed; information processing, academic learning, personal growth, social interaction, and behavioral modification. Planners should recognize that different abilities are required for giving a course, leading a discussion, facilitating personal growth, and directing a reflection-action group.

Two different situations occur in the selection of teachers. Teachers are sought for learners; learners are sought for teachers. It is often the case that a person or group of persons are looking for a teacher to give, for example, a course on sacred literature or business ethics. At other times planners are in the position of locating a group for a particular teacher who has something valuable to teach. The first case is the more common one but planners should also be sensitive to the possibility of the second situation.

The greatest source of teachers in adult religious education is from the ranks of professionally trained religious leaders and teachers: pastors, rabbis, ministers, religious sisters and brothers, and priests. A strong adult religious education program makes use of the entire leadership staff each year for at least one educational activity. These persons at times contend that since people hear them so often in the regular worship services of the religious body, they are not interested in them for adult religious education programs. My experience is that the membership wants to meet the leaders in a teaching role because this context affords more time for questions and discussion. The religious leadership also benefits from this type of experience because of the broadening of views that comes from interaction.

Though professionally trained clergy necessarily make up the majority of teachers in adult religious education, lay persons, men and women, should also be involved as teachers. The expertise and experience of these persons is especially valuable in bringing the implications of religious faith to bear on the seeking of personal, interpersonal, and socio-political values in ordinary life. In introducing lay persons to teaching in adult education programs I have often first involved them in a team teaching arrangement or a panel, forum, or symposium.

One possible source for teachers in adult religious education programs are persons who teach religion to youth. Often these persons can make the transition from relating religion to the concerns of youth to relating religion to the concerns of adults. Some teachers of youth, however, cannot make this transition. Very often in working with adults they resort to telling them what they tell their students. What is learned in such an experience is not religion for adults but religion for youth. The teacher of adults knows the life situation and experiences of adults and is able to bring religious faith to bear on this situation.

There are many opinions about the characteristics of the good teacher of adults. The lists I have seen include so many ideal characteristics that I doubt their usefulness. The brief treatment of Ingalls (1972) does highlight what I consider the essential qualities. Personal characteristics include a well-integrated personality, empathetic understanding, personal orientation toward lifelong learning, and willingness to face confrontation. Knowledge and skills requirements include cognitive knowledge, process skills, technical competence, and group management skills. My views on how these are defined are treated in various chapters of this book.

In an earlier chapter I suggested that teachers be involved as much as possible in the planning and designing process of programs in which they will participate. If this is done, evaluation of their performance as teachers will be an easy task. Evaluation of teachers and facilitators is best done in an informal manner. Adults stay away from programs which are not interesting or do not meet their needs. However, the success of a teacher (or a program) should not be determined merely on the basis of the number of persons attending and their satisfaction. Though the attractive, amusing, and entertaining teacher may hold an audience, planners should focus on the educational impact of a teacher.

Compensation for teachers is a problem that all adult education planners face. Compensation should be offered to all teachers in adult religious education programs. It is advisable for a religious body to arrive at a standard stipend for outside educators or consultants. A good norm that I have used is the rate of compensation given at adult programs in public schools and community colleges. If planners hope to attract speakers who are more in demand and who attract larger stipends, then the financing of programs becomes more complex. Some ideas on finance and budgeting are presented below.

With regard to introducing new persons as teachers for a religious body or organization, I have already suggested the practice I use. When possible schedule only one session with the planned possibility of more sessions if there is sufficient interest. Very often this is a challenge to the planners in designing the program and to the teacher or facilitator in conducting the educational activity.

The Climate for Adult Religious Learning

In this section I conceive the environment for adult religious education rather broadly to include climate, facilities, and procedures. Creating an environment that is conducive to adult learning is one of the most important functions of good management.

The *organizational climate* of the religious body is the foremost factor in the climate for adult religious education. The climate of organizations has long been the subject of social science research. Likert and Likert (1976) have found that the climate of an organization depends on the recognition of the diversity of members as a resource and not a liability. A healthy climate in their view facilitates problem solving and gives persons opportunities to be heard on all decisions that affect them.

Organizational climate is determined by a number of factors (Ingalls, 1972, p. 19). Policies need to be clearly stated. Structures adequate to the task must be developed and maintained. Caring, trust, and respect should be manifest in meetings announcements, informational literature, and advertising. Budgets and finance arrangements should be made known. Agendas, minutes, scheduling, and closing times must be arranged.

The climate of a religious body will be conducive to adult religious learning if such learning is presented as a high priority. Parish leadership determines in large part the image, visibility, and importance of such learning through their many activities. The learning climate of the liturgy or main worship service of a religious organization is crucial in determining a climate for adult religious education.

A healthy *interpersonal climate* is important for promoting adult religious learning. Fox (1973) gives eight variables for determining a healthy learning climate: *respect*—persons view one another as persons of equal worth; *trust*—people have confidence that other persons can be counted on to behave in an honest manner; *caring*—people sense that others are concerned about them; *cohesiveness*— a positive feeling by members towards the group; *continuous academic and social growth*—educators desire to improve skills, knowledge, and attitudes; *opportunity for input*—every person has the opportunity to contribute ideas and know that these will be considered; *group renewal*—the group is developing and changing rather than following routines; and *high morale*—people feel good about what is happening in the group.

Healthy interpersonal climate is fostered by a sense of welcoming which is extended to new members. Warm-up exercises are useful in promoting this atmosphere. Adults usually prefer informal learning settings to formal ones. Leaders should be sensitive to any conflicts that arise in the group and take measures to deal with them. The importance of interpersonal climate cannot be overstressed since many studies have shown that the existence of such a climate is viewed as most important by adult learners, who seek human relationships and fellowship as much as they do cognitive learning and skills.

Planners need to attend to the *physical climate* for adult religious education. Ingalls (1972, p. 17) gives four keys to physical climate setting: comfort, variety, mobility, and sensory accommodation. Physical surroundings should be comfortable. Adequate space, good lighting, and acoustics should be provided. Attention must be paid to decor, temperature, ventilation, and comfort in seating. Some light refreshments should always be served. People should know about parking and rest rooms. Name tags should be provided for the first few sessions. If audiovisual aids are used, they should be clear and understandable.

Facilities and Procedures

Most planners have difficulties in finding proper facilities for adult religious education. School facilities can be adapted for some forms of adult education: classrooms with rows of desks, large auditoriums, small seminar rooms, and lecture halls. Knowles has presented a number of creative seating arrangements for adult education (1980, pp. 164-165). Small meeting room arrangements can have the chairs arranged in a circle or tables arranged in the shape of a diamond, octagon, or maple leaf (for ease in subgrouping). Large meeting room arrangements can have tables in a fan shape, theater-in-the-round (or bowl), a semicircular theater, or chairs in small semicircles (for easy subgrouping).

Office facilities are necessary for adult religious education. It is important that records of past programs are kept and that past materials are on hand for future members of the council or committee responsible for programming. Adequate files should also be kept on what programs are available in other religious bodies and in community organizations. It is helpful for people to know about past speakers. They should have access to written and audiovisual resources, mailing lists, and persons who can be of assistance in one form or another.

Good programs have formalized *registration procedures*. It is helpful to have one member of the council in charge of this task. Another helpful practice is to make a different member of the council responsible for a particular program, including the task of registration. My policy is to make councils and committees working groups with the expectation that each person will work on at least one program each year. Preregistration is important for all programs (by mail and by phone), although opportunity to participate should be open until the last possible time.

In an earlier chapter I mentioned the importance of the *first session* in any adult education program. A great deal of time and energy should go into preparation for this initial meeting. It is important that people find this experience educational, welcoming, warm, and stimulating. People who do not attend a second session should be politely called to inquire about reasons for not attending. Helpful criticisms and suggestions often come from these personal contacts. People are also impressed with the interest of the adult education committee.

In adult education great attention is given to *attendance records, grades, and certificates.* However, these have limited value in adult religious education. It is helpful to know who attends programs and what their attitudes are toward the programs; but formal attendance records would not be appropriate. I know of no program that gives grades; these would be strong deterrents for many people. The granting of certificates is another matter. Certificates are certainly beneficial in programs that educate teachers of religion. Certificates may be helpful as signs of recognition of achievement in programs that use a school model. Such social reinforcements may signal the value that is attached to continuous learning in religion.

An important facility for adult religious education is an adult learning *resource center*. If self-directed learning is to be promoted, materials must be available for the membership of religious bodies. Efforts should be made to get many good books, cassettes, records, and films into the public library. What a library does not purchase, the organization may purchase or try to get someone to donate. Very often people are willing to donate materials for which they no longer have use. If people do not desire to donate, they will often let others use their materials. A volunteer can coordinate a learning resource center.

Educational Counseling

In the discussion on needs assessment in Chapter Eight a brief mention was made of educational counseling in adult religious education. Little attention has been given to this matter in the literature on adult religious education. The same situation exists in the general field of adult education for as Knowles notes "the notions of an educational counseling function . . . being an essential part of an institutional adult education program is so new that the role of educational counselor has not yet been clearly defined (1980, p. 172)."

If lifelong learning in religion is to become a goal of religious bodies, more assistance should be provided to persons who accept this ideal. Some of this assistance is given in informal situations. My vision is that all members of religious bodies would have the opportunity to discuss and plan their religious development with the assistance of a competent person. Something similar to this takes place in the process of spiritual direction beautifully and competently described by K. Leech in *Soul Friend* (1980).

Educational counseling is, I believe, a preferable way of describing this process, because of the connotation of authoritativeness in the term direction. Such counseling might take individual and group forms. At the heart of the counseling process is the interview. Each person who enters a program for adult education should have an opportunity for an interview about wants, needs, interests, and values. I realize how idealistic this is, given the fact that adult religious education is usually under the leadership of volunteers. Yet I feel that the reason for part of the smallness of the enterprise is the lack of one-to-one contact with people who feel a need for religious and spiritual growth.

Besides functioning on a one-to-one basis a counselor also meets with groups. Within religious organizations there are many groups that a member of the adult religious education committee can meet with to discuss needs and interests in lifelong religious learning. Many of these groups have educational objectives within their general purposes. Through a form of group counseling, some collaborative efforts may be developed with singles groups, married couples groups, parish councils, etc. These meetings should not be viewed as efforts to promote particular adult religious education, although that may be one of the effects of such gatherings.

At the present time most counseling within religious organizations is done by the leaders of the organization. Some of these persons are trained in the field of pastoral counseling. In recent years other professionally trained counselors have also entered the field of pastoral counseling. It might be beneficial for the adult education committee to have contacts with persons who do professional counseling. These contacts might result in suggestions about programs that might be offered. It might be beneficial for the pastoral counselor to be aware of what is offered in other educational programs. Counselors are often excellent resources for courses on human development.

Persons who function as counselors in schools or colleges are often good resources as adult education counselors. Such persons have the necessary background in theory, practice, personality study, and group guidance. The religious organization could also offer to provide opportunity for education in adult education and religious studies. Such persons can be valuable assets to an organization that places value on the continuing religious education of its members.

The educational counselor might take on any number of important functions: assessment of values, interests, and needs; offering suggestions on what types of programs should be offered; being aware of what services are offered in the broader community; following up those who drop out of the program; and conducting evaluations of the program. Though this role does not exist in adult religious education programs of which I am aware, it is my conviction that its existence is imperative for the development of effective adult religious education programs.

Public Relations and Promotion

Because those who participate in adult education programs usually attend on a voluntary basis, great attention must be paid to public relations and promotion of these programs. Many well-planned and designed programs have failed to attract people because they were not properly promoted. The person who fills the role of public relations and promotion on the committee is a truly vital person. An effort should be made to secure the best possible person for this position.

The fullest treatment of public relations and publicity in adult education is found in Knowles (1980, pp. 176-189). I will draw from his material a number of suggestions tht I believe are particularly important for adult religious education. I will also draw on my own practical experience in this area.

The first task of promotion is *to define the target group or clientele.* For some programs the entire organization is the clientele. For other programs a particular subgroup of the religious organization is the target for the program. Programs are also often directed to the community-at-large. Once the clientele has been clearly defined, it is easy to develop appropriate promotional strategies.

A good promotion campaign demands *careful planning.* It is good practice to plan programs for at least one year in advance. The year can be divided into different segments: September to December, January to April, May and June, July and August. Programs should be held throughout the year; but these appear to be the most useful divisions.

An adequate promotion budget should be available to the adult education committee. Some adult education committees set 15 percent of their budget for promotional purposes. Only experience can suggest the best ways to spend this budget. The usual media of promotion should be used: newspapers, television and radio, and direct mail. General publicity should begin about six weeks before the program starts. It is suggested that printed materials be in peoples' hands about three weeks before an event.

In my experience the most powerful promotion of adult religious education programs comes primarily not from these sources but from *the pulpit*. The success of programs is often due to the enthusiastic endorsement and encouragement that the leaders of the community give to these programs. The leadership has the primary task of persuading the membership of the need for lifelong religious learning and development. Perhaps this reflects a too great dependency upon the leadership. But it is a reality that I have come to accept and work with. This is one of the reasons that I suggest a strong effort in involving as adult religious educators each person in a staff leadership position in the religious organization. Leaders are more likely to be enthusiastic about programs in which they participate.

The suggestion by Knowles that adult education programs be integrated through an attractive *theme, slogan, title or symbol* is an excellent one. Adult religious education needs the kind of identity and visibility that such an integrating device gives to it. Themes that I have come across are: Lifelong Religious Learning; Adult Religious Enrichment; Renewal in Faith; God's Word Today; Challenges for Adult Faith. I think it is good practice to change the theme periodically, perhaps each year. A changing theme presents a challenge for committee members to move in different directions. A changed focus may also attract additional persons to the program.

Newspaper advertising and publicity are important means of promotion. The strategy of most committees is to get as much free publicity as possible in all media. Small newspapers are usually very anxious for items and articles about programs. It is good to establish personal contact with persons at newspapers who are in a position to handle such matters. Deadlines of various newspapers should be known. It is also helpful to have attractive action pictures prepared for publicity purposes. Most of these same suggestions are also useful for radio and television publicity and advertising.

The most costly way of advertising programs is through *direct mail*. Despite its cost, this method should be used when advertising a full range of programs. Studies have shown the effectiveness of direct mail promotion. Small folders and booklets are the most common forms of direct mail in adult education. Covers should be attractive; attention should be paid to size of type, color, layout, and drawings. Items to be included in a booklet or brochure include: name of programs; sponsoring group; learning activities; people to be served; descriptions of teachers and leaders; cost, times, and places; and registration form and procedures. Special attention should be given to writing titles of courses or educational experiences. Writers of titles and descriptions should put themselves in the place of prospective readers. The strongest selling point of programs, however, are the teachers, leaders, panelists, etc. The qualifications and achievements of these persons should be highlighted.

There are a number of other valuable methods of promoting adult religious education programs. *Posters, displays, and exhibits* serve to keep programs in the minds of the potential participants. These can be placed in a number of places: business buildings, bulletin boards in public buildings such as libraries, clubs, social agencies, and other places where interested persons may be found. Attention should also be given to the quality of these forms since the quality of programs is first judged by the quality of the advertising and publicity.

In the last stages of a promotional campaign many committees develop a *telephone committee* to publicize a program. This is easily done in a small organization. Very often all it takes to encourage participation is a call from a member of such a committee. Each person on the committee should be given only a few names to call. Those who are on a telephone committee should be prepared to answer questions on all aspects of the program.

Satisfied participants in previous programs are a valuable source of promotion. Many people are attracted to programs by friends who invite them to attend. A systematic effort can be made to invite participants to interest other persons in programs. Present participants can also suggest names of persons they feel might be interested in joining if a member of the adult education committee would call.

It is important for a committee to *evaluate promotional efforts* each year. Though it is helpful to know what efforts were most effective, this is not always possible. Participation cannot usually be tied to only one mode of promotion. Usually promotional efforts have a cumulative effect in reaching people.

Budgeting and Finance

For an adult religious education program to be put on a firm basis there is need for careful attention to budgeting and finance. The director of the program should strive to make this function a separate item in the organization's budget. Only in this way will adequate support be given for the program. Finances are an item that can be the responsibility of one member of the committee.

Knowles notes that there are different financial arrangements for various adult education programs (1980, p. 190). Some programs are completely subsidized. Other programs must show a profit. Most programs operate on both subsidies and tuition. Religious organizations with their ability to attract volunteers can usually subsidize adult education programs to some extent and charge nominal fees for their programs. This matter is discussed below.

That funding for adult religious education is a pressing problem in some religious organizations is clear from a report by Directors of Adult Religious Education in the Catholic Church (Department of Education, USCC, 1978, pp. 14-16). The directors noted that while recommendations for adequate funding are found in documents of the Church, dioceses and parishes have not provided realistic funding for hiring directors and supporting programs. The report calls for a change in priorities in parish budgets to support more education for the adult community.

Finance and budgeting demands attention to a number of principles. A budget for the year should be set. Income and expenses should be estimated. A determination should be made as to how money will be raised and expenses allocated. It is better to set rather high goals in budgeting, for budgets are invariably reduced in a budget review process. It is important that directors of adult religious education take the opportunity to present a budget to the leadership of the organization for this gives an opportunity to raise consciousness about the need for educational programs for adults.

I have found the matter of tuition or charges for educational programs a difficult one to handle. Different viewpoints exist on this matter. In some religious organizations adult religious education is totally subsidized on the principle that, given the proportionately large amount spent on education of youth, the least the organization can do is support programs for adults. It is the opinion of others that tuitions and fees should be charged on the principle that people only appreciate what they have to pay for. My view comes down in the middle; part subsidy, part fees. I have heard of very few successful programs that have operated solely on a fee basis. If attractive programs are to be offered, programs should receive subsidies from the parent organization. The decision on this matter is important and should be made with as wide consultation as possible. I have seen great resentment build up in committees over the matter of fees and subsidies.

Some important guidelines for setting fees are given by Knowles (1980, p. 192-193). Factors that should be considered are the amount of the subsidy available; the nature of the clientele served; the intensity of the motivation of the adult students; the cost of the instruction; and the standards set by other organizations in the community. In adult religious education fees should never be so high as to pose an economic barrier to participation. It is good practice to have at least one program that raises money to cover the costs of a number of programs. I believe that people are willing to pay a fee for quality programs. A parallel can be drawn with adult education in public schools and community colleges. Even though school taxes support these institutions, they still charge a fee for the courses and educational programs they offer to adults. On the other hand, it must be noted that there are adult educators who are opposed in principle to this policy, arguing that the community should support the education of adults to a greater extent than it does at present. And so the argument goes on and on.

The upshot of this discussion is that the adult religious education committee should establish a clear policy on finances and budgeting. In these days of budget cutting such a policy is essential. This policy should include, according to Knowles (1980, p. 192), the sources of authority for budget approval, limitations set on budgets, prorating of costs, degree of self-support that will be aimed for, the methods and standards of accounting, bases for deciding on fees, other sources of income, and the nature and frequency of financial reports. Although this type of policy statement is a necessity in large organizations, smaller organizations will also benefit from such a policy. It is a painful sight to see the work of adult education impeded over issues of finance and budgeting which a formulated policy could have prevented.

PART II: EVALUATION OF PROGRAMS IN ADULT RELIGIOUS EDUCATION

In secular education today there is a strong emphasis on comprehensive evaluation of programs, including student achievement. Stress on evaluation is strongest when limited resources become available for educational programs. Evaluation is thus closely connected with efforts at accountability. This stress on evaluation also extends to programs in adult education. Many of these programs receive government support and thus must be accountable to fund-giving agencies.

Formal evaluation has never been a primary concern in religious education. The field has had a number of strong advocates of evaluation, but for the most part religious educators have devoted attention to other aspects of the teaching-learning process. One can predict, however, that as resources for religious education decrease, more attention will be given to program evaluation. The field of adult religious education could benefit in a number of ways from a stronger attention to program evaluation.

In this section I treat some of the practical issues involved in evaluation. Some of these ideas are drawn from an article I published on this subject (Elias, 1979c). In this section I discuss background, theories, purposes, the role of objectives, processes, and methods.

Background

A number of religious educators have called for emphasis on evaluation of programs. Wyckoff (1966) defined evaluation as:

> a systematic comparison of some aspect of Christian education practice with the standards that should characterize its operations in that area, looking toward the identification of points at which improvement is needed (p. 144).

For Wyckoff evaluation consists of deciding on useful categories, describing the existing situation, setting up standards, and comparing the situation with the standards.

Another strong advocate of systematic evaluation in religious education is Lee (1973). In his social science approach to religious instruction the issue of evaluation is closely connected with the establishment of behavioral or performance objectives. Lee called for an evaluation that is scientific rather than impressionistic. This close connection between objectives and evaluation is found in other writers in the field of evaluation.

It is commonly stated that the field of religious education has resisted serious evaluative research and testing. Peatling (1968) gave as reasons for this neglect the contention of some that faith and the working of the Spirit cannot be measured; and that on the whole religious educators are unaware that measures exist for measuring educational goals more complex than factual recall and recognition. That the situation has improved somewhat is attested to by the quality of research reported by Peatling in his annual review of research in religious education (Peatling, 1979).

Schaefer (1972) gave attention to evaluation in his theory of program planning for adult Christian education. In his view evaluation is a general category that makes judgments about the objective, personnel, scope, process, timing, and context of the program. His major attention in evaluation is on the "validity of the planning process employed rather than with the results of the curriculum once planned (p. 68)." Although Schaefer is primarily interested in the ongoing evaluation of the planning process itself, he is aware of the importance of evaluating learning outcomes, satisfied and unsatisfied participants, and possible future directions for learning (p. 200). No discussion, however, of the nature, objectives, and methods of such evaluation is presented in his work.

Evaluation has an important place in McKenzie's treatment of program planning (1975). McKenzie stresses evaluation because he believes that too often only snap judgments are used in evaluating adult programs in religion. He recommends evaluation at the levels of program, course, and learning episode. All elements of a program are to be evaluated: objectives, context, content, methods, techniques, transactions, resources, and the relationship between objectives and outcomes (p. 83). A weakness in McKenzie's treatment of evaluation is the lack of attention to the peculiar nature of religious learning. An examination of the relationship between religious education theories and evaluation brings out a number of important issues in evaluation of outcomes of religious education.

Evaluation and Religious Education Theory

Among the various authors that differentiate among theoretical approaches to religious education, Burgess (1975) and Knox (1976) give explicit attention to evaluation of educational outcomes. Burgess examined the role of evaluation in four theories. The *traditional theological approach* does not place a strong emphasis on an attempt to measure the effects of education on students since it considers the aims of education as otherworldly and divine. The *social-cultural approach* gave evaluation a major role since it was aimed at developing skills for social and responsible living in the world. *Contemporary theological approaches* at times espouse evaluation of outcomes but shy away from stating behaviorally defined aims. These theorists are also sensitive to the danger that premature attempts to assess progress might disturb the educational process and prevent religious growth. Lee's *social science approach* strongly urges scientific, positive, and continuous evaluation of educational outcomes.

A somewhat similar assessment is given by Knox (1976) in his division of theories according to three metaperspectives: transcendist, immanentist, and integrist. The *transcendist metaperspective* coincides with Burgess's traditional theological approach. Evaluation plays a small part in this view since the aims of education are supernatural and transcendist. Tests of memory might be used but these do not touch the real aims of religious education. If an *immanentist metaperspective* is taken on religious education, then an evaluation of human experience is a valid way of testing religious education. According to this view, since the goals of religious education belong in the natural and observable order, scientific measurement is not a desecration of holy ground but a cooperation with the divine in ongoing revelation and creation. In the *integrist metaperspective*—which attempts to combine human and divine, nature and supernature—evaluation tends to focus on teacher and content rather than on students and learning.

This approach is similar to Burgess's category of contemporary theological approaches in being against fastening attention on the specifics of conduct. The approach measures success in teaching by the extent to which specific outcomes have been achieved.

From these analyses it is clear that there are differences of opinion among religious educators on the role of evaluation. Similar differences exist in general education among educators of behaviorist and humanistic persuasion. It would appear desirable to find a middle ground between leaving everything in the hands of the divine and attempting to measure every outcome with precision. Outcomes in the areas of knowledge, attitudes, and values can be assessed in general ways; most educators do this in some form. Below I will take up again the issue of measurement of religious education outcomes.

Purposes of Evaluation

Weiss (1972) distinguishes between bonafide and less legitimate purposes of evaluation. The major purpose of evaluation is to improve the program by providing information to planners about all aspects of the program. Good evaluation leads to better decisions about continuing or discontinuing programs or teachers, improving practices and procedures, and adding specific strategies and techniques. A second legitimate function for evaluation is that it provides a measure of accountability to the parent organization, leaders, and participants. Less legitimate purposes for evaluation include its use to unnecessarily postpone a decision, to duck responsibility, and merely to promote a good public image.

Evaluation of a program is indicated if any one of a number of less desirable symptoms develops in a program. From Knox's rather lengthy list of such symptoms (1969, p. 371) I have selected a number that are pertinent to adult religious education: (1) slow increase in numbers when comparable programs are increasing; (2) difficulty in attracting students from a particular population group; (3) high dropout rate during a program; (4) failure of large numbers of adults to attend from year to year; (5) complaints about teachers and learning experiences; (6) lack of any sequence among courses and experiences; (7) lack of support among leaders and policy makers. Though some of these factors might be beyond the control of the planners, the presumption is always in favor of setting up evaluation to find out what needs to be corrected in a system.

Nature of Evaluation

The review of the different positions on evaluation by theorists in religious education highlighted some problems with evaluation in religion. Once the evaluator moves beyond a concern with factual knowledge, it is extremely difficult to develop evaluative instruments that satisfy all religious educators. Evaluative instruments have built into them important assumptions about what programs should accomplish. Evaluation of programs is in terms of reactions of participants, learning outcomes, behavioral changes, and tangible results (e.g., better attendance in worship services). Difficulties exist in all these areas. What weight is to be given to participant views? What are the learning outcomes that are to be evaluated? Can an instrument validly measure behavioral changes? What tangible results count toward a successful program?

One controversial area in evaluation is the matter of assessing non-cognitive outcomes. Non-cognitive outcomes include interests, values, attitudes, preferences, and behaviors. The problems with evaluation in this area are well-known. Mehrens and Lehmann (1974) pointed out the issues involved: (1) problems of definition: how does one define honesty, goodness, faith, virtue, values? (2) non-cognitive tests are susceptible to response set, i.e., the tendency of an individual to reply in a particular direction, almost independently of content (e.g., many people favor middle-of-the-road answers.); (3) faking occurs rather often in these tests since the subjects will supply only the information that they are able and willing to report; (4) validity and reliability in these tests are less than in cognitive tests; (5) interpretation is very difficult in these tests because there are no necessarily right answers; (6) constructing and scoring of these tests is difficult because of the indefiniteness of correct answers.

Though the problems connected with measuring religious outcomes are serious, they have not dissuaded evaluators from developing instruments for measuring religious outcomes. Very few of these instruments have been developed to evaluate adult religious learning. One such instrument is REKAP—Religious Education Outcomes Inventory of Knowledge, Attitudes, and Practices

(National Forum of Religious Educators, 1978). Most of the items in this inventory are in the area of religious knowledge (fifty-eight). Eleven items test religious attitudes; twenty items test religious practices. This inventory is presented as suitable for Catholic senior high school students and adults.

The major issue in evaluating religious education outcomes lies in the definition of objectives. The matter of behavioral objectives has been touched upon a number of times in this book. With regard to objectives for learning two extremes have to avoided: vagueness in objectives and too precise definition of behavioral objectives. Leaving objectives vague often produces an aimlessness in the educational process. Defining them too precisely leads to a loss of freedom and spontaneity.

The objectives most appropriate for evaluation in religious education are the expressive objectives advocated by Eisner (1969). These do not specify the behavior that learners are to exhibit but rather describe an educational encounter. These objectives identify situations in which learners are to work, a problem to be solved, or a task to be engaged in. These objectives do not specify what learners are to get from these encounters. They are rather invitations "to explore, defer, or focus on issues that are of peculiar interest to the inquirer. An expressive objective is evocative rather than prescriptive (Eisner, 1969, p. 16)." With regard to such objectives the evaluative task is not one of applying a common standard to the product produced but one of reflecting upon what has been done in order to reveal its uniqueness and significance. The upshot of the encounter is likely to be a surprise for learner and teacher alike.

The Process of Evaluation

Evaluation of adult religious education takes place at *various times.* An informal evaluation takes place continuously in the form of judgments offered about the value of the program by leaders, teachers, and participants. It is a good practice to evaluate some aspects of a program at the halfway point. This gives ample opportunity for people to make secure judgments and also allows for modifications in programs. Most programs are also evaluated at the end. If learning outcomes are sought, this is the only proper time to have an evaluation. Crises in programs usually call for more systematic attention to evaluation.

Programs are evaluated by *different persons.* Participants are the most important evaluators of adult religious education programs. Leaders and instructors can also make important observation on aspects of a program. The director and the adult education committee have the responsibility of a more formal evaluation of the program. At times programs may also be evaluated by outside experts or consultants. This serves to put the program in a broader perspective.

The evaluation process itself begins with the *development of values* (or objectives, criteria, standards, yardsticks) with regard to expected reactions and attitudes of participants, learning outcomes, behavioral outcomes, and tangible results. Knowles recommends that criteria be developed with regard to all aspects of the program: program and operational objectives, educational objectives, organizational structure and climate, assessment of needs and interests, purposes and objectives, program design, program operation, and program evaluation (1980, pp. 205-210). What Knowles proposes here is similar to the discussion on values found in Chapter Eight of this work. Evaluative questions should include some that are precise and others that are open-ended.

Various *methods* can be used to gather evaluative data. The *reactions of participants* can be discovered through interviews, questionnaires, and checklists. Checklists are the easiest form to use since they take up little time. Their value is limited in comparison to questionnaires and interviews, which give more information. Interviews also allow opportunity for in-depth probing of reactions of participants.

A number of methods of evaluation are more appropriate for determining any *changes in individuals* through the educational process. These include controlled observation, structured investigation by peers, controlled comparisons, and objective and standardized testing. These methods are more appropriately research methods and their use in adult religious education programs would be comparatively rare.

Resources for Evaluating Programs

The best resource for planners to use for evaluating adult religious education programs is *Assessing Needs, Evaluating Programs* (n.d.), compiled by the Adult Education Office of the Archdiocese of St. Paul, Minnesota. Various types of evaluation forms are given: questionnaires, sentence completions, checklists, rating scales, and yes-or-no answers. The manual also gives a number of guidelines on the formulation of questions: (1) avoid using many questions that demand a yes-or-no answer; (2) use open-ended questions that allow for personal comments by participants; (3) employ questions on format and process of program: effectiveness of speakers, relevance of subject matter, value of group discussions, suggestions for improvements; (4) include some questions that permit the participants to indicate a particular change in behavior: what did you do as a result of participation? (5) use questions that encourage participants to be specific (p. 148).

The suggested forms included in the cited work should serve only as examples of formats for evaluations. The evaluation must suit the particular purposes of the program that is planned. The planning of evaluation is not difficult if it is viewed as an aspect of establishing values, purposes, and objectives to be achieved in a program. After a statement of these has been made, it is an obvious step to ask how would one know that such goals, purposes, and objectives have been reached. Refinement of values and objectives is the same as refinement of evaluative procedures.

CONCLUSION

This chapter has focused upon the management and evaluation of adult religious education programs. With regard to the management of programs the chapter has presented practical guidelines for such activities as selecting teachers and leaders, establishing a proper climate, preparing facilities and developing procedures, developing counseling services, promoting programs, and preparing budgets. Theoretical issues pertaining to administration and management were treated in Chapter Seven.

The second section of the chapter on evaluation of programs has included both theoretical and practical considerations. While the work of evaluation has been treated as the last activity in the entire process, it should be clear that it is implicitly included in the first stage of the investigation of values, needs, and interests and in the establishment of educational objectives. A study of evaluation indicates the complexity of program planning, design, and management. Evaluation is an area where satisfaction and objectivity are difficult to achieve. Attention to evaluation at least ensures that proper values and objectives are being sought in adult religious education.

REFERENCES

Adams, F. "Highlander Folk School: Getting Information, Going Back and Teaching it." *Harvard Educational Review,* 1973, 42 (4), 497-520.

Adult Education Office. *Assessing Needs, Evaluating Programs.* 251 Summit Ave., St. Paul, MN 55102, no date.

Agnew, M. *Future Shapes of Adult Religious Education: A Delphi Study.* New York: Paulist, 1976.

Alinsky, S. *Rules for Radicals.* New York: Random House, 1971.

Allport, G. *Becoming: Basic Considerations for a Psychology of Personality.* New Haven: Yale University Press, 1955.

Allport, G. *The Individual and His Religion.* New York: Macmillan, 1960.

Anderson, J. D., and Jones, E. E. *The Management of Ministry: Leadership, Purpose, Structure and Community.* San Francisco: Harper and Row, 1978.

Anderson, R. E., and Darkenwald, G. G. *Participation and Persistence in American Adult Education.* New York: College Board, 1979.

Archambault, R. D. "The Concept of Need and Its Relation to Certain Aspects of Educational Theory." *Harvard Educational Review.* 1957, 27 (1).

Aries, P. *Centuries of Childhood: A Social History of Family Life.* New York: Knopf, 1962.

Armstrong, D. "Adult Learners of Low Educational Attainment." Unpublished doctoral dissertation, University of Toronto, 1971.

Aslanian, C. B., and Brickell, H. M. *Americans in Transition: Life Changes as Reasons for Adult Learning.* New York: College Board, 1980.

Bandura, A. *Social Learning Theory.* Englewood Cliffs, N.J.: Prentice Hall, 1977.

Baum, G. *Religion and Alienation: A Theological Reading of Sociology.* New York: Paulist Press, 1975.

Becker, E. *The Denial of Death.* New York: Free Press, 1973.

Beckerman, M. "Adult Jewish Education: Present and Future Directions." *Religious Education,* 1973, 68 (1), 85-95.

Bellah, R. N. *Beyond Belief: Essays on Religion in a Post Traditional World.* New York: Harper and Row, 1970.

Bellah, R. "To Kill and Survive or To Die and Become: The Active Life and the Contemplative Life as Ways of Being Adult." In E. Erikson (Ed.), *Adulthood.* New York: Norton, 1978.

Berger, P., and Luckmann, T. *The Social Construction of Reality.* New York: Doubleday, 1967.

Bergevin, P., and Associates. *Adult Education Procedures.* New York: Seabury, 1963.

Bergevin, P., and McKinley, J. *Design for Adult Education in the Church.* New York: Seabury, 1958.

Bernier, J. P. "On-going Adult Christian Education at the Deanery Level: Androscoggin Deanery Project: Diocese of Portland, Maine." Unpublished doctoral dissertation, Boston University School of Theology, 1980.

Blauner, R. *Alienation and Freedom: The Factory Worker and His Industry.* Chicago: University of Chicago Press, 1964.

Blizzard, S. W. "Role Conflicts of the Urban Minister." *The City Church,* 1956, 13-15.

Bloom, B., and Associates. *Taxonomy of Educational Objectives: Part II: Cognitive Domain.* New York: McKay, 1956.

Boaz, R. L. *Participation in Adult Education, Final Report 1975.* Washington, D.C.: Center for Education Statistics, 1978.

Boshier, R. "Educational Participation and Dropout: A Theoretical Model." *Adult Education,* 1973, 23 (4), 255-282.

Bouwsma, W. "Christian Adulthood." In E. Erikson (Ed.), *Adulthood.* New York: Norton, 1978.

Bowles, S., and Gintis, H. *Schooling in a Capitalist Society.* New York: Basic Books, 1975.

Bryce, M. C. "Four Decades of Roman Catholic Innovators." In B. Kathan (Ed.), *Pioneers of Religious Education in the 20th Century.* New Haven: Religious Education Association, 1978.

Buber, M. *I and Thou.* New York: Scribner, 1958.

Burgess, H. W. *An Invitation to Religious Education.* Birmingham, Ala.: Religious Education Press, 1975.

Burns, J. M. *Leadership.* New York: Harper, 1978.

Burgess, P. "Reasons for Adult Participation in Group Educational Activities." *Adult Education,* 1971, 22 (1), 3-29.

Bushnell, H. *Christian Nurture.* New Haven: Yale University Press, 1967, first published in 1861.

Carlson, R. A. "The Time of Andragogy." *Adult Education,* 1979, 30 (1), 53-57.

Carp, A., Peterson, R., and Roelfs, P. "Adult Learning Interests and Experiences." In K. P. Cross and Associates. *Planning Non-Traditional Programs.* San Francisco: Jossey-Bass, 1974.

Clark, M., and Anderson, B. G. *Culture and Aging.* Springfield, Ill.: C. C. Thomas, 1967.

Coe, G. *A Social Theory of Religious Education.* New York: Scribner, 1917.

Cohen, S. I. "Report on the Conditions and Present Status of Adult Jewish Education in the U.S." A report prepared by the American Association for Jewish Education, October 29, 1964.

Cohen, S. I. "Adult Jewish Education—1976." *Religious Education,* 1977, 72 (2), 143-155.

Coleman, J., et al. *Youth: Transition to Adulthood.* Chicago: University of Chicago Press, 1974.

Coles, R. "Work and Self Respect." In E. Erikson (Ed.), *Adulthood.* New York: Norton, 1978.

Coolican, P. M. *Self-Planned Learning: Implications for the Future of Adult Education*. Syracuse, N.Y.: Syracuse University Educational Policy Center, 1974.

Coughlin, K. "Adult Learning Research and Adult Religious Education." *The Living Light*, 1973, 11 (2), 188-199.

Coughlin, K. *Motivating Adults for Religious Education*. Washington, D.C.: United States Catholic Conference, 1976.

Counts, G. *Dare the School Build a New Social Order?* New York: John Day, 1932.

Cremin, L. *The Transformation of the School: Progressivism in American Education, 1976-1957*. New York: Random House, 1957.

Cremin, L. A. *American Education: The Colonial Experience, 1607-1783*. New York: Harper and Row, 1970.

Cremin, L. A. *Traditions of American Education*. New York: Basic Books, 1977.

Cross, K. P. *Adults as Learners*. San Francisco: Jossey-Bass, 1981.

Crossan, J. D. *The Dark Internal: Toward a Theology of Story*. Chicago: Argus Publications, 1975.

Deboy, J. J. *Getting Started in Adult Religious Education*. New York: Paulist Press, 1979.

Department of Education. *Position Papers and Recommendations on the Parish and the Educational Mission of the Church*. Washington, D.C.: United States Catholic Conference, 1978.

Derr, R. L. *A Taxonomy of Social Purposes of Public Schools*. New York: McKay, 1973.

Dewey, J. *Democracy and Education*. New York: Macmillan, 1916.

Dewey, J. *Human Values and Conduct*. New York: Modern Library, 1922.

Dewey, J. *Experience and Education*. New York: Macmillan, 1938.

Dickinson, G., and Verner, C. "Learning Opportunities for Adults: Canada." In *Fifth Yearbook of Adult and Continuing Education*. Chicago: Marquis Academic Media, 1979.

Dollard, J., and Miller, N. *Personality and Psychotherapy*. New York: McGraw Hill, 1950.

Downs, T. *The Parish as Learning Community*. New York: Paulist, 1979.

Dulles, A. *Models of the Church*. Garden City: Doubleday, 1974.

Dunne, J. S. *The Reasons of the Heart*. New York: Macmillan, 1978.

Durka, G., and Smith, J. *Aesthetic Dimensions of Religious Education*. New York: Paulist, 1979.

Eisner, E. W. "Educational Objectives: Help or Hindrance." *School Review*, 1967, 75, 250-260.

Eisner, E. W. "Instructional and Expressive Educational Objectives: Their Formulation and Use in Curriculum." In W. J. Popham and Associates, *Instructional Objectives*. Chigago: Rand McNally, 1969.

Elias, J. L. *Conscientization and Deschooling: Freire's and Illich's Proposals for Reshaping Society*. Phila.: Westminster, 1976.

Elias, J. *Psychology and Religious Education*. Expanded Edition. Bethlehem, Pa.: Catechetical Communications, 1979. (a)

Elias, J. L. "Andragogy Revisited." *Adult Education*, 1979, 29 (4), 252-256. (b)

Elias, J. L. "Evaluation and the Future of Religious Education." *Religious Education*, 1979, 74 (6), 656-667. (c)

Elias, J. L., and Merriam, S. *Philosophical Foundations of Adult Education.* Melbourne, Fla.: Kreiger, 1980.

Erikson, E. *Childhood and Society.* Revised Edition. New York: Norton, 1963. (First published in 1950.)

Erikson, E. *Young Man Luther.* New York: Norton, 1958.

Erikson, E. *Insight and Responsibility.* New York: Norton, 1964.

Erikson, E. "Reflections on Dr. Borg's Life Cycle." In E. Erikson (Ed.), *Adulthood.* New York: Norton, 1978.

Essert, P. "The Challenge Adults Face." *International Journal of Religious Education*, 1965, 41.

Etzioni, A. *Modern Organizations.* Englewood Cliffs, N.J.: Prentice Hall, 1964.

Fichter, J. *Social Relations in an Urban Parish.* New York: Sheed and Ward, 1954.

Fowler, J. "Stages in Faith Development." In T. Hennessy, *Values and Moral Development.* New York: Paulist, 1977.

Fowler, J. "Stage Six and the Kingdom of God." *Religious Education*, 75 (3), May-June, 1980.

Fowler, J. *Stages of Faith.* New York: Harper and Row, 1981.

Fowler, J., et al. *Life Maps: Conservations on the Journey of Faith.* Waco, Texas: Word Books, 1978.

Fox, R. *School Climate Improvement: A Challenge to the School Administrator.* Englewood, Col.: CFK, Ltd., 1973.

Franklin, Benjamin, *The Autobiography of.* In L. Laboree (Ed.), *The Writings of Benjamin Franklin.* New Haven: Yale University Press, 1964.

Freire, P. *Pedagogy of the Oppressed.* New York: Seabury, 1970.

Freire, P. *Education for Critical Consciousness.* New York: Seabury, 1973.

Freud, S. *The Future of an Illusion.* In E. Jones (Ed.), *The Inter-Psycho-analytical Library*, 1953.

Fromm, E. *The Art of Loving.* New York: Harper, 1956.

Fromm, E. *The Anatomy of Human Destructiveness.* New York: Fawcett Publications, 1973.

Fry, J. R. *A Hard Look at Adult Christian Education.* Philadelphia: Westminster, 1961.

Gilligan, C. "In a Different Voice." *Harvard Educational Review.* 1977, 4.

Gilmour, S. "What Does Fowler Have to Say to Adult Educators." *The Living Light*, 1976, 13.

Girzaitis, L. *The Church as Reflecting Community: Models of Adult Religious Learning.* West Mystic, Conn.: Twenty-Third Press, 1977.

Goldman, R. *Religious Thinking from Childhood to Adolescence.* New York: Seabury, 1964.

Goldstein, J. "On Being Adult and Being an Adult in Secular Law." In E. Erikson (Ed.), *Adulthood*. New York: Norton, 1978.

Goodman, P. *The New Reformation*. New York: Vintage, 1970.

Gordon, M. *Assimilation in American Life: The Role of Race, Religion, and National Origins*. New York: Oxford University Press, 1964.

Gould, R. *Transformations: Growth and Change in Adult Life*. New York: Simon and Schuster, 1978.

Gouldner, A. *The Coming Crisis of Western Sociology*. New York: Avon, 1970.

Grabowski, S. (Ed.). *Paulo Freire: A Revolutionary Dilemma for the Adult Educator*. Syracuse: ERIC, 1972.

Grattan, C. H. *American Ideas about Adult Education, 1710-1951*. New York: Teachers College Press, 1959.

Graubard, S. R. "Preface to the Issue *Adulthood*." In E. Erikson (Ed.), *Adulthood*. New York: Norton, 1978.

Gray, R., and Moberg, D. *The Church and the Older Person*. Nashville, Eerdmans, 1977.

Greeley, A. *The Denominational Society*. Glencoe, Ill.: Scott Foresman, 1972.

Greeley, A. *The Communal Catholic*. New York: Seabury, 1976.

Greeley, A. *The American Catholic: A Social Portrait*. New York: Basic Books, 1977.

Greenburg, S. "Lifetime Education as Conceived and Practiced in the Jewish Tradition." *Religious Education*, 1973, 68 (3), 339-347.

Griffiths, W. "Implications for Administrators in the Changing Adult Education Agency." *Adult Education*, 1965, 15, 139-142.

Groome, T. H. *Christian Religious Education*. San Francisco: Harper and Row, 1980.

Gross, R. *The Lifelong Learner*. New York: Simon and Schuster, 1977.

Gruber, A. "Differences in Religious Evolution of Adolescent Boys and Girls." In *Research in Religious Psychology*. Brussels: Lumen Vitae Press, 1977.

Hall, G. S. *Adolescence*. 2 vols. New York: Appleton, 1904.

Hall, G. S. *Senescence: The Last Half of Life*. New York: Appleton, 1922.

Harevan, T. "The Last Stage: Historical Adulthood and Old Age." In E. Erikson (Ed.), *Adulthood*. New York: Norton, 1978.

Hargrove, B. *The Sociology of Religion: Classical and Contemporary Approaches*. Arlington Heights, Ill.: AHM Publishing Corporation, 1979.

Harvey, J. R. "Personal and Motivational Characteristics of Adult Learners as Related to Houle's Typology." Unpublished doctoral dissertation, University of Chicago, 1978.

Havighurst, R. J. *Developmental Tasks and Education*. New York: McKay, 1972. (First published in 1948.)

Hennig, M., and Jardim, A. *The Managerial Woman*. New York: Doubleday, 1976.

Hilgard, E. R. *Theories of Learning*. New York: Appleton-Century-Crofts, 1956.

Hoffmann, M. "Development of Internal Moral Standards in Children." In M. Strommen (Ed.), *Research on Religious Development*. New York: Hawthorn, 1971.

Holmes, U. T. *The Future Shape of Ministry*. New York: Seabury, 1971.

Holmes, U. T. *Ministry and Imagination*. New York: Seabury, 1976.

Horn, J. L. "Organization of Data on Life-Span Development of Human Abilities." In L. R. Goulet and P. B. Baltes (Eds.), *Life Span Developmental Psychology: Research and Theory*. New York: Academic Press, 1970.

Houle, C. O. *The Inquiring Mind*. Madison, Wisc.: University of Wisconsin Press, 1961.

Houle, C. O. *The Design of Education*. San Francisco: Jossey-Bass, 1972.

Illich, I. *Deschooling Society*. New York: Harper and Row, 1970.

Ingalls, J. D. *A Trainer's Guide to Andragogy*. Revised Edition. Washington, D.C.: U.S. Government Printing Office, 1972.

Jacques, E. "Death and the Mid-Life Crisis." *International Journal of Psychoanalysis*, 1965, 46, 502-514.

James, W. *The Varieties of Religious Experience*. London: Fontana, 1974, first published, 1902.

Johnstone, J. W. C., and Rivera, R. *Volunteers for Learning*. Chicago: Aldine, 1965.

Jordan, W. D. "Searching for Adulthood in America." In E. Erikson (Ed.), *Adulthood*. New York: Norton, 1978.

Jung, C. G. "The Stages of Life." In C. Jung, *Modern Man in Search of a Soul*. New York: Harcourt, 1933.

Jung, C. *Psychology and Religion*. New Haven: Yale University Press, 1938.

Jungmann, J. *Handing on the Faith: A Manual of Catechetics*. New York: Herder and Herder, 1959.

Kalish, R. A. *Late Adulthood: Perspective on Human Development*. Monterey, California: Brooks/Cole, 1975.

Kanter, R. M. *Men and Women of the Corporation*. New York: Basic Books, 1977.

Kaplan, A. *The Conduct of Inquiry*. New York: Chandler, 1964.

Katchadourian, H. A. "Medical Aspects on Adulthood." In E. Erikson (Ed.), *Adulthood*. New York: Norton, 1978.

Kaufman, G. *An Essay on Theological Method*. Washington, D.C.: Scholars Press, 1975.

Keniston, K. *Youth and Dissent*. New York: Harcourt, 1970.

Kennedy, W. B. "Christian Education Through History." In M. Taylor (Ed.), *An Introduction to Christian Education*. Nashville: Abingdon Press, 1966.

Kidd, J. R. *How Adults Learn*. New York: Association Press, 1973.

Kimmel, D. *Adulthood and Aging*. Second Edition. New York: Wiley, 1980.

Knowles, M. *A History of the Adult Education Movement in the United States*. Melbourne, Fla.: Krieger, 1977.

Knowles, M. "Andragogy Revisited: Part II." *Adult Education*, 1979, 30 (1), 52-53.

Knowles, M. *The Modern Practice of Adult Education*. Chicago: Follet/ Association Press, 1980.

Knox, A. "Continuous Program Evaluation." In N. Shaw (Ed.), *Administration of Continuing Education*. Washington, D.C.: National Association for Public School Adult Education, 1969, 368-391.

Knox, A. *Adult Learning and Development*. San Francisco, Jossey-Bass, 1977.

Knox, I. P. *Above or Within? The Supernatural in Religious Education*. Birmingham, Ala.: Religious Education Press, 1976.

Kohlberg, L. "The Implications of Moral Stages for Adult Education." *Religious Education*, 1977, 72 (2), 183-201.

Komisar, B. P. "Need and the Needs Curriculum." In B. O. Smith and R. H. Ennis, *Language and Concepts in Education*. Chicago: Rand McNally, 1960, 24-42.

Kotinsky, R. *Adult Education and the Social Scene*. New York: Appleton-Century, 1933.

Kozol, J. *The Night is Dark and I Am Far From Home*. Boston: Houghton-Mifflin, 1975.

Krathwohl, D., and Associates. *Taxonomy of Educational Objectives: Handbook II: Affective Domain*. New York: McKay, 1956.

Kuhlen, R. G. "Developmental Changes in Motivation During the Adult Years." In B. L. Neugarten (Ed.), *Middle Age and Aging*. Chicago: University of Chicago Press, 1968.

Lapidus, I. "Adulthood in Islam: Religious Maturity in the Islamic Tradition." In E. Erikson (Ed.), *Adulthood*. New York, 1978.

Lasch, C. *Haven in a Heartless World: The Family Besieged*. New York: Basic Books, 1977.

Lasch, C. *The Culture of Narcissism: American Life in an Age of Diminishing Expectations*. New York: Norton, 1979.

Lawson, K. H. *Philosophical Concepts and Values in Adult Education*. Nottingham, England: Barnes and Humby, Ltd., 1975.

Lee, J. M. *The Shape of Religious Instruction*. Birmingham, Ala.: Religious Education Press, 1971.

Lee, J. M. *The Flow of Religious Instruction*. Birmingham, Ala.: Religious Education Press, 1973.

Leech, K. *Soul Friend: The Practice of Christian Spirituality*. San Francisco: Harper and Row, 1980.

Levinson, D., and Associates. *The Seasons of a Man's Life*. New York: Ballantine, 1978.

Lewin, K. *Field Theory in Social Science*. New York: Harper and Row, 1951.

Likert, R., and Likert, J. B. *New Ways of Managing Conflict*. New York: McGraw Hill, 1976.

Lindeman, E. C. *The Meaning of Adult Education*. Montreal: Harvest House, 1961. First published 1926.

Little, L. C. *Wider Horizons in Christian Adult Education.* Pittsburgh: University of Pittsburgh Press, 1962.

Lynn, K. S. "Adulthood in American Literature." In E. Erikson (Ed.), *Adulthood.* New York: Norton, 1978.

Lynn, R. W. "A Historical Perspective on the Futures of American Religious Education." In M. Taylor (Ed.), *Foundations for Christian Education in an Era of Change.* Nashville: Abingdon Press, 1976.

McCluskey, N. G. "Religious Education in the Roman Catholic Church." In M. Taylor (Ed.), *An Introduction to Christian Education.* Nashville: Abingdon Press, 1966.

McKenzie, L. *Adult Religious Education.* West Mystic, Conn: Twenty-Third Publications, 1977.

McKenzie, L. "The Issue of Andragogy." *Adult Education,* 1977, 27 (4), 225-229.

McKenzie, L. *Adult Education and the Burden of the Future.* Washington, D.C.: University Press of America, 1978.

McKinley, J. "Perspectives on Diagnostics in Adult Education." *Viewpoints: Bulletin of the School of Education, Indiana University,* 1973, 49 (2), 69-84.

McNeil, J. *The History of the Cure of Souls.* New York: Harper, 1951.

Malia, M. E. "Adulthood Refracted: Russia and Leo Tolstoi." In E. Erikson (Ed.), *Adulthood.* New York: Norton, 1978.

Manno, B. "Distancing One's Self Religiously." *New Catholic World.* 1979, 222 (1331), 207-211.

Marcia, J. "Ego Identity Status: Relationship to Self Esteem, General Maladjustment, and Authoritarianism." *Journal of Personality,* 1967, 35, 118-133.

Maritain, J. *Education at the Crossroads.* New Haven: Yale University Press, 1973.

Marrou, H. I. *A History of Education in Antiquity.* New York: Sheed and Ward, 1956.

Marthaler, B. L. *Catechetics in Context.* Huntington, Ind.: Our Sunday Visitor Press, 1973.

Marthaler, B. L. "Socialization as a Model for Catechetics." In P. O'Hare (Ed.), *Foundations of Religious Education.* New York: Paulist Press, 1978.

Marthaler, B. "Handing on the Symbols of Faith." *Chicago Studies,* 1980, 19 (1).

Maslow, A. *Motivation and Personality.* New York: Harper, 1954.

Maslow, A. *Religions, Values, and Peak Experiences.* Columbus: Ohio State University Press, 1964.

Maves, P. "Religious Development in Adulthood." In M. Strommen (Ed.), *Research on Religious Development.* New York: Hawthorn, 1971.

Mead, M. "Why is Education Obsolete?" In R. Gross (Ed.), *The Teacher and the Taught.* New York: Delta Books, 1963.

Mehrens, W. A., and Lehmann, I. J. *Standardized Tests in Education.* Second Edition. New York: Holt, Rinehart and Winston, 1975.

Melchert, C. "Does the Church Really Want Religious Education?" *Religious Education*, 1974, 69 (1), 12-22.

Melchert, C. "What is Religious Education?" *Living Light*, 1977, 14 (3), 338-353.

Merriam, S. *Coping with Mid-Life Crisis: A Systematic Analysis Using Literature as a Data Source.* Washington, D.C.: University Press of America, 1980.

Merton, R. K. *Social Theory and Social Structure.* Rev. Ed. New York: Free Press, 1968.

Mezirow, J. "Perspective Transformation." *Adult Education*, 1978, 28 (2), 100-110.

Miles, M. *Learning to Work in Groups.* Second Edition. New York: Teachers College Press, 1981.

Miller, H. L. *Participation of Adults in Education.* Boston: Center for the Study of Liberal Education for Adults, 1967.

Miller, W. G. "The Literature on Middle Maturity with Reference to Psychology of Religion." Unpublished doctoral dissertation. Boston: Boston University, 1962.

Mills, C. W. *The Sociological Imagination.* New York: Oxford University Press, 1959.

Monette, M. L. "The Concept of Need: An Analysis of Selected Literature." *Adult Education*, 1977, 27, 195-208.

Monette, M. L. "The Language of Need in Adult Religious Education." *The Living Light*, 1978, 15 (2), 167-180.

Monette, M. L. "Needs Assessment: A Critique of Philosophical Assumptions." *Adult Education*, 1979, 29, 116-127. (a)

Monette, M. L. "Paulo Freire and Other Unheard Voices." *Religious Education*, 1979, 74 (5), 543-554. (b)

Moran, G. *The Catechesis of Revelation.* New York: Herder and Herder, 1966.

Moran, G. *Visions and Tactics: Toward an Adult Church.* New York: Herder and Herder, 1968.

Moran, G. *Design for Religion.* New York: Herder and Herder, 1970.

Moran, G. *The Present Revelation.* New York: Seabury, 1972.

Moran, G. *The Religious Body.* New York: Seabury Press, 1974.

Moran, G. *Education Towards Adulthood: Religion and Lifelong Learning.* New York: Paulist, 1979.

Morstain, B. R., and Smart, J. C. "Reasons for Participants in Adult Education Courses: A Multivariate Analysis of Group Differences." *Adult Education*, 1974, 24 (2), 83-98.

Murnion, P. A. *A Study by the Archdiocese of New York.* Archdiocese of New York, 1978.

National Forum of Religious Educators. *REKAP (Religious Education Outcomes Inventory of Knowledge, Attitudes, and Practices).* Washington, D.C.: National Catholic Educational Association, 1978.

Nelson, H., and Associates. *The Religion of Children.* Washington, D.C.: United States Catholic Conference, 1977.

Nelson, C. E. *Where Faith Begins.* Atlanta: John Knox Press, 1967.

Neugarten, B. *Personality in Middle and Late Life.* New York: Atherton, 1964.

Neugarten, B. (Ed.). *Middle Age and Aging.* Chicago: University of Chicago Press, 1968.

Neugarten, B. L. "Adult Personality: Toward a Psychology of the Life Cycle." In B. L. Neugarten (Ed.), *Middle Age and Aging.* Chicago: University of Chicago Press, 1968.

Nicholson, J. P. "A Critical Analysis of the Theological, Sociological, Educational, and Organizational Dimensions of Westerhoff's Socialization-Enculturation Paradigm." Unpublished doctoral dissertation, Fordham University, 1980.

Nieburh, R. R. *The Social Sources of Denominationalism.* New York: Holt, 1929.

Niebuhr, R. R. *Christ and Culture.* New York: Harper and Row, 1951.

Niebuhr, H. R. *The Purpose of the Church and its Ministry.* New York: Harper and Row, 1956. Reprinted in 1977.

O'Dea, T. *The Sociology of Religion.* Englewood Cliffs, N.J.: Prentice Hall, 1966.

Oden, T. C. *Kerygma and Counseling.* Phila.: Westminster, 1966. Reprinted by Harper and Row, 1978.

Parsons, T. *The Social System.* New York: Free Press, 1951.

Parsons, T. "The School as a Social System." In P. I. Rose (Ed.), *The Study of Society.* New York: Random House, 1970.

Paterson, R. W. K. *Values, Education, and the Adult.* Boston: Routledge and Kegan Paul, 1979.

Peatling, J. "The Impact of the Work of Ronald Goldman: A Prospect." *Religious Education,* 1968, 68 (6).

Peatling, J. "Research on Adult Moral Development." *Religious Education,* 1977, 72 (2), 211-224.

Peatling, J. "Annual Review of Research in Religion." *Religious Education,* 1979, 74 (4).

Peck, R. "Psychological Developments in the Second Half of Life." In B. Neugarten (Ed.), *Middle Age and Aging.* Chicago: University of Chicago Press, 1968.

Penland, P. "Self-Initiated Learning." *Adult Education,* 1979, 29 (3), 170-179.

Piaget, J. *The Moral Judgment of the Child.* Glencoe, Ill: Free Press, 1948.

Piaget, J. *Six Psychological Studies.* Edited by D. Elkind. New York: Random House, 1967.

Potvin, R., and Associates. *Religion and American Youth.* Washington, D.C.: United States Catholic Conference, 1976.

Quebedeaux, R. *The Worldly Evangelicals.* New York: Harper and Row, 1971.

Raths, L. and Associates. *Values and Teaching.* Chicago: Charles Merrill, 1966.

Rawls, J. *A Theory of Justice.* Cambridge, Mass.: Harvard University Press, 1971.

Reinhart, B. *The Institutional Nature of Adult Christian Education.* Philadelphia: Westminster Press, 1962.

Rizzutto, A. "The Psychological Foundations of Belief in God." In *Toward Moral and Religious Maturity.* Morristown, N.J.: Silver Burdett, 1980.

Rogers, C. *On Becoming a Person.* Boston: Houghton-Mifflin, 1961.

Rogers, C. *Freedom to Learn.* Columbus: Merrill, 1969.

Rohlen, T. "The Promise of Adulthood in Japanese Spirituality." In E. Erikson (Ed.), *Adulthood.* New York: Norton, 1978.

Rubin, L. *Worlds of Pain: Life in the Working Class Family.* New York: Harper and Row, 1976.

Rubin, L. *Woman of a Certain Age: The Midlife Search for Self.* New York: Harper and Row, 1979.

Rudolph, S. H., and Rudolph, L. I. "Rajput Adulthood: Reflections on the Amar Singh Diary." In E. Erikson (Ed.), *Adulthood.* New York, 1978.

Ryan, L. "Expanding Role of Adult Education in the Roman Catholic Church." Washington, D.C.: United States Catholic Conference, 1972. (a)

Ryan, L. V. "Where are We Going in Adult Education?" Washington, D.C.: United States Catholic Conference, 1972. (b)

Ryan, M. P. *Are Parochial Schools the Answer?* New York: Holt, Reinhart, and Winston, 1964.

Schaefer, J. *Program Planning for Christian Adult Education.* New York: Paulist, 1971.

Schaefer, J. *GIFT: Growing in Faith Together.* New York: Paulist, 1973.

Schaefer, J. "Update on Adult Education in Churches and Synagogues: Catholicism." *Religious Education*, 1977, 72 (2), 133-142.

Schuller, D., Strommen, D., and Brekke, M. (Eds.). *Ministry in America.* San Francisco: Harper and Row, 1980.

Sheehy, G. *Passages: Predictable Crises of Adult Life.* New York: Dutton, 1976.

Shepherd, W. C. "On the Concept of Being Wrong Religiously." *Journal of the American Academy of Religion*, 1974, 42 (1), 66-81.

Silberman, C. *Crisis in the Classroom.* New York: Random House, 1970.

Simmons, H. "Building Maps for the Journey of the Middle Years." *The Living Light.* Fall 1978.

Skinner, B. F. *Beyond Freedom and Dignity.* New York: Knopf, 1971.

Slater, P. *The Dynamics of Religion: Meaning and Change in Religious Traditions.* New York: Harper and Row, 1978.

Smart, N. *The Religious Experience of Mankind.* New York: Scribner, 1969.

Steele, F., and Jenks, S. *The Feel of the Work Place.* Reading, Mass.: Addison Wesley, 1977.

Stokes, K. "Religious Institutions." In R. Smith, G. F. Aker, and J. R. Kidd (Eds.), *Handbook of Adult Education in the United States.* New York: Macmillan, 1970.

Stokes, K. "Update on Adult Education in Churches and Synagogues: Protestantism." *Religious Education*, 1977, 72 (2), 121-132.

Stubblefield, H. "The Idea of Lifelong Learning in the Chautauqua Movement." A paper presented at the Maryland Lifelong Learning Research Conference, February 1, 1980.

Thorndike, E. L. *Adult Learning.* New York: Macmillan, 1928.

Tough, A. *The Adult Learning Projects: A Fresh Approach to Theory and Practice in Adult Learning.* Toronto, OISE, 1979.

Tracy, D. *Blessed Rage for Order.* New York: Seabury, 1976.

Tyack, D. *The One Best School System: A History of American Urban Education.* Cambridge, Mass.: Harvard University Press, 1974.

Tyler, R. W. *Principles of Curriculum and Instruction.* Chicago: University of Chicago Press, 1950.

United States Catholic Conference. *To Teach as Jesus Did.* Washington, D.C.: USCC Publications Office, 1972.

United States Catholic Conference. *A Vision and Strategy. The Plan of Pastoral Action for Family Ministry.* Washington, D.C.: USCC Publications Office, 1978.

United States Catholic Conference. *Sharing the Light of Faith: National Catholic Catechetical Directory for Catholics of the United States.* Washington, D.C.: USCC Publications Office, 1979.

Utlaut, R. L. "The Role of the Cautauqua Movement in the Shaping of Progressive Thought at the End of the Nineteenth Century." Unpublished doctoral dissertation, University of Minnesota, 1972.

Vaillant, G. *Adaptation to Life.* Boston: Little, Brown and Co., 1977.

Vaillier, J. *Catholicism, Social Control, and Modernization in Latin America.* New Jersey: Prentice Hall, 1970.

Wallace, A. *Religion: An Anthropological View.* New York: Random House, 1966.

Wallis, R. *The Road to Total Freedom: A Sociological Analysis of Scientology.* New York: Columbia University Press, 1977.

Warford, M. *The Necessary Illusion.* Phila.: Pilgrim Press, 1976.

Weber, M. *The Sociology of Religion.* Boston: Beacon, 1963, first published in 1922.

Weil, M., and Joyce, B. *Information Processing Models of Teaching.* Englewood Cliffs, N.J.: Prentice Hall, 1978. (a)

Weil, M., and Joyce, B. *Social Models of Teaching.* Englewood Cliffs, N.J.: Prentice Hall, 1978. (b)

Weil, M., Joyce, B., and Kluwin, B. *Personal Models of Teaching.* Englewood Cliffs, N.J.: Prentice Hall, 1978.

Wei-Ming, Tu. "The Confucian Perception of Adulthood." In E. Erikson (Ed.), *Adulthood.* New York: Norton, 1978.

Weiss, C. H. *Evaluation Research: Methods of Assessing Program Effectiveness.* Englewood Cliffs, N.J.: Prentice Hall, 1972.

Westerhoff, J. *Will Our Children Have Faith?* New York: Seabury, 1976.

Whitehead, E., and Whitehead, J. *Christian Life Patterns,* New York: Doubleday, 1979.

Whyte, W. F. *Men at Work.* Homewood, Ill.: Dorsey Press, 1961.

Wickett, R. E. Y. "Adult Learning and Spiritual Growth." *Religious Education*, 1980, 75 (5), 452-461.

Williamson, W. B. *Language and Concepts in Christian Education*. Phila.: Westminster, 1970.

Wilson, B. (Ed.). *Patterns of Secularization*. London: Neinemann, 1967.

Wilson, J. "Philosophical Difficulties and Moral Development." In B. Munsey (Ed.), *Moral Development, Moral Education, and Kohlberg*. Birmingham, Ala.: Religious Education Press, 1980.

Winter, G. *The Surburban Captivity of the Churches*. Garden City, N.Y.: Doubleday, 1961.

Wogaman, P. *A Christian Method of Moral Judgment*. Philadelphia: Westminster Press, 1976.

Wren, B. *Education for Justice: Pedagogical Perspective*. New York: Orbis, 1977.

Wyckoff, D. C. *Theory and Design of Christian Education Curriculum*. Philadelphia: Westminster, 1961.

Wyckoff, D. C. "Research and Evaluation in Religious Education." In M. Taylor (Ed.), *An Introduction to Christian Education*. Nashville, Tenn.: Abingdon Press, 1966.

Wyckoff, D. C. "Toward a Definition of Religious Education as a Discipline." *Religious Education*, 1967, 62 (5), 387-394.

Yankelovich, D. *The New Morality: A Profile of American Youth in the 1970's*. New York: McGraw Hill, 1975.

Yinger, J. M. *The Scientific Study of Religion*. New York: Macmillan, 1970.

Index of Principal Names

Index of Principal Subjects

VITA

John L. Elias, Ed.D, is Associate Professor of Adult Education and Director of the Division of Adult Religious Education and Development in Fordham University's Graduate School of Religion and Religious Education. He is the author of *Conscientization and Deschooling: Freire's and Illich's Proposals for Deschooling Society* (Westminster, 1976), *Psychology and Religious Education* (Cathechetical Communications, 1979), and *Philosophical Foundations of Adult Education* (Krieger, 1980).